THE ILAN STAVANS LIBRARY OF LATINO CIVILIZATION

# BORDER CULTURE

### Edited by Ilan Stavans

## GREENWOOD

AN IMPRINT OF ABC-CLIO, LLC
Santa Barbara, California • Denver, Colorado • Oxford, England

**Library of Congress Cataloging-in-Publication Data**

Border culture / edited by Ilan Stavans.
    p. cm. — (The Ilan Stavans library of Latino civilization)
  Includes bibliographical references and index.
  ISBN 978-0-313-35820-3 (hard copy : alk. paper) — ISBN 978-0-313-35821-0 (ebook : alk. paper)
  1. Mexican-American Border Region—Social life and culture.  2. Mexican-American Border Region—Social conditions.  I. Stavans, Ilan.
  F787.B658 2010
  306.0972'1—dc22

                   2009047442

13  12  11  10  9    1  2  3  4  5

This book is also available on the World Wide Web as an eBook.
Visit www.abc-clio.com for details.

ABC-CLIO, LLC
130 Cremona Drive, P.O. Box 1911
Santa Barbara, California 93116-1911

This book is printed on acid-free paper ∞
Manufactured in the United States of America

# Contents

# Series Foreword

The book series *The Ilan Stavans Library of Latino Civilization*, the first of its kind, is devoted to exploring all the facets of Hispanic civilization in the United States, with its ramifications in the Americas, the Caribbean Basin, and the Iberian Peninsula. The objective is to showcase its richness and complexity from a myriad perspective. According to the U.S. Census Bureau, the Latino minority is the largest in the nation. It is also the fifth largest concentration of Hispanics in the globe.

One out of every seven Americans traces his or her roots to the Spanish-speaking world. Mexicans make up about 65% of the minority. Other major national groups are Puerto Ricans, Cubans, Dominicans, Ecuadorians, Guatemalans, Nicaraguans, Salvadorans, and Colombians. They are either immigrants, descendants of immigrants, or dwellers in a territory (Puerto Rico, the Southwest) having a conflicted relationship with the mainland U.S. As such, they are the perfect example of *encuentro*: an encounter with different social and political modes, an encounter with a new language, and encounter with a different way of dreaming.

The series is a response to the limited resources available and the abundance of stereotypes, which are a sign of lazy thinking. The 20th century Spanish philosopher José Ortega y Gasset, author of *The Revolt of the Masses*, once said: "By speaking, by thinking, we undertake to clarify things, and that forces us to exacerbate them, dislocate them, schematize them. Every concept is in itself an exaggeration." The purpose of the series is not to clarify but to complicate our understanding of Latinos. Do so many individuals from different national, geographic, economic, religious, and ethnic backgrounds coalesce as an integrated whole? Is there an *unum* in the *pluribus*?

Baruch Spinoza believed that every thing in the universe wants to be preserved in its present form: a tree wants to be a tree, and a dog a dog. Latinos in the United States want to be Latinos in the United States—no easy task, and therefore an intriguing one to explore. Each volume of the series contains an assortment of approximately a dozen articles, essays and interviews by journalists and specialists in their respective fields, followed by a bibliography of important resources on the topic. Their compilation is

designed to generate debate and foster research: to complicate our knowledge. Every attempt is made to balance the ideological viewpoint of the authors. The target audience is students, specialists, and the lay reader. Themes
will range from politics to sports, from music to cuisine. Historical periods
and benchmarks like the Mexican War, the Spanish American War, the Zoot
Suit Riots, the Bracero Program, and the Cuban Revolution, as well as controversial topics like Immigration, Bilingual Education, and Spanglish will be
tackled.

Democracy is able to thrive only when it engages in an open, honest ex-
change of information. By offering diverse, insightful volumes about Hispanic
life in the United States and inviting people to engage in critical thinking, *The
Ilan Stavans Library of Latino Civilization* seeks to open new vistas to appreciate
the fastest growing, increasingly heterogeneous minority in the nation—to be
part of the *encuentro*.

Ilan Stavans

# INTRODUCTION

The U.S.–Mexico border is a universe onto itself. With more than 30 million people, it is a no man's land, neither American nor *mexicano*—a hybrid civilization with its own politics, language, and tradition. Nowhere else in the globe do two more polarized nations surrender their identities, giving place to a veritable New World.

This collection focuses on the culture that permeates both sides of *la frontera*. A line divides them: the Rio Grande, as it is called in English, and, in Spanish, *el Rio Bravo*. And, along with it, fences, helicopters, dogs, the border patrol, and, most recently, a towering wall designed to separate the haves from the have-nots. No matter: the border is still as porous as a sponge. It will continue thus as long as an opportunity for a better future is plentiful on one side and scarce on the other.

In truth, the border is a symbol: an end and a beginning. It is a geographical wound as well as a portable idea.

This collection is divided into two parts: the first offers theoretical disquisitions from myriad perspectives: mercantile, ideological, psychological, folkloric, and linguistic. It opens with Mario T. García's essay on *la frontera* in Chicano thought and concludes with a look at the site as a museum.

The second part is a kaleidoscope of impressionistic views. The opening chapter is a legendary study by Paul Horgan on the Rio Grande through pre-Columbian, Spanish, Mexican, and North American history. It also showcases essays by writers like Juan Villoro, Luis Humberto Crosthwaite, Cecilio García-Camarillo, Richard Rodriguez, and Guillermo Gómez-Peña. It concludes with the foreword to my book *The Hispanic Condition*.

By definition, this assortment of pieces is incomplete. My purpose has been to offer a wide range of thought-provoking approaches, some scientific in tone, others opinionated, and a few more poetic. What distinguishes the U.S.–Mexico border is its chaotic nature, the feeling it gives of having a fractured progress.

# PART I
# CONSIDERATIONS

# La Frontera:
# The Border as Symbol and Reality
# in Mexican-American Thought

## Mario T. García

For almost a century and a half the United States–Mexican border has influenced the Mexican-American experience. The result of the U.S. conquest
of northern Mexico during the mid-nineteenth century, the border separated
some Mexicans from the motherland and made them part of a new and significantly different society. Hence, people of Mexican descent, in what became the American Southwest, have had to relate in one degree or another to
the border. It is both symbol and reality in the Mexican-American experience
and has confronted each generation with questions: What does it mean to
be a Mexican in the United States? How should Mexican Americans relate
to the continual influx of Mexican immigrants? How much of Mexican culture and identity should one retain? How should Mexican Americans relate
to Mexico? These and other questions assume relevance because of the pro-
pinquity of Mexico and the heavy concentration of Mexican Americans in
the Southwest and along the U.S.–Mexican border. How each generation has
responded has determined particular political strategies for coping with the
ethnic, race, class, and cultural positions Mexican Americans have occupied
in different historical periods. An examination of the concept of the border in
Mexican-American thought provides a view of the changing nature of ethnic
and cultural nationalism among Mexicans in the United States. The meaning and ramifications of the border have varied in Mexican-American history
depending on historical epoch, whether one is an immigrant or not, levels of
acculturation, and class position and consciousness.

This study analyzes the concept of the border in the evolution of Mexican-
American thought, commencing with the first great wave of Mexican immigrants during the early twentieth century. It focuses on three influential but
significantly different community newspapers in Southern California: *La Opinión* (1926-1929), *El Espectador* (1933-1960), and *Sin Fronteras* (1975-1978). These

Mario T. García: "La Frontera: The Border as Symbol and Reality in Mexican-American
Thought," *Mexican Studies/Estudios Mexicanos*, vol. 1, no. 2 (Summer, 1985): 195–225.

three particular newspapers were chosen not only because of their regional connection, but also because each represented political views especially characteristic of a certain historical epoch. The first period is the Immigrant Era between the turn of the century and the commencement of the Great Depression when thousands of Mexicans entered the United States. These immigrants transformed earlier and smaller native Mexican communities in the Southwest into expansive and significant immigrant ones. The second period is the Mexican-American Era between 1930 and the 1960s when a generation of U.S.-born Mexicans came of political age and raised new questions about the rights and identity of Americans of Mexican descent. Finally, there is the Chicano Era of the 1960s and 1970s that is characterized by a militant but acculturated Chicano generation that sought to chart a more radical course for Mexicans in the United States. This study does not include all Mexican-American intellectual currents, but instead portrays how particular Mexican journalist-intellectuals in the U.S. reacted both in real and symbolic terms to "la frontera"—the border.

## THE IMMIGRANT ERA

Between 1900 and 1930 about a million Mexicans crossed the border seeking work or political refuge from the Mexican Revolution of 1910. Of course, Mexicans resided in the Southwest before the turn of the century, but their settlements were small and scattered. Experiencing the initial consequences of the Anglo-American conquest involving loss of lands, racial oppression, labor exploitation, and second-class citizenship, these nineteenth-century Mexicans reacted in different ways. Some refused to submit to conquest and defended themselves against Anglo control. Others, however, accommodated themselves to the transformation. Nevertheless, both groups maintained a Mexican cultural, political, and economic presence until reinforced by extensive Mexican immigration. Capitalist economic development in the region and the need for cheap labor triggered this reinforcement, which in turn overwhelmed the earlier Mexican settlements with the exception of northern New Mexico and certain locations in South Texas. Nineteenth-century Mexican communities now became predominantly immigrant ones. At no other time in Mexican American history, as during the thirty years between 1900 and 1930, have Mexican immigrants and refugees so totally dominated the Spanish-speaking Mexican condition in the Southwest and elsewhere.[1]

*La Opinión*, founded in Los Angeles in 1926 by publisher Ignacio Lozano, proved to be among the most articulate voices of the immigrant era. Ten years earlier Lozano had established *La Prensa* in San Antonio. Together, *La Opinión* and *La Prensa* became the most widely circulated and read Mexican daily newspapers in the United States although exact circulation figures no longer exist. A middle-class Catholic who had supported the overthrown dictator Porfirio Díaz, Lozano rejected the Revolution and from his sanctuary north of the border critiqued the succession of revolutionary governments. Lozano spoke for the emigré opponents of the Revolution and expressed a distinct bourgeois philosophy steeped in political and cultural nationalism. While hardly representative of the thousands of poor immigrant-workers who flocked to the U.S., Lozano nevertheless helped shape Mexican public opinion north of the border through his newspapers.[2]

As a creator and expressor of immigrant and refugee political thought, *La Opinión* related to the presence of the border. It recognized, for example, the reality of a political division between Mexico and the United States. Mexican immigrants temporarily inhabited a foreign land. Cognizant of the historic Mexican tradition in the Southwest, *La Opinión* did not consider this region, as later some Chicanos would, as an extension of Mexico or as "Occupied Mexico."[3] Mexicans were not strangers in their own land, but strangers in another land.[4] José Vasconcelos, the noted Mexican philosopher, observed in *La Opinión* that Mexicans did not regard Texas as another Alsace requiring restoration to the mother country.[5] Instead, *La Opinión* accepted the loss of these former Mexican lands to the *gringos*. *La Opinión*, however, believed that Mexican ethnicity and culture transcended the border. Ethnically, culturally, and intellectually, Mexicans in the U.S. formed an extension of Mexico even though residing in another land. *La Opinión* considered all Mexicans including those born north of the border as an organic part of Mexico. They were "México de Afuera" ("Mexico of the Outside") or "México flotante" ("floating Mexico").

*La Opinión* correctly understood that almost all Mexicans who crossed the border had no intentions of surrendering their Mexican citizenship. It applauded and encouraged this frame of mind. Most Mexicans believed that they would soon return to *la patria* once they had saved enough money and once political stability was restored. Hence, crossing the border rather than breaking with one's nationality and culture instead reaffirmed them.[6] Although *La Opinión* misread the similar ethnic and cultural persistence of European immigrants to the U.S., it nevertheless suggested that whereas Europeans were prepared to renounce their nationality and culture, Mexicans were immune to this condition owing to their shorter overland migration and the proximity of Mexico. Mexicans deflected Americanizing tendencies and consequently were less acceptable to Americans. Retaining their ethnic distinctiveness, Mexicans unfortunately encountered more exploitation and discrimination.[7]

*La Opinión* regretted this disadvantage of the Mexican immigrant experience, but also saw benefits in it. Immigration and ethnic retention helped dissolve provincialism among Mexicans. "In effect," the paper stated, "here in the United States before anything else we are Mexicans." Mexicans could remain proud of the region of their birth, but once across the border such distinctions made no sense. To help and protect one another, immigrants formed not regional but national organizations. The very names of their mutual societies, for example, smacked of national rather than regional pride: Sociedad Mexicana de Bellas Artes, Hijos de México, Cruz Azul Mexicana, Confederación de Sociedades Mexicanas. Immigration produced a "melting pot" where Mexicans lost their provincialism, but instead of becoming Americans they united as Mexicans.[8] The immigrant experience also dissolved the political and religious differences that had so badly hampered nationhood in Mexico. "We have the right to be whatever we want," *La Opinión* concluded, "but we also have the obligation above everything else to be Mexicans."[9]

Moreover, such ethnic unity transcended nationality and citizenship. *La Opinión* considered all Mexicans whether holding Mexican or U.S. papers to be one people. All were part of the Mexican nation. *La Opinión* commentator Rodolfo Uranga noted that no prejudices should mar relationships between Mexican nationals and Mexican Americans. Rather, friendship and solidarity should be promoted. "All are members of the same *raza*," he observed. While those *"de aquí"* were legally U.S. citizens, they retained the same religion, language, and customs as Mexican nationals. "In spirit they are Mexicanos." Anglos, of course, lumped all Mexicans together and hence Uranga encouraged a united Mexican front against discrimination.[10] He allowed that among Mexican Americans diverse opinions existed concerning Mexican immigration. Some supported restrictions. All, however, denounced the racism against Mexicans voiced by supporters of the Box Bill intended to place Mexicans on immigrant quotas. Uranga stressed the imperative of ethnic defense. He cautioned Mexican nationals not to criticize Mexican Americans for speaking incorrect Spanish or for using certain Anglicisms in their vocabulary. Mexican nationals should correct Mexican Americans through example and not by ridicule. In fact, many Mexican Americans spoke better Spanish than some Mexicans. "On the whole, there is no difference between them and us. We all speak, think, and feel the same."[11]

Unlike those in Mexico who viewed the immigrants and refugees as traitors for leaving their homeland, *La Opinión* regarded them as true patriots. Rather than taking something away from Mexico, Mexican immigrants contributed much value to *la patria*. They would return having learned new skills and work discipline that Mexico desperately needed for its development. They might face much hardship in the U.S., but *La Opinión* encouraged immigrant-workers to sacrifice for the sake of what they could offer to Mexico. *La Opinión* almost interpreted Mexican life north of the border as a form of purgatory. One suffered temporarily here, but paradise awaited upon return. Mexican immigrants would also be a vanguard bringing political salvation to Mexico. Having learned how to reconcile their political, religious, and regional differences while living in another country, repatriated Mexican immigrants and refugees would introduce an often missing ingredient in Mexican politics: tolerance. Consequently, the border and its crossing by Mexicans symbolized for *La Opinión* not despair but hope for Mexico's future.[12]

This future, however, needed nurturing. *La Opinión* recognized that Mexican political and cultural nationalism in the U.S. could only be sustained in the short run. It did not worry about the immigrant generation that had displayed no inclination to discard its Mexican citizenship and pride in being Mexican. Indeed, those few who became U.S. citizens were regarded as traitors. Yet, as the immigrant experience became prolonged and a new generation of U.S.-born Mexicans appeared, Americanization would begin to take its toll. This would occur due to involuntary circumstances as well as conscious efforts by Americanizing institutions.[13] *La Opinión* warned against the consequences of "de-Mexicanization." It considered naïve, for example, a suggestion by Mexican labor leader Luis Morones that Mexican workers in the U.S. seek protection under the American Federation of Labor. Mexican workers might be exploited, *La Opinión* contended, but they were better off than in Mexico. More importantly, the newspaper found it unacceptable for Mexican workers to move toward becoming U.S. citizens—a prerequisite for AF of L membership—in return for union benefits. *La Opinión* believed that the best solution for Mexican immigrant-workers lay in a marked improvement in Mexico's economic and political fortunes that would permit Mexicans to return home.[14]

*La Opinión* admonished Mexican workers to beware of American welfare organizations that, in return for assisting Mexicans, expected them to accept Americanization. This would involve loss of both citizenship and religion. The paper observed that such conversion ironically would not lead to a better status for Mexicans since they would still be treated as inferior aliens.[15] These were hardly alarmist warnings, Uranga stressed. Americanization had already spilled over into the Mexican side of the border with unhealthy results. Havens of Mexican culture in the past, these bordertowns had now adopted questionable U.S. tastes in architecture, music, dance, and even the use of *chicle,* chewing gum. Unfortunately, while many Mexicans equated Americanization with superior civilization, Mexican bordertowns, rather than becoming more civilized, had become barbaric. In contrast, Mexican immigrants had civilized bordertowns on the U.S. side by their infusion of Mexican culture.[16] However, retaining a strong Mexican cultural influence north of the border would not be easy. Adults had to remember that while they might not fall under Americanizing influences, their children and grandchildren would. If the diaspora lasted long enough, succeeding generations would be lost forever to Mexico.[17]

To prevent this, Mexicans in the U.S. had to promote their culture. Uranga noted the success of Jewish immigrants in retaining their identity and encouraged Mexicans to do likewise by establishing their own cultural institutions.[18] He promoted, for example, the formation of Spanish-language libraries either through private donations or by the Mexican government through its consulates.[19] Libraries, however, would not be enough. Uranga and *La Opinión* feared the effects of Mexican children attending U.S. public schools. This could only be countered by a separate Mexican educational system north of the border. *La Opinión* applauded the opening of such schools throughout the Southwest where children could learn Mexican cultural traditions and absorb a love of Mexico.[20] In reporting the inaugural of the José María Morelos school in Burbank, California, Uranga observed that despite its modest appearance what mattered was its rich spirit. At the same time, he disputed those who believed that Americans objected to separate Mexican schools or who felt it unwise for Mexicans to duplicate good American schools. Uranga argued that in fact Americans supported such schools and that in no location had these Mexican schools caused problems. Of course, he admitted, Americans would object to anti-Americanism. But this would not be the case. Mexican schools would acknowledge the benefits to be derived from the U.S. and would stress the value of Mexican culture rather than the dangers of Americanization. Uranga agreed that U.S. public schools were good, but that as more Mexicans crossed the border no reason existed why they could not form a comparable system.[21]

In educating Mexican children north of the border, *La Opinión* considered indispensable the retention of the Spanish language. "We who are proud of our nationality," it noted, "should understand and always keep fresh in mind this incontrovertible truth: nationality begins with language and language either strengthens or weakens nationality."[22] Hundreds of thousands of Mexicans now lived in the U.S. and *La Opinión* worried that within many families young children received their primary schooling in English and expressed themselves outside the family in that language rather than in Spanish. *La Opinión* saw nothing wrong in their learning English, but not at the expense of the mother tongue. The speaking and writing of Spanish had to be fostered.[23]

Cultural retention or "boundary maintenance" also involved other expressions. Uranga, for example, sponsored Mexican music. He publicized the organization of Mexican bands and promoted Mexican musical concerts. Music, he believed, kept alive the spirit of the culture. "It Mexicanizes our sentiment." Moreover, Mexican music exposed Anglos to the refined cultural tastes held by Mexicans. Anglos knew about political instability and economic underdevelopment in Mexico, but unfortunately little about its music and culture. "Let us make the music of Mexico," he exhorted, "a second religion."[24]

Viewing the immigrant experience as an opportunity to create a "new" Mexican, *La Opinión* believed that *barrios* needed to be self-reliant political and cultural enclaves. In this process, the Mexican government had to play a major role through its consuls. Immigrants and refugees looked to Mexico City, not Washington, for protection and redress of grievances. Uranga called on Mexican consuls to sponsor less commerce and more protection and services for Mexicans regardless of political or religious beliefs.[25] He lamented that in many communities consuls spied on their co-nationals and bred discord. "The divisions that exist within our country," Uranga stressed, "should not go beyond our borders, and if they do, they should not persist."[26] Instead, consuls needed to provide ethnic self-protection and their consulates needed to be transformed into centers of Mexican unity. *La Opinión* likewise encouraged mutual societies to assist Mexicans in times of need. Uranga suggested that Mexicans build and maintain their own clinics and hospitals. Mexicans needed to show compassion toward their "compañeros." Uranga scolded Mexicans in Colorado who, knowing about a worker named Antonio Casillas who had been sentenced to die for a crime, refused to visit him or attempt to convince officials to commute his execution. As the Great Depression dawned, *La Opinión* called on Mexicans to protect one another from increased efforts to deport them across the border to turn over their jobs to unemployed Anglos. To avoid mass deportations, it cautioned its readers in Mexico about entering the United States and urged the Mexican government to institute economic incentives to encourage Mexican repatriation.[27]

Until they returned, Mexicans in the U.S. had to conduct themselves honorably. Recognizing their vulnerability as aliens as well as insisting on law and order, *La Opinión* lectured Mexicans on obeying U.S. laws. By so doing they hopefully would eliminate certain grounds for prejudice against them and create respect for Mexicans. Uranga noted that Anglos accused Mexicans of possessing three vices: thievery, delinquency, and uncleanliness. He considered such charges to be on the whole false, but conceded that they contained a germ of truth. "It is impossible, we know, for 'México de Afuera' to be perfect; it is formed by humans, and all humans—without exception of race or color—are far from being perfect." Mexicans could better themselves. Uranga especially urged Mexican business and professional leaders to uplift their poorer compatriots. In addition, La Opinión cautioned Mexicans to avoid U.S. domestic politics. Reflecting its own aversion to "radicalism," the newspaper frowned on Mexican involvement in Los Angeles' disturbances concerning the controversial Sacco-Vanzetti case. La Opinión warned that those arrested in such disorders could not expect much help from either the newspaper or the consul. It concluded that the most appropriate decorum for Mexicans consisted of staying out of trouble, obeying the laws, and above all working hard.[28]

If La Opinión favored Mexican nationalism north of the border, it also encouraged its version of Pan-Americanism. Vasconcelos explained that Mexicans in the U.S., having experienced a *choque*—the shock of accommodating to Anglos and other ethnic groups—had, as a result, not only become more Mexican but more "Latino"—Latin American. "One hears more about '*latinidad*' in *México de Afuera* than in *México de Adentro*, 'Mexico of the Inside.'" Vasconcelos believed in identifying with the rest of Latin America.[29] La Opinión displayed a hostility to Yankee material and cultural imperialism not from a Marxist perspective, but from a conservative elitist one that stressed Hispanic cultural superiority. It called on Mexicans in the U.S. to be proud of this legacy and to associate with *La Raza*—the people of Latin America. Mexicans had to counter Anglo-American hegemony by counterposing Latin American unity. The "Colossus of the North" had to be checkmated by the "Colossus of the South." *México de Afuera* formed the front-line defense.[30] While speaking from a conservative emigré point of view, La Opinión, nevertheless, reflected certain realities of Mexican life north of the border. Mexican immigrants for the most part saw their experiences as transitory. They hoped to return to *la patria* and a better life. Theirs was a "Mexican Dream" not an "American Dream." They accommodated to life in the U.S. by attempting to reproduce a Mexican world for themselves, Consequently, La Opinión's political and cultural nationalism appealed to many immigrants. Unfortunately, many never returned including Ignacio Lozano himself. As La Opinión feared, the longer Mexicans remained apart from Mexico the more acculturation threatened them, especially their children. If the border proved to be centripetal for most immigrants, it was centrifugal for many of the succeeding generation.

## THE MEXICAN-AMERICAN ERA

The 1930s witnessed a new and expansive generation of U.S.-born Mexicans who came of political age. They utilized various terms of self-definition including Spanish American and Latin American, but increasingly identified as Mexican American. They saw themselves in relationship to life north of the border. Mexican Americans, certainly through their leadership and major organizations such as the League of United Latin American Citizens

(LULAC), the American G.I. Forum, and even more militant groups such as the Spanish-Speaking Congress and the Asociación Nacional Mexico-Americana (ANMA), broke with an immigrant consciousness while upholding a tradition of ethnic defense. Politics for Mexican Americans meant the politics of U.S. citizenship and not the politics of Mexico. More acculturated than immigrants, Mexican American leaders demanded civil rights and equal opportunities. World War II created increased labor demand in the Southwest. By providing Mexican Americans access to more skilled jobs, exposure to unionization, and even breakthroughs into lower-middle-class professions, the war only served to accelerate Mexican American aspirations for a better life in the United States. Seeking a place in American society, Mexican Americans pursued a pluralistic world view that would allow them to be accepted as U.S. citizens while remaining proud of their ethnic origin.[31]

Ignacio L. (Nacho) López was among the best-known journalist-intellectuals of the Mexican-American era. Born in Guadalajara but nationalized and raised in the U.S., López published and edited *El Espectador* from 1933 to 1960 in the Pomona Valley of Southern California. A weekly tabloid, *El Espectador* could not compete with *La Opinión* in circulation. Still, it played an influential role in mobilizing Mexican-American political action in the Pomona Valley as well as presenting an alternative viewpoint to *La Opinión* which, despite its continued publication after 1930 (it is still publishing today), has historically directed more to recent arrivals from Mexico and to those who remain largely *Mexicano* in sentiment. By contrast, through his editorials, essays, and general direction of *El Espectador*, López reflected and shaped a Mexican-American consciousness.[32]

López, like *La Opinión*, accepted the political reality of the border. He, however, recognized that a new generation of Mexicans in the U.S. permanently resided north of it. Mexico, not the U.S., was foreign to many Mexican Americans. While *La Opinión* saw Mexicans on both sides of the border as an organic whole, López discerned political, cultural, and economic cleavages separating Mexican Americans both from Mexico and from Mexican immigrants. Mexican Americans were not *México de Afuera* but "Americans of Mexican descent."

The border and the return to Mexico held no attraction for López. For Mexican Americans, there was no retreat to Mexico. The more enterprising aspired to the "American Dream." López appreciated the permanency of Mexican Americans in the United States. Having attended American schools, he desired to make something of himself in his adopted country. López absorbed the values and ideals of the United States. He did not at the same time reject his Mexican cultural traditions. Yet a U.S. experience, not a Mexican one, shaped much of his politics. López and many of the Mexican American activists and intellectuals of his generation can be seen as political sons and daughters of the New Deal era and of the U.S. involvement in World War II. As part of a generation engaged in a campaign to overturn obstacles to full equality, López helped advance the notion that the Mexican-American struggle lay north of the border. By participating in Mexican-American issues, such as the desegregation of public facilities and schools plus the movement into electoral politics, López spoke more for the attainment of the fruits of the American Revolution than of the Mexican Revolution. Hence, the sense of permanency—the U.S. as home country—influenced the political ideology and activism of Mexican Americans.

As permanent residents of the U.S., López and other Mexican Americans in the Pomona Valley waged protracted struggles against discrimination and segregation. Prejudice, of course, affected all Mexicans and López did not differentiate between Mexican Americans and Mexican nationals in the securement of equal treatment. He did believe, however, that Mexican Americans had more at stake in desegregation. Besides combatting affronts to their ethnic dignity, Mexican Americans saw desegregation as a means to equal opportunities with Americans and recognition as full-fledged U.S. citizens.

Unlike *La Opinión*, López understood that Mexican Americans could not reconcile their exploited conditions by believing that a better life awaited in Mexico. Mexican-American life might be a purgatory, but heaven would be found north not south of the border. *La Opinión*'s caution about Mexicans not engaging in civil conflict in the U.S. had no relevance to Mexican Americans. López preached direct action to combat prejudice. He challenged discrimination in public facilities such as movie theaters, swimming pools, and restaurants as among the most objectionable forms of separation. In 1939, for example, López personally led a boycott of the Upland Theater in Upland, California for segregating Mexicans in the first fifteen rows. The boycott succeeded and the theater agreed to complete integration. "In this manner the first step is taken," López noted, "in the Mexican community's defense of its dignity and in its struggle for civil rights."[33]

Both *La Opinión* and *El Espectador* advocated education for Mexican children north of the border. However, where *La Opinión* supported a separate Mexican system to prevent acculturation, López encouraged Mexican Americans to integrate the public schools. He believed in ethnic pride and cultural retention, but appreciated that in order for Mexican Americans to advance they had to learn English and have access to quality education. This could only be achieved by dismantling the dual public school system of the Southwest that relegated Mexican children to inferior public "Mexican schools" and instead integrating both Mexicans and Anglos in the same schools. Writing in *El Espectador* Eugenio Nogueras also pointed out the contradiction of "Mexican schools" in California. Such schools belonged in Mexico not the United States.[34] Moreover, López upheld school integration not only as a right but pedagogically correct. Integration facilitated the learning of English; segregation impeded it. Integration also socialized children to live with one another and to respect each other. López saw in integrated public schools the perfect vehicle for achieving democratic rights for Mexican Americans.[35]

*El Espectador* supported ethnic solidarity as did *La Opinión* but not at the expense of equal opportunities for Mexican Americans. While *La Opinión* had supported self-sufficient Mexican enclaves that would breed Mexican nationalism, López rejected what he considered self-segregation. He opposed, for example, any form of segregated housing. In 1950 he editorialized against construction of a housing tract in Whittier exclusively for Mexican-American

veterans. He admitted that some Mexican Americans supported such housing because it meant better homes, but aligned himself with those who opposed it on the principle that segregation was unacceptable. The housing tract
constituted an effort to pacify Mexican Americans while denying them the
opportunity to purchase homes in Anglo neighborhoods. Offended at such
discrimination, especially when the country asked for unity because of the
Korean conflict, López concluded:

> It is not the anglo-saxon who will reap the repercussions of this case of segrega-
> tion . . . it will be those of us who have yet to understand that the only way to
> end discrimination and segregation is for us to integrate fully into society . . .
> making us part of the community and not trying to live in an exclusive world
> reserved only for ourselves.[36]

In the pursuit of integration and equal opportunities, López broke with
the idea of an organic unity of the Mexican people on both sides of the border
supported by La Opinión. He did not believe, for example, that the economic
interests of Mexican Americans and Mexican nationals necessarily coincided.
López defended braceros and undocumented workers, but recognized that
they replaced and dislocated resident Mexican-American workers. The right
to a decent job was both a human and civil right and, in certain cases, López
found himself defending local workers against Mexican nationals. In the Pomona Valley and throughout California, unscrupulous employers pitted one
set of workers against the other and where possible employed the cheaper
braceros or alambristas. Employers persistently declared that they could not
find enough domestic agricultural workers and hence the need for braceros.
Yet this claim always worked against Mexican-American farmworkers. When
local growers requested braceros in February of 1949, López replied that in his
opinion braceros were not needed due to the availability of domestic workers
who often had to go without work during certain seasons. There were not
enough jobs for both Mexican Americans and braceros. Often, when braceros
arrived and discovered insufficient work, they abandoned their camps and
sought employment illegally. However, López viewed with greater alarm the
fact that the use of braceros lowered wage standards, especially for Mexican
Americans who could not compete with the cheaper labor.[37]

In many instances, undocumented workers rather than braceros harmed
Mexican-American interests. El Espectador noted various cases of employers illegally hiring alambristas, through illicit contraband traffic in what the
newspaper termed "human meat." López supported the elimination of undocumented immigration and questioned the neutrality of immigration and
border patrol officers who often seemed invisible when growers desired undocumented workers. "The only ones who can solve this problem," López
proposed, "are the resident workers of this region who must take this issue
to the highest officials and have them understand that this problem is one
of the gravest facing labor in California and is the problem of thousands of
Mexican Americans who live exclusively by doing farm labor."[38] He lamented
opposing the employment of Mexican nationals and believed this dilemma

to be a modern and tragic version of the Cain and Abel biblical story. Yet Mexican nationals replaced Mexican-American workers and López called for an end to this displacement. "It is unjust for those from the outside to come and take bread away from our children, even if this is justified on the laws of Supply and Demand. The resident workers of this country should have priority over any other group—even if this involves the painful case of that other group being of our own race and tongue."[39] The migration of Mexican workers across the border was a complex issue, but López suggested that the solution lay in Mexico establishing new agricultural centers that would be productive enough to retain workers in their own country.[40]

Politically, *El Espectador* differed from *La Opinión*. Whereas *La Opinión* applauded co-nationals retaining their Mexican citizenship and saw political organization as a means to ethnic solidarity and protection from American cultural contamination, López advocated the political integration of Mexican Americans within the United States. A fervent disciple of American democracy, López consistently encouraged his readers to vote. Voting expressed citizenship. During World War II, López reminded Mexican Americans that the war and the preservation of democracy would be won both in the battlefield and in the polling booth. "Remember that it is a patriotic obligation," he wrote, "to vote in the elections, register if you have not done so."[41] Through voting Mexican Americans could better assimilate into the political life of the nation. Unfortunately many Mexican Americans possessing the right to vote did not do so: "We refer to that large number of American citizens of Hispanic descent, men and women, who being able to vote and to actively participate in the civic life of their community fail to do so because they have not registered to vote."[42]

López viewed voting in more than idealistic terms. He realized that an electoral strategy could advance Mexican-American working and living conditions. In 1938 López editorialized concerning what Mexicans in the United States could do to improve their lives north of the border. Mexicans had two choices. They could either accept their second-class status, as many had done for almost 100 years and through at least five generations, or they could begin to struggle to achieve equality. López believed the time had arrived to demand the Mexicans' rightful place in American society. He observed that Mexicans now formed a sizeable population in the Southwest, particularly in Southern California. Statistics, however, would not generate changes. Mexican Americans alone could do this by directly participating in politics and, in a word, by voting. "If you want economic and social power," he told his audience, "then first acquire political power."[43] López even suggested that Mexican nationals in California think seriously about becoming American citizens so that through voting they could improve their material status. Mexican Americans should not complain about discrimination, López lectured, and then not vote. Only by voting in large numbers would Mexican Americans achieve respect and reforms.[44] "The vote is our most sacred right," López sermonized, "and at the same time the most powerful political weapon."[45] Indeed, the vote "in the final analysis is the panacea for all our ills."[46] Politicians only understood organized political pressure. If Mexican Americans could achieve this through voting, they would be surprised at the "miracles" their votes would bring:

paved and lighted streets, better police and fire service, better treatment by public officers, and more Mexican Americans in government.[47]

*El Espectador* also had to confront the cultural question in the United States. However, unlike *La Opinión* which preached Mexican cultural nationalism, *El Espectador* opted for biculturalism and a modified form of Mexican-American nationalism. López supported the integration of Mexicans into the mainstream of American society, but not at the expense of cultural heritage. He took pride in being of Mexican descent and believed in pragmatic cultural retention. Moreover, López understood that the racial and cultural discrimination that bred insecurity among Mexican Americans had to be countered by ethnic pride. "Respect and pride in one's heritage," he advised young Mexican-American graduates in 1957, "is essential in order to feel proud in being American."[48] Hence, López cultivated a bicultural world view among Mexicans in the Pomona Valley. He promoted Mexican cultural traditions and accepted a process of acculturation that would pave the way for integration. Fearful of too much acculturation, especially among youth, Lopez recognized cultural pluralism as a viable alternative. As one writer in *El Espectador* put it: "Continue united for unity builds strength and continue to be proud of being both in the United States and of having Mexican blood in your veins."[49]

López advocated Mexican cultural retention in several ways. Linguistically, he affirmed the use of Spanish and the development of a bilingual population. *El Espectador* itself was a predominantly Spanish-language organ. The paper also served as an outlet for local poets who published their Spanish-language poems and *corridos* (ballads) in its pages. "Journalism has been my mission in life," López proclaimed in 1956. "And I have nothing to complain about. In publishing a Spanish language newspaper we have contributed in a small way to fostering among our readers a love of our beautiful language and of our culture which gives it life."[50] *El Espectador* paid particular attention to the celebration of the 16th of September—Mexican Independence Day—and Cinco de Mayo, the Mexican victory over an invading French army in 1862. López consistently prompted the Mexican communities to organize festivals for these key Mexican holidays. "The most important gift that we can leave our children," López editorialized, "is pride in being Mexican." If parents retained their cultural traditions and passed them on to their offsprings, the "Mexican soul" would survive north of the border.[51]

López, however, also recognized the importance and, indeed, the inevitability of acculturation. *El Espectador* reflected and even influenced this process. The paper's periodic use of a bilingual format underlined the cultural and linguistic changes experienced by Mexican Americans. Between 1938 and 1959, López launched at least five bilingual versions of *El Espectador*. Each ran for several months before reverting again to a Spanish-language copy. Bilingualism in *El Espectador* consisted of an English-language page aimed at the growing number of Mexican-American youth in the public schools. "These young adults and children," López wrote in 1938, "preferring to read in English, in order to understand it better, and also because many cannot read in Spanish, have no interest in our newspaper. Hence, it is our intention (by publishing this English section) to interest our Mexican youth in *El Espectador*."[52] Nine years later, Larry Probasco, a World War II veteran and the second editor of the paper's English section, stressed the importance of learning English. It formed the common denominator linking all ethnic groups in the United States. One spoke English not just out of necessity but because it was a privilege.[53]

Supporting Mexican cultural traditions while understanding the attraction and pragmatic necessity of acculturation, López proposed a type of dual cultural citizenship. Mexican Americans could and should benefit from both cultures. Dual cultural citizenship was not only a goal but a growing reality. Adult Mexicans remained highly loyal to their language and culture, but among the young various forces pushed them to accept cultural compromises or what López termed "naturalization." However, this need not be feared. "Naturalization" remained distinct from forced Americanization that had been tried earlier and failed. López opposed forced Americanization but accepted acculturation as inevitable and pointed out that customs, diet, marriage, education, jobs, and even wars helped socialize Mexican Americans to life in the United States.[54]

Acculturation was not wrong, but it had to be balanced. It should neither deprive Mexican Americans of their cultural heritage nor of their ethnic identity. Acculturation could and should not be prevented, but this transformation could be eased by a sensitivity on the part of both Mexican Americans and Anglos to the benefits of cultural pluralism. World War II had proved, López editorialized in 1946, that people and nations had to cooperate and treat each other with respect. This also had to apply domestically in the postwar era. "The great hope for realization of a better world, instead of a planet of shattering holocausts," he wrote, "lies in our will to merge viewpoints and differing customs—to come to know its varying people as friends and neighbors. To have such opportunities here in our own communities is something we should seek ardently."[55] López recalled the unique cultural roots of California and of the distinct Spanish-Mexican heritage of the state. Cultural pluralism was real in California, but had to be more than simply the stereotypical "Colorful Mexican." Mexican Americans had to be accepted as full citizens and integrated into all levels of California society. Only in this manner could a viable cultural pluralism flourish and a united society be forged or the "one world" López referred to:

> The time has come—indeed it had to come—for 'one world' in our home communities. It is the time for friendliness and courtesy, for the merging of viewpoints and differing customs, for the sharing of civic responsibilities and problems. Not as newcomers, but as co-workers over many decades of community history, the descendents of Spain and Mexico, bearers of a great cultural heritage, come to take their place in civic life. They are ready to help bear its burdens and rejoice in its triumphs.[56]

## THE CHICANO ERA

Yet, despite certain advances, Mexican Americans such as Ignacio López failed to fully integrate Mexicans north of the border although this accommodating tendency continues to represent an important part of Mexican-

American political thought. Consequently, out of the frustrated aspirations of the Mexican American era a new and more militant politics emerged in the 1960s: the Chicano Movement. A product of the historic exploitation of Mexicans in the U.S., Chicanos as a generation were likewise the result of a decade of social conflict and questioning of American values and culture. Black civil rights struggles, the Black Power Movement, anti-war protests, ethnic revivals, radical feminism, and youth alienation and rebellion influenced the birth of the Chicano generation. Chicanos rejected the politics of compromise and accommodation and, attracted to Third World struggles, called for political and cultural self-determination. Ironically more Americanized, educated, and occupationally mobile than their parents, Chicanos despaired of their acculturation and of American middle-class materialism. Instead, they sought roots and a new identity through the path of Chicano cultural nationalism and revived an image of a lost homeland in the Southwest: Aztlán.[57]

Cultural nationalism, however, soon proved to be politically and intellectually stifling for some Chicanos. It did not explain class contradictions among Mexicans in the United States. Culture and identity, they argued, could not be divorced from the predominant working-class character of most Mexicans. Cultural nationalism apart from class struggle could degenerate into an opportunistic reactionary movement. Hence, by the early 1970s an important wing of the Chicano Movement gravitated toward a synthesis of nationalism and working-class struggle. A leader of the Chicano left was CASA—General Brotherhood of Workers. Organized in Los Angeles by longtime community organizer Bert Corona in the late 1960s for the protection of undocumented Mexican workers, CASA had been captured in the mid-1970s by young radical activists and intellectuals. Maintaining an emphasis on the increasing numbers of undocumented workers, CASA also saw itself as a political vanguard and symbolized an important evolution to the left by young Chicano intellectuals, students, and particular sectors of workers. Moreover, in its development CASA inherited a radical current present in Mexican-American thought and expressed by earlier movements such as the followers of the anarcho-syndicalist Ricardo Flores Magón during the 1910s, the militant Spanish-Speaking Congress (1938–1943), and the Asociación National Mexico-Americana (ANMA) during the cold war years of the early 1950s. In its analysis of the Mexican position in the U.S. and through its monthly and modestly circulated newspaper *Sin Fronteras* (1976–79), CASA interpreted the border differently from *La Opinión* and *El Espectador*.

As its title indicated, *Sin Fronteras* (Without Borders) rejected the idea of a border. A political border existed, but *Sin Fronteras*, unlike *La Opinión* and *El Espectador*, considered it to be only an artificial creation that in time would be destroyed by the struggles of Mexicans on both sides of the border. In its version of the "National Question," *Sin Fronteras* regarded the Mexican War as a colonial conquest that had imposed a subordinate status on Mexicans. It sympathized with Chicano historians such as Rodolfo Acuña who proposed a theory of internal colonialism to explain the Chicano condition.[58] However, *Sin Fronteras* went one step further and included Mexicans south of the border as part of the colonized. "Occupied Mexico" was on both sides of the border. Yankee political, economic, and cultural colonialism victimized all Mexicans, whether in the U.S. or in Mexico. Like *La Opinión*, *Sin Fronteras* accepted Mexicans as one people, whether U.S. citizens or Mexican nationals and irrespective of which side of the border they lived on. "Presently, when we speak of the Mexican population, we speak of approximately 80 million people situated on both sides of the border," CASA proposed. "This means that we are the largest Spanish-speaking population in the World."[59] *Sin Fronteras* shunned terms such as Chicano and Mexican American that implied differences among Mexicans and, instead, used only the term "Mexicano." It rejected the narrow nationalistic concept of Aztlán, but agreed with the 1969 Plan de Aztlán that "we do not recognize capricious borders on the Bronze Continent."[60]

*La Opinión*, of course, had sponsored the organic unity of all Mexicans based on ethnic and cultural ties. *Sin Fronteras* differed by focusing on the national and class character of Mexicans. That is, Mexicans because of conquest were an oppressed nation and as a fundamentally working-class people they also formed an exploited class under capitalism. Consequently, the "Mexican worker" rather than *La Opinión's* "universal Mexican" constituted the foundation for the organic unity that transcended the border. Mexicans were one people on both sides of the border because they were products of the same nation, Mexico, and possessed a common class character. Victims of oppression, Mexicanos could achieve liberation and self-determination only by engaging in a borderless struggle to defeat American international capitalism.[61] "Thus it is our responsibility," CASA stressed, "to fight exploitation and national oppression for our rights as workers and as a people."[62]

Because of this organic unity, *Sin Fronteras* in the 1970s concentrated on what it believed to be the most pressing issue facing Mexicans in the U.S.: the plight of the undocumented worker. It noted that those calling themselves Chicanos or Mexican Americans could not escape several fundamental factors that bound all Mexicans together. For example, Mexicans from both sides of the border were racially and ethnically one people. In his analysis of the Chicano Movement, Carlos Vásquez observed that it had progressively evolved to include undocumented workers. "A segment of the Chicano Movement deepened its commitment to national identity and to class struggle and unified their efforts with those of the undocumented worker," he wrote. "Not as a solidarity to strangers, but as a direct responsibility to members of the same nationality, of the same people."[63] Vásquez criticized those Chicanos who, lacking historical and class consciousness, distanced themselves from the struggles of the undocumented. These Chicanos ironically withdrew from their own families, since many members often possessed no documents.[64] Unlike Ignacio López who discerned political, economic, and cultural differences between Mexican Americans and Mexican nationals, *Sin Fronteras* idealistically dismissed such differences as minor and called on Mexicanos north of the border to reject such divisive proposals. "[We] should not only resist the government's attempt to divide us by creating the conception that we are a different nationality from our compatriots born south of the border," CASA member Nativo López stressed. "We must also resist and combat these false notions among our people which are perpetuated by self-proclaimed vanguards, some intellectuals and assimilationists."[65]

Besides a common nationality, Chicanos and Mexican Americans needed to identify with the undocumented because any Mexican possessed a historic right to migrate to the Southwest. "To Mexicans," *Sin Fronteras* proclaimed, "it [migration] means we are concretely repopulating lands stolen from us in the Invasion of 1846. . . ."[66] CASA further emphasized that since most Chicanos and Mexican Americans descended from earlier immigrants, they should not now turn their backs against more recent arrivals.[67]

Chicanos and Mexican Americans likewise needed to pragmatically recognize that undocumented workers formed an indispensable component of the Mexican working class in the United States. Liberation and self-determination could not be achieved without the participation of the undocumented. Moreover, Chicanos and Mexican Americans as a predominantly working-class people possessed the same class position as the undocumented. Class interests, along with ethnic ones, produced one people. "Workers, with or without documents," CASA's Political Commission acknowledged, "only create the wealth that enriches the exploiting class. They [Mexicanos] are the exploited, and this is the common interest they have as a universal class."[68] Reversing *La Opinión*'s emphasis that Mexican workers in the U.S. would return to their homeland and introduce modernizing changes, *Sin Fronteras* believed that undocumented workers coming in the opposite direction could become a political vanguard among Mexicans north of the border. "The immigrant workers bring with them enormous experiences of struggle from their own countries," political exile José Jacquez Medina wrote:

> An example of this is the concept of a 'strike' which immigrant workers have. When they participate in a strike, they are the first to openly propose the total shut-down of the factory and the placing of the red-and-black flags over the gates. When north American workers tell them that it is against the law to do that, they usually answer that the only strike they know is when the workers stop the factory totally and do not allow scabs to replace them.[69]

Finally, Chicanos and Mexican Americans had to understand that their capitalist exploiters eyed all Mexicans as the same. It made no sense for Chicanos and Mexican Americans to separate themselves from the undocumented since racism and class oppression affected them all. "Because we compose the majority of Latin workers in this part of the country," one CASA member explained, "racism is aimed at the Mexican worker. Although this capitalist government claims that we are all equal under the law, we are actually in an inferior position. In reality, there is no difference between those born here and those recently arrived, between those who have lived here for years."[70]

Because of this inescapable organic unity, *Sin Fronteras* urged Chicanos to protect undocumented workers from the anti-alien hysteria spreading during the 1970s. CASA in particular attacked President Carter's immigration plan as repressive legislation. The plan intended to curtail the right of Mexicans to enter the U.S. and would discriminate against all Mexicans north of the border. Like *El Espectador*, but for different reasons, *Sin Fronteras* opposed any reinstitution of the Bracero Program suggested by some proponents of immigration "reform." Ignacio López had primarily criticized the Program for harming Mexican American farmworkers, while *Sin Fronteras* considered it a system of "rented slaves" for the profit of agribusiness.[71] Moreover, *Sin Fronteras* disdained immigration legislation that sought to arbitrarily divide Mexicans. "Taken in parts or in its totality," Nativo López argued, "Carter's program is an affront to the very livelihood, the very existence of Mexican people, born on either side of the border, regardless of generation."[72]

Any Mexican who collaborated with Carter's plan, *Sin Fronteras* warned, betrayed his ethnic heritage and participated in the victimization of his own people. Such collaborators played the role of colonial administrators.[73] *Sin Fronteras* considered, for example, that Carter's appointment of Leonel Castillo as Director of the Immigration and Naturalization Service (INS) fit this description. "If he becomes an apologist for the INS," it suggested, "he will be serving the interests of those who took our lands, who keep us in the condition under which we live, and who suck the lifeblood of Mexico with their multinational corporations and international investments."[74]

Instead of restricting immigration and deporting undocumented workers, *Sin Fronteras* advocated unconditional amnesty for all Mexicans in the U.S. without papers. Mexicans producing wealth through their labor had earned the right to live and work here. Amnesty also validated the Mexicans' historic presence in the Southwest. "Amnesty," CASA member Felipe Aguirre underscored, "signifies the tacit acknowledgement of those rights taken away through violence, along with lands, and the agression [sic] upon their culture, customs, and language of the Mexican people."[75] *Sin Fronteras* believed immigration restrictions and deportations against Mexicans to be historical hypocrisy. To consider Mexicans illegal in the Southwest was preposterous and a farce. "U.S. imperialists invaded and robbed our (Mexican) lands, put up fictitious borders and now want to treat us as illegals," stated Antonio Rodríguez, national coordinator of CASA. "It takes more than a treaty [of Guadalupe Hidalgo, 1848] to separate our people: no government can legislate our right to live in our own lands. We demand complete and total amnesty for all immigrants, and an end to deportations."[76]

Self-determination, however, could not be limited to Mexicans north of the border. It could be accomplished only through the unified struggles of Mexicans on both sides. The same conditions, for example, that caused unemployment and sub-employment on one side produced it on the other. "Mexico is a classical example of North American economic intervention," Jacquez Medina stressed.[77] "We have seen," columnist Magdalena Mora noted, "that the exploitation of workers is not limited by borders. Thus, the resistance of workers cannot be limited by national boundaries. Their struggle is one."[78] Mexican workers in the U.S. needed to join the anti-imperialist struggles of their "compañeros" in the factories and fields of Mexico. *La Opinión*, of course, had also opposed U.S. imperialism, but in support of a Mexican national bourgeoisie and not a society controlled by workers favored by *Sin Fronteras*. "Mexican people on both sides of the border," Jacquez Medina observed, "victims of worsening conditions, begin to understand that solutions to their problems are not found in the governments nor systems which rule on both sides of the border."[79] Only the workers themselves could solve their problems by establishing a workers' state transcending the border. *Sin Fronteras* boldly concluded: "NO BORDER STOPS WORKERS' STRUGGLES."[80]

To achieve workers' unity, the borderless struggle for political liberation had to be accompanied by a movement for cultural self-determination. *Sin Fronteras*, like *La Opinión* and *El Espectador*, feared the dangers of Americanization. It disagreed, however, with *La Opinión* that self-enclosed Mexican cultural enclaves could be maintained. Instead, it pragmatically believed with Ignacio López that acculturation could not be avoided and that at best a bicultural, bilingual condition could be achieved. Yet, while López interpreted biculturalism as accommodation within the U.S. system, *Sin Fronteras* accepted it as a cultural base for national self-determination. Mexicanos had to protect their historic culture and language not only because of their heritage, but because they needed to form cultural links between Mexican Americans and Mexican nationals in the U.S. and between Mexicans on both sides of the border. Carlos Vasquez noted that a positive feature of the Chicano Movement had been its emphasis on cultural self-determination. Unfortunately, the movement had not always put this into practice. Vasquez pointed out that many Chicano newspapers utilized English and avoided a bilingual format. Hence, they regrettably separated themselves from a large Spanish-speaking audience.[81] *Sin Fronteras* published bilingually. Moreover, without the right to use Spanish, many Mexican workers in the U.S. could not adequately defend themselves. *Sin Fronteras* particularly protested efforts by some labor unions in Southern California to prohibit Spanish at their local meetings. This discriminated against Mexican members on the basis of language. "If members don't understand English, then they can't raise questions or engage in discussion; and if they can't do that, then corrupt union leaders will never be stopped."[82]

Consequently, cultural retention and promotion was needed to prevent such efforts by U.S. institutions or by unsympathetic Mexican Americans to deprive Mexicanos of a common culture and language as a way of dominating them. "[We] must view all plans to assimilated [sic] us or portray us as assimilated as a conscious act to weaken our unity and our strength in numbers," *Sin Fronteras* editorialized:

> It means that all attempts to divide us according to legal status, place of birth, language dominance, or whatever must be resisted. It does not matter whether it comes from the state or it comes from some of our own misguided and confused people who try to hide their assimilation and deculturation in pseudo-revolutionary rhetoric about multi-nationalism.[83]

*Sin Fronteras* urged cultural maintenance, but did not advocate a separate Mexican educational system as earlier advanced by *La Opinión*. It aligned itself with *El Espectador*'s position favoring the right of Mexican-American students to equal educational opportunities in the public schools. However, *Sin Fronteras* also insisted on bilingual, bicultural education. Ignacio López and many other Mexican Americans of his era believed bilingual education singled out Mexican Americans as different and hence they opposed it. They considered Spanish-language retention to be the responsibility of the home and community institutions. Chicanos in the 1960s rejected this view as assimilationist. Instead, they stressed bilingual education both as a methodology to assist Spanish-speaking students and for the cultivation of cultural nationalism. *Sin Fronteras* agreed and supported its implementation in the Los Angeles public schools. The issue of busing to desegregate schools only enhanced *Sin Fronteras'* concern over bilingual education. Busing posed a difficult issue for CASA. It did not want to side with the opponents of busing, yet CASA feared that busing could disperse the Mexican community and harm bilingual programs in predominantly Mexican-American schools. "Would forced busing be equivalent to forced assimilation?" it asked.[84] Discounting that true integration could be achieved under a racist capitalist system, *Sin Fronteras* aimed to protect the cultural integrity of Mexicanos as a way of advancing liberation struggles. Busing could endanger this effort. Mexicanos did not want integration, *Sin Fronteras* argued; they wanted cultural self-determination and public education had to reflect this desire. "Busing does not resolve the demands of the Mexican people," Antonio Rodríguez explained:

> It does not guarantee the respect to the practice and cultivation of our national rights, as reflected in the demand for bilingual and bicultural education. Without those rights equal education does not exist for us. The use of our language and culture forms part of the democratic struggle for our political survival faced with brutal Yankee cultural aggression and its attempt to destroy the use of our national language.[85]

*Sin Fronteras* supported busing only if it did not adversely affect bilingual programs.

More radical than either *La Opinión* or *El Espectador*, *Sin Fronteras* pursued different long-range goals. *La Opinión* had looked toward the eventual return of Mexicans to their homeland south of the border and a better life under a Mexican capitalist state. *El Espectador* had hoped for the integration of Mexican Americans in an American bourgeois pluralist society. *Sin Fronteras*, however, believed in the achievement of socialism by Mexicano workers on both sides of the border. Mexicanos would re-possess their lost lands in the Southwest and join with their compatriots in Mexico to establish a greater Mexican workers' state. Meanwhile, the struggles for the protection of the undocumented, for union democracy, for bilingual education, among others, formed a transitional phase for raising the political consciousness of Mexican workers and preparing them to achieve socialism and true democracy. In these efforts, Mexicano workers united with the larger working-class movement in the U.S. while retaining their right as a people to national self-determination.[86] "Although Mexican workers form part of the working class," CASA explained, "the oppression of the Mexican people goes beyond that experienced by other members of the working class under capitalism. We suffer both as workers and as a people."[87]

As socialists, CASA members encouraged a broader internationalist perspective. Besides rejecting a border between Mexico and the U.S., *Sin Fronteras* also preached the borderless solidarity of all oppressed peoples, especially in Latin America and the Third World. This internationalism went beyond the more limited and elitist Pan-Americanism advocated by *La Opinión*. Mexicano workers, according to *Sin Fronteras*, could defeat U.S. imperialism not only by uniting with their brothers and sisters in Mexico, but by joining with other workers throughout the world fighting the same enemy. "The revolutionary trend demands the intensification of the militant international solidarity and the support of the just struggles of national liberation which are being fought throughout the world," CASA's Political Commission concluded. "The international alliance of Capitalism must be opposed by proletarian internationalism and the people's international solidarity."[88] CASA sided with the Cuban Revolution and supported other movements for national liberation in Latin America. "Our organization is made up of Mexican and Latin American people that defeated colonialism," Antonio Rodríguez stated on his way to a Havana conference in solidarity with Puerto Rican independence. "We are part of a people that daily suffer racism, discrimination, exploitation under the same imperialists who today maintain Puerto Rico as a colony."[89] *Sin Fronteras* recognized no borders between oppressed people in Latin America and called attention to its motto: "Somos Uno Porque América Es Uno [sic]."

## CONCLUSION

The different interpretations of the border by *La Opinión*, *El Espectador*, and *Sin Fronteras* captured an important spirit within each of their historical periods. Although possessing unequal circulation and reaching by and large different audiences, these newspapers reflected and shaped intellectual currents among opinion-makers and political activists, but, of course, could not speak for all Mexicans. *La Opinión*, for example, was distributed and read throughout the United States. On the other hand, *Sin Fronteras* influenced primarily students, intellectuals, and young workers. Yet, each newspaper gives testimony to significant political and intellectual changes within the Mexican communities north of the border. In its early years *La Opinión* spoke for the immigrants and political refugees who dominated most Mexican communities in the early twentieth century. As such, *La Opinión* served and continues to serve as an immigrant institution. *El Espectador* articulated the voice of a people in search of their place in the United States. Finally, *Sin Fronteras*, which ceased publication by the late 1970s, transmitted the concerns of an important segment of the new Chicano generation of the 1960s and 1970s that sought to reconcile a renaissance of Mexican nationalism with working-class ideological affiliation in the hope of militantly defending the interests of Mexican workers on both sides of the border. Each of these newspapers stressed central themes of the Mexican experience in the U.S.: conquest, subjugation, immigration, racism, cultural nationalism, acculturation, integration, ethnic revival, alienation, and class consciousness. Other ethnic groups in the country possessed somewhat similar intellectual traditions; yet, with the limited exception of French Canadians in the U.S., they did not confront a two-thousand-mile border between the United States and the mother country that daily reinforced these themes. Moreover, the persistence of such themes from one generation to another among Mexicans attests to continued class and racial barriers confronting Mexicans as well as the constant and relatively easy migration of Mexicans as economic refugees across the border into the United States. In a fascinating departure from almost all other ethnic experiences in this country, second and third generation U.S.-born Mexicans of varying class positions continue to co-exist with thousands of recent arrivals from Mexico. Consequently, different states of consciousness also co-exist: an immigrant consciousness steeped in Mexicano ethnic and cultural nationalism plus an abiding attachment to Mexico; a Mexican-American consciousness centered on integration and acculturation; and a Chicano consciousness stressing ethnic revival with elements of Marxism. These three political tempers and varying sub-tempers interacted with one another in the 1980s and continue to influence Mexican-American political thought.

Clearly, with such heterogeneity no consensus has surfaced on the meaning of the border among Mexicans north of it. Still, each generation has had to directly or indirectly relate to *la frontera*. No viable political strategy among Mexican Americans nor public policies affecting Mexican Americans can possibly succeed without being cognizant of the border. Unending immigration, Mexico's nearness, and the concentration of Mexicans in the Southwest have all given the border, as both symbol and reality, a major place in Mexican-American thought.

## NOTES

1. For the post–Mexican War period and the Immigrant Era see for example: Mario Barrera, *Race and Class in the Southwest: A Theory of Racial Inequality* (Notre Dame: University of Notre Dame Press, 1979); Albert Camarillo, *Chicanos in a Changing Society: From Mexican Pueblos to American Barrios in Santa Barbara and Southern California, 1848–1930* (Cambridge: Harvard University Press, 1979); Lawrence Cardoso, *Mexican Emigration to the United States, 1897-1931* (Tucson: University of Arizona Press, 1980); Arnoldo De Leon, *The Tejano Community, 1836-1900* (Albuquerque: University of New Mexico Press, 1982) and *They Called Them Greasers: Anglo Attitudes Toward Mexicans in Texas, 1821–1900* (Austin: University of Texas Press, 1983); Mario T. García, *Desert Immigrants: The Mexicans of El Paso, 1880–1920* (New Haven: Yale University Press, 1981); Richard Griswold del Castillo, *The Los Angeles Barrio, 1850–1890: A Social History* (Berkeley: University of California Press, 1979); Leonard Pitt, *The Decline of the Californios: A Social History of the Spanish-Speaking Californians, 1846–1890* (Berkeley: University of California Press, 1966); Mark Reisler, *By the Sweat of Their Brow: Mexican Immigrant Labor in the United States* (Westport, CT: Greenwood Press, 1976); Robert J. Rosenbaum, *Mexicano Resistance in the Southwest: The Sacred Right of Self-Preservation* (Austin: University of Texas Press, 1981). For an economic history of the U.S.-Mexican border see Raul Fernandez, *The United States–Mexican Border: A Politico-Economic Profile* (Notre Dame: University of Notre Dame Press, 1977). For a good case study of border life see Oscar J. Martínez, *Border Boom Town: Ciudad Juárez Since 1848* (Austin: University of Texas Press, 1978).

2. For a short content analysis of *La Opinión* see Francine Medeiros, "*La Opinión*, A Mexican Exile Newspaper: A Content Analysis of Its First Years, 1926–1929," *Aztlan*

11 (Spring 1980): 65-88. *La Opinión,* of course, is still being published today, but for this study only the issues from 1926 to 1929 covering part of what I term the "immigrant era" were considered.

    3. See *Sin Fronteras* for the 1970s.

    4. See David Weber, ed., *Foreigners in Their Native Land* (Albuquerque: University of New Mexico Press, 1973).

    5. *La Opinión,* 10 June 1928, p. 37. The types of questions posed by *La Opinión* indirectly dealt with what is termed the "National Question." That is, do Mexicans in the U.S. constitute a separate nation, a national minority, or an oppressed nationality? One writer suggests that the debate on the "National Question" is only of recent origin; however, Mexicans in the U.S. in one form or another have addressed this question for some time, even though in a less theoretical fashion than in recent years. See Antonio Ríos Bustamante, *Mexicans in the United States and the National Question* (Santa Barbara: Editorial La Causa, 1978).

    6. *La Opinión,* 15 Nov. 1926, p. 3.

    7. *Ibid.,* 25 Aug. 1927, p. 3.

    8. *Ibid.,* 20 Feb. 1927, p. 1.

    9. *Ibid.,* 3 Jan. 1927, p. 3.

    10. *Ibid.,* 10 Sept. 1927, p. 1.

    11. *Ibid.,* 18 March 1928, p. 1.

    12. *Ibid.,* 15 Nov. 1926, p. 3; 1 Jan. 1927, p. 3; 6 Nov. 1928, p. 1.

    13. *Ibid.,* 29 Nov. 1926, p. 3.

    14. *Ibid.,* 25 Aug. 1927, p. 3.

    15. *Ibid.,* 5 Nov. 1927, p. 3.

    16. *Ibid.,* 3 Oct. 1928, p. 1.

    17. *Ibid.,* 26 March 1927, p. 3.

    18. *Ibid.,* 30 Oct. 1926, p. 1.

    19. *Ibid.,* 19 Sept. 1926, p. 1; 28 Oct. 1926, p. 1; 18 March 1927, p. 1.

    20. *Ibid.,* 24 Aug. 1927, p. 1.

    21. *Ibid.,* 2 March 1928, p. 1.

    22. *Ibid.,* 21 March 1928, p. 3.

    23. *Ibid.*

    24. *Ibid.,* 8 Dec. 1927, p. 1; 6 March 1928, p. 1.

    25. *Ibid.,* 9 June 1927, p. 1.

    26. *Ibid.,* 20 Aug. 1927, p. 1.

    27. *Ibid.,* 2 April 1928, p. 1; 3 March 1927, p. 1; 28 Jan. 1928, p. 1; 16 Nov. 1926, p. 1; 15 Feb. 1928, p. 3; 23 Jan. 1928, p. 3; 6 Jan. 1928, p. 3; 4 March 1927, p. 3; 11 Feb. 1927, p. 3; 14 June 1927, p. 3.

    28. *Ibid.,* 27 Feb. 1928, pp. 1 and 6; 13 Aug. 1927, p. 3; 11 Oct. 1926, p. 3; 8 Oct. 1926, p. 3; 4 March 1928, p. 1.

    29. *Ibid.,* 10 June 1928, pp. 3 and 10.

    30. *Ibid.,* 12 Oct. 1927, p. 3; 7 June 1927, p. 3; 9 June 1927, p. 3; 1 Dec. 1927, p. 3; 12 Dec. 1927, p. 3; 31 Jan. 1928, p. 3.

    31. For the Mexican American Era see for example: Carl Allsup, *The American G.I. Forum: Origins and Evolution* (Austin: Center for Mexican-American Studies, The University of Texas, 1982); Luis Arroyo, "Chicano Participation in Organized Labor: The CIO in Los Angeles, 1938–1950, An Extended Research Note," *Aztlán* 6 (Summer 1975): 277–303; Albert Camarillo, "Research Note on Chicano Community Leaders: The G.I. Generation," *Aztlán* 2 (Fall 1971): 145–150; Richard A. García, "The Mexican American Mind: A Product of the 1930s," in Mario T. García and Francisco Lomeli, eds., *History, Culture, and Society: Chicano Studies in the 1980s* (Ypsilanti: Bilingual Press, 1983), 67–94; Edward Garza, "L.U.L.A.C." (Master's Thesis, Southwest State Teachers College, 1951); Ralph Guzman, *The Political Socialization of the Mexican American People* (New York:

Arno Press, 1976); Beatrice Griffith, *American Me* (Boston: Houghton Mifflin, 1948); Pauline K. Kibbe, *Latin Americans in Texas* (Albuquerque: University of New Mexico Press, 1946); Raul Marin, *Among the Valiant: Mexican Americans in World War II and Korea* (Los Angeles: Borden Publishing Co., 1963); Alonso S. Perales, *Are We Good Neighbors?* (San Antonio: Arles Graficas, 1948); Guadalupe San Miguel, "Mexican American Organizations and the Changing Politics of School Desegregation in Texas, 1945 to 1980," *Social Science Quarterly* 63 (December 1982): 701–715; Frances Jerome Woods, *Mexican Ethnic Leadership in San Antonio, Texas* (Washington, D.C.: Catholic University of America Press, 1949).

32. For a short biography of López, see Ignacio López Collection Folder of Information in Ignacio López Collection in Special Collections, Stanford University. The López Collection consists of original as well as microfilm copies of *El Espectador*.

33. *El Espectador*, 17 Feb. 1939, pp. 1 and 2; 24 Feb. 1939, pp. 1 and 7; 3 March 1939, pp. 1, 9, and 11.

34. *Ibid.*, 13 Dec. 1947, p. 2.

35. *Ibid.*, 23 Oct. 1942, p. 1.

36. Ibid., 11 Aug. 1950, pp. 2 and 3.

37. Ibid., 18 Feb. 1949, p. 17. Also see 5 Oct. 1945, pp. 1, 2, and 10; 7 Dec. 1945, pp. 1 and 4; 5 April 1946, p. 1; 10 Jan. 1947, pp. 1 and 8; 28 May 1948, p. 1; 13 May 1949, p. 1; 25 Aug. 1950, p. 2; 28 Sept. 1951, p. 1; 25 April 1952, pp. 1 and 7; 20 July 1956, p. 8; 29 March 1957, p. 1.

38. *Ibid.*, 1 Sept. 1952, p. 2.

39. *Ibid.*, 6 Oct. 1950, pp. 1 and 15.

40. *Ibid.*, 22 June 1951, p. 1.

41. *Ibid.*, 3 July 1942, p. 1.

42. *Ibid.*, 27 Jan. 1939, p. 1.

43. *Ibid.*, 18 Feb. 1938, p. 3.

44. *Ibid.*, 19 May 1939, p. 2; 7 March 1950, p. 1; 28 April 1950, p. 1.

45. *Ibid.*, 8 Sept. 1950, p. 2.

46. *Ibid.*, 3 Nov. 1950, p. 3.

47. *Ibid.*, 22 Feb. 1952, pp. 1 and 8.

48. *Ibid.*, 14 June 1957, p. 1.

49. *Ibid.*, 24 April 1959, p. 2.

50. *Ibid.*, 17 Aug. 1956, p. 1.

51. *Ibid.*, 16 Sept. 1949, p. 1.

52. *Ibid.*, 4 Nov. 1938, pp. 1 and 7.

53. *Ibid.*, 13 June 1947, p. 4.

54. *Ibid.*, 7 July 1949, p. 1.

55. *Ibid.*, 1 March 1946, p. 12.

56. *Ibid.* For a leftist contrast on the Mexican American Era see Emma Tenayuca and Homer Brooks, "The Mexican Question in the Southwest," *The Communist* 18 (March 1939): 257–268. Tenayuca and Brooks saw all Mexicans north of the border as one people, but no longer an organic part of Mexico. They called for a united front of Mexicans and progressive Anglos to achieve basic democratic rights.

57. For the Chicano Era see F. Chris García, ed., *La Causa Política: A Chicano Political Reader* (Notre Dame: University of Notre Dame Press, 1974); Juan Gómez Quiñones, *Mexican Students Por La Raza: The Chicano Student Movement in Southern California, 1967-1977* (Santa Barbara: Editorial La Causa, 1978); Carlos Muñoz, "The Politics of Protest and Chicano Liberation: A Case Study of Regression and Cooptation," *Aztlán* 5, nos. 1 and 2 (Spring and Fall 1974): 119–141; Armando Rendón, *Chicano Manifesto* (New York: Macmillan, 1971); Gerald Paul Rosen, *Political Ideology and the Chicano Movement: A Study of Political Ideology of Activists in the Chicano Movement* (San Francisco: R and E Research Associates, 1975); Richard Santillan, *La Raza Unida* (Los Angeles: Tlaquilo

Publications, 1973); John Shockley, *Chicano Revolt in a Texas Town* (Notre Dame: University of Notre Dame Press, 1974); Stan Steiner, *La Raza: The Mexican Americans* (New York: Harper, 1970).

58. See Rodolfo Acuña, *Occupied America: The Chicano's Struggle Toward Liberation* (San Francisco: Canfield Press, 1972). For other views on Chicano internal colonialism see Mario Barrera, Carlos Muñoz, and Carlos Ornelas, "The Barrio as an Internal Colony" in García, ed., *La Causa Política*, pp. 281–301; Robert Blauner, *Racial Oppression in America* (New York: Harper and Row, 1972); Tomas Almaguer, "Toward the Study of Chicano Colonialism," *Aztlán* 2 (Spring, 1971): 7–21; Guillermo Flores, "Race and Culture in the Internal Colony: Keeping the Chicano in His Place" in Frank Bonilla and Robert Girling, eds., *Structures of Dependency* (Stanford: Nairobi Bookstore, 1973); and Mario T. García, "Internal Colonialism: A Critical Essay," *Revista Chicano-Riqueña* VI (1978): 38–41.

59. See "Who We Are" special supplement to *Sin Fronteras* (no date), p. 1.

60. *Sin Fronteras*, July, 1977, p. 10. For a comparison of CASA's position on the "National Question" with that of other left organizations, see Rios Bustamante, *Mexicans in the United States*. Also see August Twenty-Ninth Movement, *Fan the Flames: A Revolutionary Position on the Chicano National Question* and "The Struggle for Chicano Liberation," special issue of *Forward* 2 (August 1979). For a discussion of CASA's political action see Richard A. García, "The Chicano Movement and the Mexican American Community, 1972–1978: An Interpretive Essay," *Socialist Review* 8 (July-October 1978): 117–136 and Tomas Almaguer, "Chicano Politics in the Present Period: Comments on García," in *Ibid.*, pp. 137–141.

61. *Ibid.*, Sept. 1975, p. 6.

62. "Who We Are," p. 4.

63. *Sin Fronteras*, July 1977, p. 10.

64. *Ibid.*

65. *Ibid.*, Aug. 1977, p. 9.

66. *Ibid.*, Jan. 1977, p. 8.

67. *Ibid.*, May 1977, p. 4.

68. *Ibid.*, Sept. 1975, p. 7.

69. *Ibid.*, March 1977, p. 8.

70. *Ibid.*, Aug. 1977, p. 10.

71. *Ibid.*, Dec. 1976, p. 8.

72. *Ibid.*, March 1977, p. 9.

73. *Ibid.*

74. *Ibid.*, May 1977, p. 8.

75. *Ibid.*, Dec. 1976, p. 9.

76. *Ibid.*, Sept. 1975, p. 1.

77. *Ibid.*, Feb. 1977, p. 9.

78. *Ibid.*, Jan. 1976, p. 8.

79. *Ibid.*, Sept. 1977, p. 9.

80. *Ibid.*, May 1977, p. 10.

81. *Ibid.*, Feb. 1977, p. 10; June 1977, p. 8; Sept. 1977, p. 10.

82. *Ibid.*, Sept. 1975, p. 3.

83. *Ibid.*, June 1977, p. 8.

84. *Ibid.*, Feb. 1977, p. 8.

85. *Ibid.*, April 1977, p. 9.

86. *Ibid.*, Jan.-Feb. 1978, p. 9; Dec. 1976, p. 9.

87. *Ibid.*, "Who We Are," p. 5.

88. *Sin Fronteras*, Jan. 1976, p. 7.

89. *Ibid.*, Sept. 1975, p. 2.

# THE GREAT WALL OF CAPITAL

## Mike Davis

When delirious crowds tore down the Berlin Wall in 1989 many hallucinated that a millennium of borderless freedom was at hand. Globalisation was supposed to inaugurate an era of unprecedented physical and virtual-electronic mobility. Instead neoliberal capitalism has built the greatest barrier to free movement in history.

This Great Wall of Capital, which separates a few dozen rich countries from the earth's poor majority, completely dwarfs the old Iron Curtain. It girds half the earth, cordons off at least 12,000 kilometres of terrestrial borderline, and is comparably more deadly to desperate trespassers.

Unlike China's Great Wall, the new wall is only partially visible from space. Although it includes traditional ramparts (the Mexican border of the United States) and barbed wire–fenced minefields (between Greece and Turkey), much of globalised immigration enforcement today takes place at sea or in the air. Moreover borders are now digital as well as geographical.

Take, for example, Fortress Europe, where an integrated data system (upgrading the Strasbourg-based Schengen network) with the sinister acronym of PROSECUR will become the foundation for a common system of border patrol, enforced by the newly authorised European Border Guards Corps. The EU has already spent hundreds of millions of euros beefing up the so-called Electronic Curtain along its expanded eastern borders and fine-tuned the Surveillance System for the Straits that is supposed to keep Africa on its side of Gibraltar.

Tony Blair recently asked his fellow EU leaders to extend white Europe's border defences into the heart of the Third World. He proposed "protection zones" in key conflict areas of Africa and Asia where potential refugees could be quarantined in deadly squalor for years. His model is Australia, where right-wing prime minister John Howard has declared open war on wretched Kurdish, Afghan and Timorese refugees.

After last year's [2003] wave of riots and hunger strikes by immigrants indefinitely detained in desert hell-holes like Woomera in south Australia, Howard used the navy to intercept ships in international waters and intern refugees in even more nightmarish camps on Nauru or malarial Manus Island off Papua New Guinea.

Blair, according to the *Guardian*, has similarly scouted the use of the Royal Navy to interdict refugee smugglers in the Mediterranean, and the RAF to deport immigrants back to their homelands.

If border enforcement has now moved offshore, it has also come into everyone's front yard. Residents in the U.S. Southwest have long endured the long traffic jams at "second border" checkpoints far away from the actual lines. Now stop and search operations are becoming common in the interior of the EU. As a result, even notional boundaries between border enforcement and domestic policing, or between immigration policy and the "war on terrorism," are rapidly disappearing. "Noborder" activists in Europe have long warned that the Orwellian data systems used to track down non-EU aliens will be turned against local anti-globalisation movements as well.

In the U.S., likewise, trade unions and Latino groups regard with fear and loathing Republican proposals to train up to 1 million local police and sheriffs as immigration enforcers.

Meanwhile the human toll of the new world (b)order grows inexorably. According to human rights groups, nearly 4,000 immigrants and refugees have died at the gates of Europe since 1993—drowned at sea, blown up in minefields, or suffocated in freight containers. Perhaps thousands more have perished in the Sahara en route. The American Friends Service Committee, which monitors the carnage along the U.S.-Mexico border, estimates that a similar number of immigrants have died over the last decade in the furnace-hot deserts of the Southwest.

In the context of so much inhumanity, the White House's recent proposal to offer temporary guest-worker status to undocumented immigrants and others might seem a gesture of compassion in contrast to the heartlessness of Europe or the near fascism of Australia.

In fact, as immigrant rights groups have pointed out, it is an initiative that combines sublime cynicism with ruthless political calculation. The Bush proposal, which resembles the infamous Bracero programme of the early 1950s, would legalise a subcaste of low-wage labour without providing a mechanism for the estimated 5 to 7 million undocumented workers already in the U.S. to achieve permanent residence or citizenship.

Toilers without votes or permanent domicile, of course, is a Republican utopia. The Bush plan would provide Wal-Mart and McDonald's with a stable, almost infinite supply of indentured labour.

It would also throw a lifeline to neoliberalism south of the border. The decade-old North American Free Trade Agreement, even former supporters now admit, has proven a cruel hoax—destroying as many jobs as it has created. Indeed the Mexican economy has shed jobs four years in a row. The White House neo-Bracero proposal offers President Vicente Fox and his successors a crucial economic safety valve.

It also provides Bush with an issue to woo the swing-vote Latinos in the Southwest next November. Undoubtedly, Karl Rove (the president's grey eminence) calculates the proposal will sow wonderful disarray and conflict among unions and liberal Latinos.

Finally—and this is the truly sinister serendipity—the offer of temporary legality would be irresistible bait to draw undocumented workers into the open where the Department of Homeland Security can identify, tag and monitor them. Far from opening a crack in the Great Wall, it heals a breach, and ensures an even more systematic and intrusive policing of human inequality.

# Establishing Shots of the Border: The Fence and the River

## Claire F. Fox

For the first time the world is completely divided up, so that in the future only redivision is possible, i.e., territories can only pass from one "owner" to another, instead of passing as ownerless territory to an "owner."

—V. I. Lenin, 1916[1]

In spring 1992, Terry Allen, a multimedia artist known for his exploration of the mythology of the U.S. Southwest, was invited to do an installation at The Ohio State University's Wexner Center for the Arts as part of that institution's artist-in-residence program. The Wexner Center installation, entitled *a simple story (Juarez)*, was the continuation of a project begun over twenty years ago, which has included record albums, a radio play, photographs, video, sculpture, collages, prints, and drawings. At the Wexner Center the artist constructed three sets: a cantina ("Melodyland"), an airstream trailer encased in the wooden hull of a ship ("The Perfect Ship"), and a gas station ("Stations"). These sets loosely correspond to episodes in *a simple story's* scripted narrative, which tells of four characters, Sailor, Spanish Alice, Chic Blundie, and Jabo, whose destinies become intertwined.[2] *A simple story* traces the journeys of the quartet from Southern California to Cortez, Colorado, where Jabo and Chic murder newlyweds Sailor and Alice in a trailer, and eventually part ways after they escape to Juárez.

Allen does not fix *a simple story's* characters or their location in time or space. Instead, the fragmented episodes of *a simple story's* narrative function as traces of memory that forge a connection among the depopulated sets of the installation. Allen built the sets at two-thirds human scale and theatrically illuminated them with the flicker of video monitors and neon signs. In her afterword to the published script accompanying the exhibition, Curator Sarah Rogers-Lafferty described the video images projected at "Stations" as "hypnotic." She wrote, "These images capture what is perhaps the most

Claire F. Fox: "Establishing Shots of the Border: The Fence and the River," first published as Chapter 2 of *The Fence and the River: Culture and Politics at the U.S.-Mexico Border.* Minneapolis: University of Minnesota Press, 1999.

pivotal characteristic of this circular tale—the sense of endless journey, and escape to find oneself that haunts all the details of the story."[3] Rosetta Brooks, the reviewer for *Artforum*, also perceived Allen's border to be atmospheric and psychological; for her, *a simple story* was a nostalgic fantasy about the western U.S. frontier:

> The installation recalled the kinds of buildings seen in many small, formerly frontier towns across the West. The frontier has always had a special force in the American psyche; the dream of surviving it, of passing through the wilderness to the promised land, seems to strike a chord in the hearts of this continent's Anglo population.[4]

It is telling that these critics stress the installation's existential antiheroes and overlook images of other bodies depicted in one of the videos projected at the "Stations" set, which features 360-degree pans taken from El Paso/Juárez's pedestrian bridge.[5] The bridge is crowded with people, while below, through chain-link fence, the viewer sees *indocumentados* crossing the river on make-shift inner-tube rafts.

The bodies of border residents and panoramic views of urban El Paso/Juárez are nagging reminders that photographic "evidence" of the contemporary U.S.–Mexico border can rarely support the mythological vision of the border as a no-man's land sparsely populated by deviants and drifters. This latter border nonetheless appears to have been the early inspiration for Allen's project. Honky-tonk songs, written and recorded by Allen in the early 1970s, were the first in-stallments in the *Juarez* cycle, songs like "Texican Badman": "in Juarez / Gonna meet me a fine señorita / Gonna tip her my hat when I meet her / Gonna take her out / And dine her on tortilla / And if you love her / You bought her / If you didn't you oughta / Get a little off that daughter / In Juarez."[6]

I begin with this example from Allen's *Juarez* project because it so vividly stages the extreme polarization of border images in U.S. popular culture that evolved during the project's own twenty-year history. The border featured in Allen's video is a familiar visual accompaniment to descriptions of the gnaw-ing social issues affecting today's border cities, such as pollution, rapid urban-ization, and immigration. The border of fiction and fantasy evoked by Allen's sets is the highly eroticized milieu of outlaws and whores, where embattled individuals confront themselves through confrontations with "the Other."

Many artists who explore U.S.–Mexico border issues have critiqued both of the stereotypical image repertoires captured by Allen's installation, often through repetition, hyperbole, parody, and other formal devices. "Border art" has become a common phrase to describe projects like Allen's, though it is difficult to define border art as a movement, because the term does not posit a shared political tendency, aesthetic project, or site of production. Some artists and critics, for example, celebrate the U.S.–Mexico border's capacity to juxta-pose and absorb disparate cultural elements, while others criticize the former perception as an appropriative fascination with the daily life and experience of border dwellers. Both the cosmopolitan and the regionalist position have played a role in the complex process of setting criteria for this genre. In exhibi-tions, curators formulate various responses as to whether border art describes art about the border, art by people living on the border, or simply art located on the border. In the case of *La Frontera*, an exhibition about the U.S.–Mexico border experience co-organized by the Centro Cultural de la Raza and the Museum of Contemporary Art, San Diego, concerns about the organizing role of the latter mainstream art institution led several prominent artists working in the region to decline representation in the show.[7] In comparison, artists from around the world are invited along with local artists to submit projects for *inSITE*, a large-scale exhibition of site-specific art that has taken place in 1992, 1994, and 1997. Playing upon the "sister cities" trope so prevalent during NAFTA negotiations, the exhibition is held in Tijuana and San Diego, with sponsorship coming from a combination of corporate-funded regional arts institutions as well as government sources.[8] The result, as George Yúdice has commented, "is an almost ironic combination of artworks that raise political issues about immigration, race, and national and cultural identity, and that garnish, so to speak, a celebration of dubious economic arrangements brought about by NAFTA."[9] Border art has also commonly found itself included as one tendency within much larger geographic or cultural frames, such as multicultural, Chicano/a, folk, Mexican, and pan-American art.[10]

For the purpose of this chapter, I use a content-based approach to border art because I am interested in examining recent permutations of two stereotypical "establishing shots" of the border: the fence and the river. In narrative film and video the establishing shot is typically a two- to three-second take of a building exterior or landscape that is inserted at the beginning of a scene. Rarely are establishing shots imbued with special meaning; in fact they are meant to be unobtrusive keys that help the viewer to locate action within a larger space, before the ensuing scene systematically fragments that space into smaller units through medium shots and close-ups. I use the phrase *establishing shot* liberally in the analysis that follows, referring to how the border as a place has been registered not only in film and video, but also in photography, literature, and other media.

In many recent images of the border, such as those featured in videos about NAFTA, corporate chain-link fences and waste-water canals have become prominent aspects of the mise-en-scène, indeed much more so than the low-key establishing shots typical of mainstream narrative film and video. Both chain-link fences and waste water can be related to more conventional establishing shots of the border that U.S. audiences have come to know through commercial cinema and popular culture—namely, panoramic views of the Rio Grande/Río Bravo and lengths of barbed wire fence extending across vacant landscapes. Through their fusion or conflation of national and corporate territories, the "new border establishing shots" explore the relationship between nation-states and transnational corporations, and in the process, document changing spatial configurations in the border region.

## THE FENCE AND THE RIVER IN ART AND POPULAR CULTURE

Throughout this century, the U.S.–Mexico border has taken on various guises in U.S. visual culture. While General Pershing chased Pancho Villa across Northern Mexico, U.S. postcard photographers represented the border as an obelisk-shaped boundary marker or an imaginary line drawn in the sand.[11] Narratives stressing the historical and social continuity of the border region, like Les Blanc's documentary film *Chulas Fronteras* (Beautiful borders) and Aristeo Brito's novel *El diablo en Texas* (The devil in Texas), challenged the obstacle posed by the national boundary through recurrence to tropes like the binational bridge and the ferry boat.[12] And Chicano/a scholars and activists have, in distinct historical periods, imagined communities called Aztlán and the Borderlands, which erased the border in the first instance, and valorized it as a liminal zone in the second.[13] In the contemporary era, generally speaking, the Rio Grande/Río Bravo and the fence are the two primary icons used to establish the location of a narrative in the border region. Their cultural entrenchment as constitutive of "the border" is perhaps most clearly witnessed in the way that they metonymically mark those Mexican workers who traverse them as either *mojados* ("wets") or *alambristas* ("wire-crossers").

For U.S. and Mexican audiences alike, the border fence has great symbolic currency. As one of Néstor García Canclini's *tijuanense* informants told him, "El alambre que separa a México de los Estados Unidos podría ser el principal monumento de la cultura en la frontera" ("The fence that separates Mexico from the United States could be the principal monument of culture on the border").[14] Chicano artist Willie Herrón used chain-link fence as a central element in his graphic design for the *Chicano Art: Resistance and Affirmation (CARA)* catalogue, which was produced in conjunction with the traveling art exhibition of the same name organized by UCLA's Wight Art Gallery. The chain-link leitmotif of the catalogue reclaims what is in most urban neighborhoods a commonplace marker of private property, and converts it into the emblem of a particular cultural experience. But Herrón and the curators made a distinction between international and intranational borders in their conceptual framework for the show.[15] Herrón introduced a section of artwork about civil liberties, for example, with an image of barbed wire, while he used chain-link fence to introduce a section featuring urban Chicano/a art. His iconography was echoed by some of the artists included in the show. Graphic posters by Rupert García (¡*Cesen Deportación!* 1973) and Malaquías Montoya (*Undocumented*, 1981), for example, both emphasized the harshness of barbed wire to protest the plight of undocumented workers.[16] The group Asco on the other hand, of which Herrón was a founding member, featured chain-link fence in its 1990 installation at the Wight Art Gallery (included in the *CARA* show through photodocumentation).[17] In the Asco piece reproduced in the *CARA* catalogue, chain-link distances the spectator from a recessed space filled with media images and precariously balanced TV sets.

The national spectrum of Chicano/a art presented in the *CARA* catalogue gives the impression that the barbed wire border is slightly more hostile than the inner-city chain-link fence because the former represents the state, while the latter only represents private property. Barbed wire is an icon of the alienated *indocumentado* and the experience of crossing national borders, while the chain-link fence connotes both marginality within the nation and a communal experience focused around the barrio. A recent example from the art world that affirms this logic is the 1996 controversy involving a sculpture commissioned by the University of New Mexico from Chiricahua Apache artist Bob Haozous. His work about border crossings, entitled "Cultural Crossroads of the Americas," was approved in maquette form by the University, but the final version was rejected because the artist had added razor wire to the top of the piece, a thirty-foot-tall metal billboard structure featuring silhouetted pre-Columbian and modern urban images. According to the artist, the university wanted the piece to reflect all North American borders, including the Canadian one, while he wanted it to be a statement about the U.S.–Mexico border in particular.[18]

Other artists who treat the U.S.–Mexico border in their work do not uphold this distinction between domestic and international border markers, however. Chain-link is evidently the fence of choice for many border artists, although it is rarely used as a primary fencing material on the borderline itself. In fact, in 1987 photographer Peter Goin found that chain-link ran along no more than fifteen miles of the border's almost two-thousand-mile length.[19] It is not surprising that chain-link should be so common in art about the border experience, because as border cities become increasingly urbanized, they have come to share much of the same spatial imagery that was attractive to groups like ASCO in East Los Angeles. When Terry Allen was interviewed about all the chain-link in his installation, for example, he talked about it as an icon of "the new border":

> I remember the first time I went to Juárez, to the border, those fences weren't there . . . on the bridge and whatever . . . and now it's just like this incredible visual . . . all the chain-link fencing. . . . You can't look at anything without a grid kind of being in front of you.[20]

Many artists who work with U.S.–Mexico border imagery explore the metaphoric possibilities of chain-link as both barrier and permeable interface, as abstract grid and everyday landscape. Peter Goin's 1987 photoessay, *Tracing the Line: A Photographic Survey of the Mexican/American Border*, scrupulously catalogued the entire length of the border, and exposed many of the fence's vulnerabilities in the process. Other well-known photographers of the border such as Don Bartletti, Douglas Kent Hall, Jay Dusard, Max Aguilera-Hellweg, Jeff Wall, Susan Meiselas, and Sebastiao Salgado have used the fence in their photographic compositions, often to foreground interactions between Mexicans and Anglos.[21] The Border Art Workshop/Taller de Arte Fronterizo (BAW/TAF) of San Diego/Tijuana often highlights border conflict and collaboration in installations and performances featuring chain-link. In BAW/TAF installations dating from the mid-1980s, the chain-link fence appeared as a Moebius strip, as an object of contemplation for "disinterested" spectators, and as constituting the very body of the *alambrista*.[22] The chain-link fence was set ablaze on the cover of BAW/TAF's 1991 catalogue, and stood amidst a garbage-strewn wasteland on the cover of Terry Allen's 1992 catalogue for *a simple story (Juarez)*.[23]

Together, the fence and the river have played an important role in the way that maps of the North American continent have been drawn in this century. During the U.S. militarization of the border at the time of the Mexican Revolution, the continent of North America was anthropomorphized through visual gags in which Mexico became the lower body joined to the United States as the upper body, while the borderline served as a geographical waistline.[24] In the NAFTA era, one essayist recast these hierarchical territories as a "Freudian map," in which Canada was the superego, the United States was the ego, and Mexico was the unconscious.[25] Guillermo Gómez-Peña's 1985 poem (revised 1995) entitled "Freefalling toward a Borderless Future" drew a similar map in which the gonads once again fell to Mexico:

Standing on the map of my political desires
I toast to a borderless future
(*I raise my glass of wine toward the moon*)
with...
our Alaskan hair
our Canadian head
our US torso
our Mexican genitalia
our Central American cojones
our Caribbean sperm
our South American legs ...[26]

According to Rolando J. Romero, the association of Mexico with the lower body is still very prevalent in contemporary U.S. popular culture, as in the double entendre of Taco Bell's advertising slogan, "Make a run for the border." The command is ambivalent, invoking at once stereotypes of Mexico as filthy and unsafe, while also urging U.S. consumers to liberate their repressed oral and anal erotic drives through sampling Taco Bell's cuisine.[27] Romero illustrates his argument with a lengthy passage from Joseph Wambaugh's police novel *Lines and Shadows*, in which the border is described as the point where the United States and Mexico meet one another "asshole to asshole." In this passage, *indocumentados* passing from Mexico to the United States through a drainage pipe are referred to as "turds," and the flow of human beings back and forth between the countries is compared to diarrhea.[28]

Such scatological imagery comes up repeatedly when any number of invasions from the south are discussed in U.S. media. The image of Mexico as lower body is in turn associated with Mexico's food and drinking water, and with the much publicized pollution that plagues the Rio Grande/Río Bravo and border *acequias* in recent years.[29] These tropes have also been taken up by some border writers and videographers in order to denounce the underlying political and economic factors that foster disease and poverty in Mexico. Images of shit, death, and organic waste, for example, are recurrent in the work of Luis Alberto Urrea, a San Diego/Tijuana-based journalist and activist, whose two chronicles of life among Tijuana's poorest residents, *Across the Wire* and *By the Lake of Sleeping Children*, have done much to call attention to issues of social justice in the border region.[30] Urrea's compassion for the people about whom he writes is counterbalanced by a hard-boiled, often dryly humorous prose and lack of sentimentality in his depiction of daily life on the border.

His frequent asides to the reader and foregrounding of his role as translator to non-Spanish speakers clearly indicate that he writes for a U.S.-based audience that knows little about this world and can be ruffled by descriptions such as this one of a sign in a bathroom at a Tijuana orphanage:

PLEASE DON'T SHIT ON THE FLOOR / PLEASE DON'T WIPE YOUR ASS WITH YOUR FINGERS / PLEASE DON'T WIPE YOUR FINGERS ON THE WALL.

Ancient brown fingerprints and smears angle away from this notice, trailing to faint shadow. They look like paintings of comets, of fireworks.[31]

In a more self-conscious and historically oriented manner than Urrea's writing, Debbie Nathan's essay, "Love in the Time of Cholera: Waiting for Free Trade," examines the erotic and repulsive fascination with the Rio Grande/Río Bravo; the author associates the spread of contagion northward with the spread of free trade southward.[32] Nathan, an El Paso–based journalist and activist, intricately weaves vignettes detailing the response to free trade on the part of journalists, health, and business professionals.[33] The framing narrative is about the author's relationship with Perla, a fruit vendor from Juárez who, over the course of her four-year relationship with the author, has developed the propensity to interrupt Nathan and her husband during their moments of love-making. This time Perla seeks Nathan out because her son Chuyito has been sick for days with diarrhea. "Can this be the famous cholera?" Perla asks Nathan.

Throughout the essay, Nathan foregrounds her own relative advantage in the transactions she makes with Perla—loans that will never be repaid, limes and avocados bought from Perla to garnish tonight's supper, an old washing machine that finds a new home in Perla's one-room, cinder-block house built at the foot of a TV antenna on a Juárez hillside. Perhaps most important of these transactions in terms of this essay is the service that Perla performs as Nathan's informant and guide. At one point, Nathan decides to make the daily crossing with Perla from Juárez to El Paso. The women change clothes behind bushes before entering the river. Nathan writes,

We all scooted behind thorny bushes and weeds to change, and immediately I noticed that among the bushes, human and animal urine and feces were everywhere. I hopped around barefoot, trying to avoid them. It was impossible. I felt nauseous. I wanted to wash but the river was no relief. A rat floated past. We crossed, discarded our rags, then ran across I-10. I was wild with fear for the children. We made it, though, then entered a wet sewer tunnel, bent over like crones, stumbling through the dark. Someone spotted a light and we climbed up through the hole. Suddenly we were in my neighborhood.[34]

When Nathan's essay was published in January 1993, cholera had arrived on the border, and NAFTA was soon to follow. According to the author, by that time every acequia in Juárez had tested positive for the cholera bacterium.[35] Nathan's essay is an attempt to show how the transformations that have taken place along the border in recent decades might be registered through an experimental and fragmented writing style.[36] The border-crossing passage, nevertheless, is central to the essay. It enables the author to link the social conditions of Perla's Juárez to those of Nathan's El Paso, and this experience provokes the narrator to think through the relationships of individual actors within a global economic system. For me, Nathan's essay serves as a bridge between the visual strategies taken up by the border artists discussed previously and the didactic impulse of videos about the border produced by grassroots organizations.

## SPIN-OFFS OF THE FENCE AND THE RIVER: VIDEOS OF THE NAFTA ERA

Benedict Anderson proposes that the representation of a world in which spatially dispersed events occur simultaneously and yet are causally related to one another is concomitant with the consolidation of national literatures. He bases this idea upon his theorization of literate citizens as individuals bound to a given geographical unit through their mutual relationship of horizontal fraternal comradeship.[37] Nathan ironically appeals to a conceptual framework similar to that of Anderson's nation in her essay, but she does so in order to imagine a very different community: her border is at once international and a local space, and her relationship with Perla is not based on the solidarity of male citizens but rather on the uneven economic relations of female neighbors. The spatial and social contiguity of border metropolises like El Paso/Juárez makes them a logical place from which to imagine such cross-border alliances and to question nationalist projects.

In the last decade, however, the impulse to organize across borders has been emanating from other parts of North America as well, spurred on by resistance to the 1989 U.S.–Canada Free Trade Agreement (USCFTA) and, more recently, to NAFTA. Cathryn Thorup of the Center for U.S.–Mexican Studies has described the 1990s as a new era of U.S.–Mexico relations in which

> it is possible that conflict may become more class-, issue-, and interest-based [rather] than bilateral in nature. Instead of "U.-S." interests facing off against "Mexican" interests on a given issue, a constellation of U.S. and Mexican interest groups will confront an opposing constellation of U.S. and Mexican interest groups.[38]

As the decade draws to an end, Thorup's prediction for increasing transnational organization describes the path taken by many nongovernmental organizations, labor, ethnic, and single-issue movements in the United States and Mexico. Transnationalism, however, has not completely superseded the bilateral model of conflict and resolution.

International organization on the part of progressive and grassroots organizations is a necessary response to transnational capital's flight to Mexico and other low-wage havens in the wake of the world financial crisis of the 1970s. This flight witnessed businesses recycling strategies that were already quite familiar on a domestic level, such as outsourcing, heightened division of skilled and unskilled labor, and tiered wage scales. The old technique of whipsawing—that is, pitting the laborers of one plant against those of another in order to force wage cuts[39]—has crossed national borders, so that capital easily mobilizes racist and nationalist rhetoric to turn labor forces against one another, rather than against their employers. In order to resist these developments, activists themselves face the challenge of building geographically dispersed networks.

Both labor and management increasingly use video as an organizing tool in these struggles because of its relatively low cost and accessibility, and its ability to reach illiterate audiences across linguistic boundaries. In its most promising manifestations the turn toward video has permitted workers on both sides of the U.S.–Mexico border to become producers of their own narratives and to forge ties with workers in other locations.[40] Throughout the continent, over forty documentary videos (and some films) about NAFTA and border issues have been produced in the last twenty years, and many more continue to be made. Their producers are independent documentarists, educators, labor unions, and religious, environmental, and women's groups, many of whom are affiliated with trinational coalitions.

As with border art, this body of videos may be seen as symptomatic of a growing interest in the border region and NAFTA rather than as evidence of a unified movement. Although the works often share common visual and rhetorical strategies, significant differences exist among them in terms of production, distribution, and consumption. The videos range in production values from slick, high-budget documentaries that have aired on public television to short subjects intended for church and union-hall viewing. Their scope, too, varies from those like *The Global Assembly Line*, which present a systematic analysis of transformations in the global economy,[41] to shorts such as *What's the Cost of Your Blouse?*, an eighteen-minute video narrated entirely through still photographs, that recounts three local struggles among workers in San Francisco, El Paso, and Nogales, Sonora.[42]

It is important to distinguish among the political histories of these videos, including their sources of funding and the activities and orientation of their creators, a subject that goes beyond the scope of this chapter. Briefly, some of the videos document "solidarity visits" to Mexico by U.S. and Canadian delegations, while others result from long-term activist projects in the border region. This distinction loosely corresponds to historical markers, also. While the videos produced prior to NAFTA's passage tend to refer to the border in the context of binational politics, more recent productions often chronicle campaigns by border activist groups regarding specific issues such as labor, the environment, and immigration. My comments focus primarily on the preNAFTA videos. The year 1994 marks an important watershed for these productions because it was an election year in Mexico. The videos produced prior to this date support a continental political program that favors the Partido de la Revolución Democrática (PRD), liberal U.S. Democrats, and the Canadian Liberal Party, and opposes Salinas de Gortari, Reagan, Bush, Clinton, and Mulroney. The 1994 PRD presidential candidate Cuauhtémoc Cárdenas (currently Regente of Mexico City) in particular emerges as a potential savior of Mexico from total colonization by the United States. The conclusion of Dermot and Carla Begley's *Mexico: For Sale* presents an extreme example of this position. The closing sequence features a medium close-up of Cárdenas in slow motion as he makes his way through a crowd of followers, and then cuts to a close-up of Emiliano Zapata's face as the last lines of the "Corrido de Libre Comercio" drift by: "Ándale prietita, hay que zapatear / Que si no hay comercio siempre en Mexico es igual" ("Go on little dark girl, you have to dance / If there's no trade, it's still the same in Mexico").[43]

Unfortunately, many of the videos find it difficult to escape the restrictive binary logic of mainstream NAFTA debates in which free trade and protectionism were posed as the only two alternatives for citizens in all three countries. Instead they combine populist elements of both of these options in rather contradictory fashions. This ambiguous political stance is particularly true of the Canadian productions and certain U.S. productions embraced by the mainstream labor movement. The videos marshal international solidarity across borders in the interest of establishing a mutually beneficial nationalism that would ultimately leave borders firmly in place and pressure runaway shops located on the border to come "home." Bruce Campbell, a former research analyst for the Canadian Labor Congress, summarizes this sort of "friendly protectionism" when he argues that

> a different arrangement [from NAFTA] would have to attach *primacy to the rights of national development over the rights of transnational corporations*. It would have to foster upward convergence of social and environmental standards instead of a … dynamic which pits worker against worker, community against community [emphasis mine].[44]

All of these videos base their forecasts about NAFTA in part upon an interpretation of the U.S.–Mexico border region. One filmmaker, determined to make an objective documentary about NAFTA, told me that it was much easier for him to find articulate anti-NAFTA spokespersons for his film than pro-NAFTA ones, because the anti-NAFTA side could draw upon thirty years of documentation about the Border Industrialization Program to back up its arguments.[45] Many of the videos dramatize delegations from the United States and Canada making "fact-finding" trips to border maquiladoras and *colonias* in order to better understand economic transformations in their own regions. No matter what local struggles these videos address, they share a common tendency to portray the U.S.–Mexico border as a prototype for the future economic development of the continent.

Primitivo Rodríguez of the American Friends Service Committee outlines this perspective succinctly in the documentary *Leaving Home*: "What we witness at the border is what we will see more and more all over the place, so the border is in a sense one of the greatest, nearest laboratories of what the future might provide."[46] Although Rodríguez makes his comment within the context of border environmental activism, his words echo those of people in academic disciplines such as cultural studies who, like Néstor García Canclini, have found in the border region "uno de los mayores laboratorios de la posmodernidad" ("one of the greatest laboratories of postmodernity").[47] The laboratory metaphor signals a certain intellectual frame of reference belonging to many academic think tanks that have mushroomed in the border region in the last thirty years with emphases on quantitative social scientific research and public policy formulation. San Diego–based artist David Avalos noted with some irony in his essay contributed to the *La Frontera* catalogue that it took the foundation of two high-profile research institutions, the University of California's Center for U.S.–Mexican Studies in San Diego and the Tijuana-based Colegio de la Frontera Norte, to bring border issues to the attention of a wider public.[48]

By appropriating the border-as-laboratory image, the videos replicate the observer/observed dynamic of much traditional documentary cinema, in which the testimony of local witnesses is mediated through "expert" talking heads, and both of these in turn are subsumed by a voice-over narrator's authoritative commentary. Often in their ambitious attempt to establish a "North American" oppositional language about labor and environmental abuses, the videos portray the border region as the worst-case scenario. Humanitarian arguments about fair trade and "what's best for Mexicans" are intercut with imagery that depicts the Mexican side of the border as abject. At times, the voyeurism of U.S. and Canadian observers in these narratives panders to sensationalism, as in Repeal the Deal Productions' *We Can Say No!* in which a delegate from Canada recounts through melodramatic voice-over that on a "fact-finding" trip to the border,

> we saw a lagoon of black, bubbling toxic waste created from open dumping by a group of corporations in an industrial park. We followed it to where it met up with an open ditch full of untreated raw sewage and to where this toxic soup ran into what was a small river, past squatters' camps, where children covered in open sores drank Pepsi Cola out of baby bottles.[49]

Rarely is a native of the upper or middle class (save Salinas) seen in these videos; Mexico is most often personified in stock shots of the "poor but dignified people."

As in the work of the artists discussed previously, the videos foreground the river and the fence to distinguish Mexican territory from that of the United States, along with a host of clichéd auxiliary signifiers such as national flags, musical motifs, cowboy hats versus sombreros, and so on. But the videos also introduce two second-tier icons related to the fence and the river, namely, the corporate fence and *aguas negras* (waste water or sewage). The international fence and the Rio Grande/Río Bravo demarcate national space, while the latter two signifiers divide *colonias* from maquiladoras on the Mexican sides of border cities. In many of these videos, the distinction between national and corporate boundary lines collapses altogether, or the importance of national borders becomes secondary to the boundaries of factories and industrial parks. In *Leaving Home*, for example, a highly compressed image superimposes the names of *Fortune 500* companies doing business in Mexico against a background of chain-link fence, through which one can see one of the international bridges connecting Mexico and the United States.

The chain-link fence is also a focal point where ambivalence about continental solidarity becomes manifest. In the case of the NAFTA videos, corporate fences come to figure prominently in the narratives for very obvious practical reasons. Camera crews—especially anti-NAFTA ones—are not generally permitted to film inside maquiladoras, so the videographers shoot the outside of the factory through the fence, or they interview workers from a particular plant against the fence in front of their place of employment.[50] At any rate, shooting the corporate compounds of such familiar names as Zenith, Ford, and Green Giant as though they were fortresses or citadels puts U.S. spectators in the rather ironic position of constantly gazing at a U.S.-identified space from which they are barred access, while being situated in a space coded by the video as being "Mexican." This dynamic is particularly evident in a video entitled *Stepan Chemical: The Poisoning of a Mexican Community*, distributed by the San Antonio–based Coalition for Justice in the Maquiladoras, and produced by Ed Feigen of the AFL-CIO.[51] (This is the same video that Ross Perot brandished before Al Gore in order to shame the "environmentalist" vice president in the November 1993 NAFTA debate.) *Stepan Chemical* is an exposé about groundwater contamination in a Matamoros *colonia* called Privada Uniones by a manufacturing plant of the U.S.–owned Stepan Chemical Company. The plant literally borders the homes of Privada Uniones residents, and has been blamed for an epidemic of health problems including anencephaly, a birth defect which causes babies to be born without brains.[52] The camera work illustrates the proximity of the two spaces constantly, through rack focus, high-angle pans taken from rooftops that sweep from factory to *colonia*, and hidden camera footage of illegal toxic waste dumping by Stepan, shot through chain-link fence from the backyards of Privada Uniones homes. About halfway through the video, the camera cuts to a high-contrast still of the Stepan fence with the menacing subtitle, "El Lado Oscuro de la Frontera" ("The Dark Side of the Border"). Playing with a language familiar to U.S. audiences, where the border is often portrayed as seamy and lawless, the Stepan Chemical video suggests that the dark side of the border is to be found within the plant's boundaries and back in Chicago, where Stepan Chemical portrays itself as a company with a conscience, and the Stepan family is active in Democratic Party politics and philanthropic causes.

The videos do not always portray corporate citadels as impregnable. Cinefocus Canada's video *NAFTA: Playing with a Volatile Substance* and the American Labor Education Center's *$4 a Day? No Way!* both feature footage of plant occupations, in which workers are shown dancing, cheering, and decorating the fences that surround their factories.[53] The latter video is about a movement on the part of Mexican workers at Ford's Cuautitlán plant to disaffiliate from the *oficialista* Confederación de Trabajadores Mexicanos (CTM) and to elect their own union representatives. When CTM-hired thugs dressed in Ford uniforms showed up at the plant on January 8, 1990, they shot ten Ford workers, killing one, Cleto Nigmo. The video's theme of "extending hands across borders" refers to the trinational organizing efforts in the automotive industry undertaken by progressive elements within the U.S., Canadian, and Mexican labor movements in the wake of Nigmo's murder.

As with the fence imagery, the videos demonstrate considerable compression between images of the Rio Grande/Río Bravo and those of the *aguas negras*, or raw sewage flowing from border industries and *colonias*. Along certain stretches of the border, as in Ciudad Juárez, a concrete waste water canal runs parallel to the river channel itself. Almost all of the NAFTA videos feature a segment on environmental degradation of the border region, and others make environmental issues their focal point. One of these, entitled *Dirty Business: Food Exports to the United States*, is quite well-known and received an award at the 1991 National Educational Film and Video Festival.[54]

The framing narrative of the documentary depicts a middle-class couple in a U.S. supermarket selecting some broccoli. The narrator's voice-over introduction questions whether U.S. consumers really know where their food comes from. Then the film cuts to a shot of child laborers on the back of a cabbage truck in Irapuato, Guanajuato, in southern Mexico, where Birdseye, Green Giant, and other food companies have relocated much of their frozen vegetable empires, in order to take advantage of the long growing season and cheap wages. By the documentary's close, we learn that these companies use *aguas negras* to irrigate their crops, along with a great deal of information about child labor, diarrhea and parasites, slaughterhouse run-off, and other problems endemic to Irapuato.

*Dirty Business* subtly concludes twice: first, with a voice-over statement addressed to "everyone," and second, with another addressed to paranoid U.S. consumers. The narrator states that protections for children and the environment, decent wages and living conditions, and safe, clean food should be basic rights for everyone," as the film returns the viewer to the supermarket of the opening sequence and continues, "As multinational companies continue exporting from this polluted environment, consumers may well wonder about the quality, safety, and social costs of food production in Mexico."

*Dirty Business* stems from the context of nearly a decade of labor struggles taking place in Watsonville, California, the "frozen food capital of the United States," around the issues of wage cuts and job relocation on the part of the big food processors. In contrast to other NAFTA videos that concentrate on job loss among Anglo and African-American workers in the U.S. manufacturing sector, the Watsonville workers are primarily Mexicans and Chicanos/as with very close ties to Mexican communities in the United States and Mexico. The video is the result of a solidarity visit to Irapuato on the part of Watsonville's frozen food and canning workers, who found it difficult at the time to forge an extensive network because their Mexican counterparts had no union.[55] *Dirty Business* missed a potentially interesting angle in declining to explore the equivocal position that Chicanos/as occupied throughout the NAFTA debates: pitted against Mexicans for relatively low-wage and labor-intensive jobs, on the one hand, and promoted as a vital link in cross-border organizing efforts, on the other.[56]

The narrative of *Dirty Business* never reflects upon its own production history, and perhaps this is one reason why organized labor found it easy to endorse the video in its efforts to lobby Congress for its "Buy American" protectionist agenda. In early November 1993, right before the NAFTA vote, I was residing in Milwaukee, and my Congressman, Jerry Kleczka, sent a newsletter to me featuring a still photograph and a case study lifted straight from the video. "I just can't seem to get the picture you see on this page out of my mind," he wrote. "This is the Jolly Green Giant—or Gigante Verde—a symbol of the forces at work luring American companies south of the border."[57] In this broader U.S. context, the three-way metonymical association that the video draws among Mexican labor, Mexican products, and *aguas negras* becomes very striking, as it once again invokes scatological images of Mexico culled from popular stereotypes. Ross Perot, who as I have noted was also influenced by an anti-NAFTA video, made this association in his inimitable way during the NAFTA debate:

> When you look . . . at the man who works for Zenith in Mexico and you compare him to his counterpart who works for Zenith in the United States, this poor man makes $8.50 a day. You know what his dream is? To someday have an outhouse. Do you know what his big dream is? To someday have running water.[58]

## BORDER TRAFFIC: PEOPLE, GOODS, IDEAS

During the 1992 U.S. election campaigns, fear of Mexican immigration to the United States was invoked by both Democrats and Republicans, who resorted to coded (and at times explicit) racism in order both to justify and to denounce NAFTA. In the media coverage of NAFTA prior to the Congressional vote in November 1993, free-trade proponents argued that exporting low-wage jobs to Mexico would keep Mexicans from "stealing" U.S. jobs, while protectionists simply wanted to dig trenches and build walls to keep Mexicans out.[59] As I have argued in the case of *Dirty Business*, however, fear of immigrants is only one example of a larger phenomenon, for there is considerable anxiety in the United States about *anything* identified as Mexican crossing the border.

In her essay "Passports," Susan Buck-Morss traces this ambivalence about borders and migrants to medieval European anxieties about the plague, which through the centuries became mapped onto modern industrial demands for cheap migrant labor. The precursor to the visa, according to Buck-Morss, was the *pestpass*, which permitted healthy people to enter communities during epidemics. Passports have their origin in the same era, when they were developed as a means of controlling military desertion. Buck-Morss writes,

> In the application of this ideology [associating aliens with contamination] to control migrant labor, there emerges most clearly the structural contradiction which is inherent in the modern age: Throughout the process of industrialization, capital has needed a highly mobile labor force, and the more docile and submissive the better. Increasingly, as labor has organized to resist exploitation, an absolutely crucial source of supply has been foreign migrants whose precarious status as non-citizens has made them willing to accept whatever the conditions or wages they are given.[60]

Buck-Morss goes on to argue that passports really took on their present form after World War I, as fear of communist revolution within industrialized nations that had ethnically and racially diverse labor forces, like the United States, arose among capitalist classes. One strategy of President Wilson and the League of Nations was to make Bolshevism, an international movement, seem like a national movement through the creation of formal border apparatuses. Buck-Morss explains that this transformation was achieved through a dissimulation of sorts:

> By creating a place of passport control and a practice of passing through it, it gave the appearance that state boundaries were substantive, that they really existed— that a particular state apparatus "owned" a part of the world, in the same way that a private citizen [owned] his home, a capitalist his business, a farmer his field, a person his or her own body—except that the state owned all of these first.[61]

The invention of borders as we now know them paved the way for the deportation and persecution of workers in the United States who expressed "foreign" ideas, such as communism and anarchism. In Buck-Morss's words, "Class warfare was recast as international warfare. This was the legacy of Versailles."[62] It bears remembering that another backdrop of the Peace Conference in Versailles, from the North American perspective, was the Mexican Revolution, which not only threatened extensive U.S. and European investments in Mexico, but also marked the first large-scale exodus of poor Mexican immigrants to the United States. During this period, Mexicans joined Chinese as "undesirable aliens" entering the United States from Mexico, and precursors to the Border Patrol were established as federal institutions separate from the Immigration Service (now the Immigration and Naturalization Service). A 1919 anecdote from the biography of Jeff Milton, one of the Border Patrol's early heroic figures, illustrates the extent to which the origin and mission of today's Border Patrol arose from an interpretation of borders as both physical and ideological barriers. While serving as a Mounted Chinese Inspector for the Immigration Service in the Arizona/Sonora desert, Milton was told to report immediately to Ellis Island where he was charged with guarding Emma Goldman, Alexander Berkman, and "247 more alien radicals who were so sure that Revolutionary Russia was the promised land." He eventually escorted them by boat to Hangö, Finland, before returning to duty in Arizona.[63]

Citing empirical evidence, economist Paul Krugman challenges the notion that the state and private property can be conflated through an analogical model. He begins his book about the fashion of pseudo-economic theory in the era of free trade, *Pop Internationalism*, with a criticism of the Clinton administration's rhetoric of "competitiveness" among nations. Such a claim, argues Krugman, rests upon a facile assumption that both nations and corporations play a zero-sum game. Krugman counters, "The bottom line for a corporation is literally its bottom line: if a corporation cannot afford to pay its workers, suppliers, and bondholders, it will go out of business." He continues, "Countries, on the other hand, do not go out of business. They may be happy or unhappy with their economic performance, but they have no well-defined bottom line."[64] The willingness of many prominent politicians, advisers, academics, and voters to believe such rhetoric, nevertheless, suggests that the state puts on a rather convincing show of masquerading as a corporation. If borders are one example of the state's attempt to dissimulate private property, then one could view the NAFTA-era border establishing shots as exposing a type of capitalist spatial organization that has been fundamental to the existence of the border apparatus in the modern era. The NAFTA videos foreground the latent duality of borders, which would cast them at once as the communal property of the body politic and as the domain of a state that regulates ("owns") the movement of its citizens. Instead of showing a brief establishing shot of a single border, the videos create a spatial patchwork of fences and rivers traversing the border region and dividing "foreign" from "local," and "workers" from "factories."[65] The spatial dispersal of national boundaries and their diminished presence vis-à-vis transnational capital along the U.S.–Mexico border does not indicate that the nation-state is defunct, as those who have noted the implementation of immigration blockades along the border will attest. But it may mean that nation-states will work in tandem with capital to enforce a division of labor even among different borders.

While the U.S.–Mexico border became increasingly industrialized in the early 1990s, the Mexico-Guatemala border was apparently selected as the avant-"rear-garde" of U.S. immigration control. The Mexican government reported that in 1993 it deported a record number of Central Americans (deportations financed in part by U.S. funds), while the U.S. Immigration and Naturalization Service sent its own agents to train the Guatemalan police. In the words of a priest who aids refugees on the Mexico-Guatemala border: "Tecún Umán [Guatemalan border city] has been converted into a hell, where everything you can imagine is permitted. . . . There is prostitution, alcoholism, drug addiction, money laundering."[66] Another priest states, "There are more [human rights] violations here in one day than there are in a year [on the U.S.–Mexico border]."[67] The "old border" establishing shots of Terry Allen's sets have not disappeared; they have simply become the "new border" establishing shots farther south.

## NOTES

1. V. I. Lenin, quoted in Neil Smith, *Uneven Development: Nature, Capital and the Production of Space*, 88.

2. The characters are introduced as follows. Sailor: "A Texas boy/Just returned from duty/With the navy in the Pacific/On leave in the port of San Diego"; Spanish Alice: "A Mexican prostitute/Working the bars in Tijuana/And looking for ways/into the USA"; Jabo: "A Juarez-born pachuco/Living in Los Angeles/Decides to go home/By way of a joy ride/Up into southern Colorado"; and Chic Blundie: "Jabo's L.A. girlfriend/An enigma/Rock-writer/And occasionally . . . Jabo himself" (Terry Allen, *a simple story (Juarez)*, 7].

3. Sarah Rogers-Lafferty, "Afterword," in Allen, *simple story*, 77.

4. Rosetta Brooks, "From the Middle of Nowhere: Terry Allen's Badlands," 86.

5. "The Perfect Ship" has a white mannequin inside of it, and the video projected in that set is a long-take of a woman's legs as she walks across the bridge from the United States into Mexico.

6. Allen, *simple story*, 6.

7. Patricio Chávez and Madeleine Grynsztejn, *La Frontera/The Border: Art about the Mexico/United States Border Experience*, 38. In her catalogue essay, Grynsztejn acknowledges the work of several important artists who were conspicuously absent from the show.

8. See Sally Yard, ed., *inSITE94: A Binational Exhibition of Installation and Site-Specific Art*, and *inSITE 94 Guide*, and Danielle Reo, ed., *inSITE 97 Guide*. The first *inSITE* exhibition featured local artists; the second featured artists from around the globe. The third seems to strive for a balance of sorts between the previous two shows; it features artists from North and South America and the Caribbean.

9. George Yúdice, "The Cultural Impact of Free Trade in the United States," unpublished ms. (March 1995), 27. Forthcoming as a chapter in *We Are Not the World: Identity and Representation in an Age of Global Restructuring* (Durham: Duke University Press).

10. A few examples of such exhibitions include *The Decade Show: Frameworks of Identity in the 1980s* (New York: Museum of Contemporary Hispanic Art, The New Museum of Contemporary Art, and the Studio Museum in Harlem, 1990); *Art of the Other Mexico: Sources and Meanings* (Chicago: Mexican Fine Arts Center Museum, 1993); *Chicano Art: Resistance and Affirmation, 1965–1985* (Los Angeles: Wight Art Gallery, UCLA, 1991); *Mito y magia en las Américas: Los ochenta* (Monterrey: Museo de Arte Contemporáneo de Monterrey, 1991); *About Place: Recent Art of the Americas* (Chicago: The Art Institute of Chicago, 1995); and *1993 Festival of American Folklife, July 1–July 5* (Washington, DC: Smithsonian Institution, 1993). Lucy R. Lippard's book *Mixed Blessings: New Art in a Multicultural America* is also an important early contribution to this current.

11. Paul J. Vanderwood and Frank N. Samponaro, *Border Fury*.

12. *Chulas Fronteras*, dir. Les Blanc; Aristeo Brito, *The Devil in Texas/El diablo en Texas*.

13. On Aztlán, see Rudolfo Anaya and Francisco Lomelí, eds., *Aztlán: Essays on the Chicano Homeland*; and Carlos Muñoz, Jr., *Youth, Identity, Power: The Chicano Movement*. On the Borderlands, see Héctor Calderón and José David Saldívar, eds., *Criticism in the Borderlands: Studies in Chicano Literature, Culture, and Ideology*; and Gloria Anzaldúa, *Borderlands/La Frontera: The New Mestiza*.

14. Néstor García Canclini, *Cultural híbridas: Estrategias para entrar y salir de la modernidad*, 300.

15. Richard Griswold del Castillo, Teresa McKenna, and Yvonne Yarbro-Bejarano, eds., *Chicano Art: Resistance and Affirmation, 1965–1985*, flysheets, 248, 256.

16. Griswold del Castillo et al., eds., *Chicano Art*, 35, 255.

17. Griswold del Castillo et al., eds., *Chicano Art*, 49, 286. In the early 1970s, ASCO entered into polemics with certain Chicano/a artists who favored the revival of Aztec and pre-Columbian myth as subject matter for their work; ASCO in contrast preferred to refashion the contemporary visual languages of mass media, urban street life, and popular culture that they found in their native East Los Angeles.

Another founding member of ASCO, Harry Gamboa, Jr., has used the chain-link motif in the post-ASCO years. The climactic scene of his 1993 video, *L.A. Familia*, which deals with the disintegration of a Chicano family in Los Angeles, is staged on a chain-link enclosed pedestrian bridge spanning an eight-lane freeway. The video was included in the exhibition "Identity and Home" (Museum of Modern Art, New York, 8 November 1993–9 January 1994).

18. Roberto Rodríguez, "(Barbed) Wired for Controversy"; Nancy Traver, "NM, Artist, University Divided over Sculpture Topped with Wire."

19. For the record, many fencing materials are currently in use on the U.S.–Mexico border. They include barbed wire, chain-link, metal webbing, wire cable, and steel-reinforced concrete. Newer barriers that have increasingly been implemented in the past five to ten years are drainage ditches and corrugated steel walls constructed from

military surplus landing mats. As pressure from U.S. nativist groups and the fencing proposals of right-wing politicians Pat Buchanan and Newt Gingrich have gained
momentum, more imposing fencing materials are found in urban and densely crossed
zones. So far the areas affected are San Diego/Tijuana, Tecate, Calexico/Mexicali, San
Luis Río Colorado, Nogales, Douglas, and Naco, and a fence is currently being erected
in Sunland Park/Anapra. The passage of the Illegal Immigration Reform and Immigrant Responsibility Act of 1996 calls for constructing second and third fences behind
the main fence in San Diego/Tijuana.

See James S. Griffith, "The Arizona-Sonora Border: Line, Region, Magnet, Filter";
Peter Goin, "Following the Line: The Mexico-American Border"; People Against the
Wall, *People against the Wall, El Paso, TX, Sunland Park, NM and Anapra, Chih.*, unpub-
lished ms., 1996 (available from Border Rights Coalition, El Paso); and Marisa J. Demco,
"Bolstering INS Enforcement."

20. *A Conversation with Terry Allen and Dave Hickey*, video.

21. For work of this type by Bartletti, see the Oakland Museum, *Between Two Worlds:
The People of the Border, Photographs by Don Bartletti*; for Hall, see Douglas Kent Hall,
*The Border: Lift on the Line*; and Allen, *simple story*; for Dusard, see Alan Weisman, *La
Frontera: The United States Border with Mexico*; for Aguilera-Hellweg, see Museum of
Contemporary Hispanic Art et al., *Decade Show*, 56–57, plate 1; for Salgado's, see Sal-
gado, "The Border." Jeff Wall's photos were featured in the exhibition *About Place* at
the Art Institute of Chicago and in a solo exhibition at the Museum of Contemporary
Art, Chicago, both in 1995. Susan Meiselas's unpublished photoessay is titled "The
U.S.-Mexico Border" (1990).

22. I refer to the installations "Border Realities III," February 1987; "Fence Border
line boundary," January 1987; and "Aztep," February 1986. These are illustrated in Jeff
Kelley, ed. of English text, *The Border Art Workshop (BAW/TAF), 1984–1989*, 26, 43, 27.

23. BAW/TAF, *Tallér de Arte Fronterízo, 1984–1991*, cover.

24. For several examples of political cartoons anthropomorphizing the continents
of North and South America, see George Black, *The Good Neighbor*.

25. Morris Berman, "Shadow across the Rio Grande," 90.

26. Guillermo Gómez-Peña, *The New World Border*, 2–3. *Cojones* means "balls."

27. Rolando J. Romero, "Border of Fear, Border of Desire," 38.

28. Joseph Wambaugh, quoted in Romero, "Border of Fear," 37–38.

29. Bruce Selcraig, "Poisonous Flows the Rio Grande."

30. Luis Alberto Urrea, *Across the Wire: Life and Hard Times on the Mexican Border*, and
*By the Lake of Sleeping Children: The Secret Life of the Mexican Border*.

31. Urrea, *Lake of Sleeping Children*, 70. Urrea also quotes from Wambaugh's novel
(6).

32. Debbie Nathan, "Love in the Time of Cholera: Waiting for Free Trade."

33. Nathan relocated to San Antonio in 1998.

34. Nathan, "Love," 15.

35. Nathan, "Love," 12.

36. Debbie Nathan, personal interviews, fall 1992.

37. Benedict Anderson, *Imagined Communities: Reflections on the Origin and Spread of
Nationalism*.

38. Cathryn Thorup, "The Politics of Free Trade and the Dynamics of Cross-Border
Coalitions in U.S.-Mexican Relations," 15.

39. Kim Moody and Mary McGinn, *Unions and Free Trade: Solidarity vs. Competition*,
14–15.

40. Professor Fran Ansley, University of Tennessee College of Law and the Tennessee Industrial Renewal Network, personal interview, 10 September 1993; Professor
Fran Ansley, letter to the author, 17 June 1997. For further information on grassroots
video in Latin America, see *Media Development*, spec. issue, "Video for the People";

and Pat Aufderheide, "Film and Video in the Cultural Struggle of Latin America," and "Latin American Grassroots Video: Beyond Television."

Transnational corporations also use video as a means of communicating with their workers. In testimony delivered before the Trade Staff Policy Committee hearings in Atlanta, Georgia, Shirley Reinhardt, a former GE worker, recalled the company's treatment of its workers right before it initiated a period of massive layoffs: "At the same time the company was threatening us, they were also sweet-talking us. I especially remember the video they made which was shown to all the workers at the plant right before the time for the union election. The video showed a lot of local spots in Morristown. It was like they were trying to say how 'at home' the company was here in our little town, what a difference they made to the whole community. (And of course they *do* make a difference.) They had also gone around and taken photographs of every worker at the plant. When they finally showed the video to us, there we were up on the screen, each one a part of the picture. In fact, the video said that we were all a part of the 'GE Family.'" (Citizens Against Temporary Services, "Testimony Prepared for the Trade Staff Policy Committee, Office of the U.S. Trade Representative, Atlanta, Georgia, Thursday, August 29, 1991," unpublished ms. [available from the Tennessee Industrial Renewal Network], 3).

41. *The Global Assembly Line*, dir. Lorraine Gray.

42. *What's the Cost of Your Blouse?* dir. Sydney Brown and Betty McAfee.

43. *Mexico: For Sale*, dir. Dermot and Carla Begley.

44. Bruce Campbell, quoted in David Brooks, "The Search for Counterparts," 95.

45. Personal interview, 16 July 1993. The director preferred to remain anonymous.

46. *Leaving Home: A Road Trip into Our Free Trade Future*, prod. We Do the Work.

47. García Canclini, *Culturas híbridas*, 293.

48. Avalos writes, "The formation of these border laboratories was duly noted by the local media as academic events of international significance"; see David Avalos, "A Wag Dogging a Tale."

49. *We Can Say No!* dir. Mark Cameron.

50. Two documentaries broadcast on public television, *Global Assembly Line* and *Leaving Home*, as well as the BBC's *Mexico: For a Few Dollars More* evidently were able to shoot inside the maquiladoras; *Leaving Home* also features footage of the interior of a plant taken from a concealed, handheld video camera.

51. *Stepan Chemical: The Poisoning of a Mexican Community*, dir. Mark R. Day.

52. Stepan was one of ninety-two companies in the Brownsville/Matamoros area named in a lawsuit that was filed by twenty-seven families who had been affected by such birth defects. The case was finally settled out of court for an undisclosed sum in September 1995 ("Anencephaly Suit Settled, Many Questions Remain," 6).

53. *NAFTA: Playing with a Volatile Substance*, prod. Cinefocus Canada; *$4 a Day? No Way!* prod. American Labor Education Center.

54. *Dirty Business: Food Exports to the United States*, dir. Jon Silver. Though Irapuato is not on the border, it is interesting to note that as early as 1984 Paco Ignacio Taibo II had dubbed it a maquiladora town in his *Irapuato mi amor*.

55. Kim Moody, *An Injury to All*; Moody and McGinn, *Unions and Free Trade*, 48.

56. Several of the videos besides *Dirty Business*, such as *Leaving Home* and *What's the Cost of Your Blouse?* acknowledge the position of Mexican Americans in the North American economy, but do not engage in an analysis of their perspectives as U.S. citizens or residents.

57. Hon. Jerry Kleczka, "Special Report on NAFTA." The spin that Kleczka put on this video is difficult to distinguish from the anti–free trade campaign launched in 1997 by major produce growers and Republican Representative Sonny Bono. Bono proposed legislation called the Import Produce Labeling Act that would require all Mexican produce sold in the United States to be labeled as such. Florida growers produced

their own video entitled *The True Cost of Winter Vegetables*, which recurred to familiar images of waste water and raw sewage in Mexican agricultural areas (see "Video Evidence for Import Labeling Bill").

58. Ross Perot, quoted in "The NAFTA Debate."

59. The 1992 U.S. elections witnessed a strange spectrum of positions on NAFTA, which did not neatly correspond to party lines. The extreme right wing of the Republican Party, such as Pat Buchanan and David Duke (one of whom advocated building a great wall between the United States and Mexico, and the other of whom participated in a "Light Up the Border" vigilante photo-op), shared the protectionist camp with Ross Perot and "Rust Belt" and pro-labor Democrats, while the center left and center right of the two major parties tended to support NAFTA.

For an excellent overview of the U.S. political parties' stances on free trade, written from a liberal position, see Alan K. Henrikson, "A North American Community: 'From the Yukon to the Yucatan.'"

60. Susan Buck-Morss, "Passports," 68.

61. Buck-Morss, "Passports," 75.

62. Buck-Morss, "Passports," 77.

63. J. Evetts Haley, *Jeff Milton: A Good Man with a Gun*, 378–81. For a modern story emphasizing similar themes, see Debbie Nathan's essay on the deportation hearing of Margaret Randall entitled "Adjustment of Status: The Trial of Margaret Randall," 90–108.

64. Paul Krugman, *Pop Internationalism*, 6.

65. Moreover, this way of seeing boundaries carries over to the videos' portrayal of U.S. and Canadian space. A segment of *Leaving Home*, for example, charts the closure of a Zenith plant in Springfield, Missouri, and its subsequent relocation to Mexico. Shots of the plant taken from outside chain-link fence are coupled with this voice-over observation from John Piney, a former Zenith worker: "We can kind of relate to what's happening to us now because we took this work away from Chicago."

66. Quoted in Tracy Wilkinson, "Dreams Die on Mexico's Second Border," A10. The priest is Raúl Hernández of the Catholic Church's Episcopal Conference in Guatemala.

67. Quoted in Hayes Ferguson, "Seeking a Better Life—in Mexico," A10. The priest is Fr. Ademar Barilli.

# Lola Casanova: Tropes of *Mestizaje* and Frontiers of Race

## Robert McKee Irwin

On 23 February 1850, a young *criolla* beauty named Dolores Casanova was making the short trip along with some relatives from her hometown of Guaymas to Hermosillo by carriage. Although the travelers were armed and prepared for a possible attack, they were unable to defend themselves from an assault by Seri Indians. Tensions had been high recently between the Seris and the Mexicans, and such attacks were not out of the ordinary. On this occasion, a bloody battle resulted, in which many of the traveling party were killed. Several of the survivors were kidnapped by the Indians, among them lovely Lola Casanova. One of the leaders in the assault, the young Seri Coyote Iguana, was attracted to Dolores. While she did not return his affection immediately, he eventually won her over during her captivity. Not only did Lola consent to give up her comfortable life in Guaymas and stay with the primitive Seris but she also accepted Coyote Iguana's proposal for marriage. She later bore several of his children.

This legend, subject over the years to many variations, usually ends without Lola's return to Guaymas. Lola is something of an anti-Malinche, and her story is an alternative paradigm of *mestizaje* that goes against well-known national tropes. Its recasting of race relations in the borderlands is in fact so shocking that despite the originality and romantic appeal of the story, it has never gotten a foothold into the realm of national culture in Mexico. Not even in the borderlands has it been sanctioned as a major legend of regional identity.

On the other hand, although it may still provoke a certain degree of astonishment or repugnance in some, it continues to fascinate multiple audiences. Lola Casanova, over a century and a half later, remains a popular icon of Mexican borderlands culture, her legend playing out the region's deep-rooted racial tensions. More important, her story contests liberal idealizations of nineteenth-century Mexican culture that would close a blind eye to these

Robert McKee Irwin: "Lola Casanova: Tropes of *Mestizaje* and Frontiers of Race," first published as Chapter 3 of *Bandits, Captives, Heroines, and Saints: Cultural Icons of Mexico's Northwest Borderlands*. Minneapolis: University of Minnesota Press, 2007.

acute tensions that continued to provoke violence in the borderlands throughout the century.

## NATIONAL MYTHS OF *MESTIZAJE*:
## LOS HIJOS DE LA CHINGADA

*Mestizaje*, although not a popular identity trope in Sonora nor a central rallying point for Mexican national identity until after the revolution of 1910, was
gradually gaining acceptance in elite national culture in the second half of the
nineteenth century. By the turn of the century certainly, mixed-race Mexicans
were increasingly visible in Mexican national culture. However, *mestizaje* in
late-nineteenth-century Mexican literature followed a very limited range of
defining tropes to which the legend of Lola Casanova in no way conformed.

The first and most basic trope of *mestizaje* in Mexican cultural production
is that of the rape of Mexico by Spain. This encounter is typically represented
allegorically through the figures of Hernán Cortés and La Malinche (aka Malintzin or Doña Marina). She was the indigenous maiden originally given to
Cortés as a gift, who later would become his translator and lover. While on
the one hand this representation of interracial relations implies the violence of
armed conquest, with La Malinche being part of the spoils of war, on the other
hand, she has traditionally been seen as a traitor to Mexico for collaborating
with the enemy invaders. These interpretations are problematic, of course,
because Mexico did not exist as such prior to the conquest, nor did Malintzin
see herself as representing indigenous Mesoamericans as a whole. Indeed it
is hard to charge her with responsibility to any group since her own people
had betrayed her by giving her away as they would a jewel. Meanwhile, the
Aztecs, toward whose fall she did conspire, were in fact despised by many
indigenous peoples of Mesoamerica for their own imperialist aggressions.

Nonetheless, the representation of *mestizaje*, whether through La Malinche
or other figures, traditionally followed the same paradigm. The male partner
was white and the female indigenous. The female and her offspring were
then incorporated into white colonial (and later national) culture. Although
the new generation was not white, it was no longer exotically indigenous.[1]
La Malinche appears repeatedly in nineteenth-century novels. Interestingly,
the conquest of the Aztecs comes up as a theme first in Cuban, not Mexican,
literature. The New World's first historical novel, *Jicoténcal*, was published in
1826 in Philadelphia and was written probably by a Cuban, possibly Félix
Varela.[2] It featured two indigenous protagonists who become involved in
one way or another with Cortés: the traitor Doña Marina (his lover) and the
Tlaxcaltec heroine Teutila (the defiant object of his desire). Simultaneous with
the various romantic and erotic interactions between the Spaniards and the
Tlaxcaltecs and other indigenous Mesoamericans, there occurs a series of debates among the Tlaxcaltecs that result in their ultimate collaboration with
the Spaniards, which in turn leads to the defeat of the Aztecs. In this novel's
scenario of interracial relations, heterosexual bonding between whites and *indios* (and their product: *mestizaje*) is imagined as taking shape in any of several
ways: by treachery and possibly rape (Cortés's treatment of Teutila), by treason and conspiracy with the enemy (La Malinche's collaboration with Cortés),
or possibly even by love (the Spaniard supporting player Diego de Ordaz's

noble affection for Teutila). In any case, should such a bond be realized, it is a given that the woman must give up her indigenous culture and identity, as Doña Marina does—and Teutila does not—and assimilate into Spanish culture. *Mestizaje* is about assimilation and civilization, about the gradual acculturation of indigenous Mesoamerica into Spanish or (now in the nineteenth century) *criollo* culture.

Multiple variations of the story of La Malinche appear in a number of other historical novels of the conquest of the Aztec empire, all with significant Mexican distribution in the nineteenth century, including the Cuban Gertrudis Gómez de Avellaneda's *Guatimozín* (1845),[3] the Yucatecan Eligio Ancona's *Los mártires de Anáhuac* (1870), and Ireneo Paz's *Amor y suplicio* (1873) and *Doña Marina* (1883).[4] The political goals of the authors may vary; nonetheless, the notion of a white male having his way with an indigenous female was commonplace in Mexican letters by the late nineteenth century, so much so that Mexican *mestizaje* came to be understood almost exclusively in these terms. When Ireneo Paz's grandson Octavio Paz articulated Mexican national identity as *mestiza* and designated Mexicans as "los hijos de la Malinche" in 1950 (59–80), these notions were already well engrained in the Mexican literary imaginary.

However, an alternative vision of *mestizaje* appeared in Mexican literature in the same era, one that was not constructed as an interracial bond between white *criollo* male and indigenous female. Ignacio Altamirano was Mexico's leading promoter of national literature in the late nineteenth century, and his greatest national novel is *El Zarco*.[5] *El Zarco*, like the novels by Ancona and Paz, deals with interracial romance but with a totally new formulation: this time the indigenous protagonist is male. Although he is portrayed as "ugly like the Indian he is" (67), Nicolás is the novel's romantic hero. Moreover, despite being ugly to some, including the (*criolla*) protagonist Manuela, he is a hard-working and successful blacksmith and good husband material (according to Manuela's mother). Manuela, however, is dazzled by the good looks and flashy clothes of the blue-eyed bandit known as El Zarco, so she runs off with him, only to discover that he is spineless, selfish, and callous. Nicolás is not white but lives in Yautepec, a place where "the entire population speaks Spanish, as it is composed of mixed races. Pure Indians have disappeared completely there" (4).

Like Altamirano, Nicolás is an Indian but is not an Indian. He looks like one and is identified as one, but he lives like any *criollo*. He is reasonably well educated, earns his living through *criollo* institutions, dresses *criollo*, and speaks only Spanish. It only makes sense that he would court a *criolla* like Manuela. Altamirano promotes a new trope of interracial romance that is finally realized when Nicolás marries Manuela's adopted sister Pilar. The lesson of the novel is that a good *criolla* like Manuela is better off not with flashy blond *bandidos* ("who are demons vomited forth from hell" [10], in the opinion of Manuela's mother), but with a good man like Nicolás, regardless of his race. After all, he is not a primitive savage but an "hombre de bien," an honest, upstanding citizen. And once again, as with La Malinche, it is the indigenous protagonist that gives up his culture and assimilates into *criollo* culture.

Here, of course, is the key to the shock value of the legend of Lola Casanova. The trope of *mestizaje* is not parallel with that of the familiar Malinche story in which the indigenous maiden is violated by the Spanish invader. Here the dangerous invader is the indigenous captor, and the violated maiden is white. This terror of a white virgin possibly being raped by indigenous savages, of course, provides the dramatic tension of a totally different trope of interracial relations: the captivity narrative. Before analyzing Lola Casanova's cultural meanings, it is worth looking at the racial ideologies promoted in nineteenth-century romantic narratives of captivity.

## TERROR ON THE FRONTIER:
## WHITE DAMSELS AND SAVAGE RAPTORS

American captivity narratives have in common the general scheme of fair white maidens being abducted by barbaric indigenous American captors.[6] The sexual violence implied in such narratives fed racial tensions among whites by portraying indigenous Americans as dangerously violent, animalistically irrational, and with a propensity to rape helpless females. In erudite literature and popular legend alike, such a threat became a national allegory that implied a need to subjugate indigenous insurgents in order to prevent the brutal violation of white civilization by unruly savages (Faery 10). Despite their predictable basic structure, each captivity narrative took its own shape and presented unique cultural nuances. Let us look at a few examples that circulated in the nineteenth-century borderlands.

On 27 July 1860, *La Estrella de Occidente*, Sonora's official state newspaper, printed the translation of a report originally published in the *Republican* of Saint Louis. Dated 9 April 1860, Tubac, Arizona, it recounts the "horrific details of the captivity, savage barbarity and sufferings of Mrs. Larina A. Page" (4). She was alone with a young female Mexican servant at her home in Arizona while her husband was out supervising Mexican laborers on his land when a band of Apaches attacked, ransacking the house and kidnapping the two women, tying them up and forcing them to walk behind them as they rode off on horseback.

They went on in this fashion for a full day, the women exhausted from being forced on at a rapid pace and terrorized with frequent threats that they would be killed. When Mrs. Page could no longer keep up, she narrates, "my savage captors resolved to kill me to put an end to their impatience. They stripped off my clothes including my shoes, leaving me in nothing but a shirt" (4). They then threw her down onto a rock, stoned her, "and soon left me there assuming I would die" (4). Although they had torn open her shirt, putting her "practically in a state of nakedness" (4), they had shown her only contempt and had never approached her sexually.[7] She then began walking, despite being injured and nearly frozen in the snowy mountains, until sixteen days later she finally reached home.

This captivity narrative is interesting for several reasons. First, it is told in the voice of the surviving victim herself, but more important it is told by an Anglo-American woman and is reprinted for a Sonoran audience. It is troubling that the fate of Mrs. Page's Mexican servant is forgotten. Clearly, in the context of the United States, it is the captivity of a (white) Anglo-American woman that is

horrifying, not that of a (nonwhite) Mexican American. Apparently for the presumably white Sonoran reader, the fate of the presumably nonwhite Mexican
servant was also of little consequence. That the white woman, Mrs. Page, sur-
vives is a comfort. In addition, for the Mexican reader, it is a tale from the other
side of the border and therefore removed from the day-to-day life of Sonorans
in Ures, Guaymas, or Hermosillo.[8] It also has a happy ending. The Indians are
savage and cruel, but they are not murderers or even rapists—at least according
to Page.

It is also significant that the captors were Apaches, a people residing primarily on the U.S. side of the border. The 1850s was a particularly tense time
along the U.S.–Mexico border due to the frequent raids of U.S.–based Apaches
into Sonora. The "guerrilla warfare" waged by the Apaches made northern Sonora "practically uninhabitable" and set in motion a series of serious conflicts
between Mexico and the United States (Tinker Salas 62). The situation was
such that "on the Mexican side, both in Chihuahua and Sonora, the Apaches
had absolute control and no one dared take them on" (Antochiw 406). The
Sonorans were bound by the Treaty of Guadalupe Hidalgo from waging war
with the Apaches across the border into U.S. territory until the 1880s (Tinker
Salas 64); instead, they began offering rewards for delivering adult Apaches,
dead or alive.[9] It was legal to "keep" children under fourteen "to educate in social principles."[10] Government-sponsored headhunting, of course, exacerbated
tensions. Meanwhile, "most Sonorans, including top leaders . . . contended that
Americans openly colluded with Apaches in their attacks on Mexico" (Tinker
Salas 64). The rhetoric of manifest destiny in the United States was felt strongly
in Mexico's Northwest, especially during the 1850s, when filibuster raids were
commonplace and the hope for Sonora and Baja California to become the next
two new U.S. territories was widespread in the U.S. Southwest. The mining
speculator Sylvester Mowry wrote in 1864, "[The] Apache Indian [is] preparing
Sonora for the rule of a higher civilization than the Mexican" (quoted in Tinker
Salas 64). The thinking was that the Apache raids would drive the Mexicans
out of Sonora "leaving to us (when the time is ripe for our possession) the territory without its population" (Mowry, quoted in Park 54).

This captivity narrative, then, would have reminded Sonoran readers of
a danger lurking beneath its surface. A retelling of the kidnapping of Larina
Page emphasized that Apaches were not necessarily exclusively in cahoots
with the *gringos* at the expense of Mexicans. However, it also reminded Sonorans of the everyday danger posed by the marauding Apaches for Sonorans, whom they considered their absolute worst enemies. The historian
Joseph F. Park writes:

> In 1859 . . . the [Apache] chief, Francisco, asked if the Apaches would still be per-
> mitted to steal from Sonora if the United States took the state from Mexico. The
> [U.S.] agent said that he thought not, and the old chief replied that "as long as
> he lived and had a warrior to follow him, he would fight Sonora, and he did not
> care if the Americans did try to stop him, he would fight till he was killed." (52)

It was a reminder of imminent danger, but a danger once removed.

A second borderlands captivity narrative presents a totally different set of lessons for a different audience. On John Russell Bartlett's exploratory journey to the region under the auspices of the United States and Mexican Boundary Commission in the early 1850s, he came across "a party of New Mexicans" in possession of "a young female and a number of horses and mules [all of which] had been obtained from [Piñal Apache] Indians" and all of which they planned to sell (303). Bartlett fussed at the New Mexicans, who "belonged to a people with whom the system of peonage prevails, and among whom, as a general thing, females are not estimated as with us, especially in a moral point of view" (306-7). Bartlett then proclaimed, "I therefore deemed it my duty—and a pleasant one it certainly was, to extend over her the protection of the laws of the United States, and to see that, until delivered in safety to her parents, she should be 'treated with the utmost hospitality' that our position would allow" (307). While the girl, whose name was Inez González, informed her rescuers that "[n]o improper freedom was taken with her person" (308) when with the Apaches, it is not made clear what "moral" conflicts had occurred with her purchasers, nor what Bartlett, so pleased to find himself in the role of hero to the damsel in distress, meant to imply with the word "hospitality," delivered as it was *entre comillas*.

In any case, the story of her captivity with the Apaches is as follows. While on an excursion to a fair at a neighboring town in northern Sonora, where she lived, the party with which she traveled was attacked by a band of Apaches who killed everyone except Inez, her two female servants, and a young boy. The other captives were sold separately, so she was left alone with her captors, who did not violate her but did rob her of her clothing "save a skirt and under linen" (308).

Once purchased by the New Mexicans, she was soon rescued by Bartlett, who made sure she was properly clothed. In addition, "she received many presents from the gentlemen of the Commission, all of whom manifested a deep interest in her welfare, and seemed desirous to make her comfortable and happy. But with all the attentions extended to her, her situation was far from enviable in a camp of over a hundred men, without a single female" (309). Once again, Bartlett maintains the sexual tensions central to a captivity narrative, while always simultaneously emphasizing the captive's safety with her benevolent *gringo* rescuers (many of whom had been soldiers during the U.S. invasion of Mexico only a few years earlier).

As they traveled down into Sonora, Bartlett continued to dote on his rescued captive. He dined with her daily, and in the Burro Mountains he adoringly named a spring after her: Ojo de Inez. Soon, they arrived at Santa Cruz, which would be the scene of Inez's dramatic reunion with family and friends, who had thought they would never see her again:

> The joy of the father and friends in again beholding the face of her whom they
> supposed was forever lost from them, was unbounded. Each in turn (rough
> and half naked as many of them were), embraced her after the Spanish custom:
> and it was long ere one could utter a word. Tears of joy burst from them all; and
> the sun-burnt and brawny men, in whom the finer feelings of our nature are

wrongly supposed not to exist, wept like children, as they looked with astonishment on the rescued girl. (399)

Bartlett establishes himself not only as friend to the Indian-like ("rough
and half naked") Mexicans but as their rescuer, a larger-than-life benevolent
patriarch to the Mexican people. Given the constant conflict regarding the
exact location of the border, the cross-border Indian raids, livestock rustling
and smuggling, and cross-border escapes of runaway slaves, not to mention
filibuster invasions, such an image would hardly have been bought by most
Mexicans (and in particular *fronterizos*). But Bartlett wrote in English for a U.S.
readership that would not take much convincing to be persuaded that Mexico
would be better off having the United States managing its affairs and protect-
ing its virgins.

The legend of Lola Casanova is different from either of these types of borderlands captivity narratives. First, the United States is absent from the foreground. Neither the victim nor any other protagonist in her drama is from
that country. Still, it is clearly a drama of the contact zone. In the background
lies the major social problem of the northwestern borderlands in the late
nineteenth century: Mexico's inability to populate the region due to conflicts
with indigenous groups and its consequent vulnerability to U.S. aggression,
or stated another way, its inability to properly fortify its border against ever-
threatening Yankee imperialism until it subjugated all insurgent indigenous
groups. The legend of Lola Casanova served as a harsh reminder that the
Seris, who remained a major problem along the northwest coast of the state
until late in the nineteenth century, had to be conquered once and for all.

Second, there is no happy ending this time—at least not for *los fronterizos
criollos*. While Lola herself might have fallen in love and come to enjoy life
among the Seris,[11] such an idea was unthinkable for Sonorans for whom the
Seris were primitives, savages, and well-established enemies to *criollo* Mexicans.[12] There is no heroic tale of escape or rescue. It is a story of defeat of *criollos* of Guaymas at the hands of *indios bárbaros*.

Third, and importantly, whether by consent or by force, Lola had sexual
relations with Coyote Iguana and eventually became mother to at least one
child by him. Neither Larina Page nor Inez González admitted to being sexually violated. Should it have become known that the presumably virgin Lola
had been raped or impregnated by a Seri, she would have been shamed if not
ostracized by her peers and would likely have been unable to ever marry. In
short, this captivity narrative is beyond tragic: it is utterly shocking.

While Coyote Iguana may have spoken Spanish, he is no Nicolás. The historian Cynthia Radding has shown that for decades indigenous Sonorans had
been assimilating into the mainstream. In nineteenth-century Mexico in general, and Sonora in particular, racial terminology often reflected not blood
ties or ethnic heritage but "connotations of economic and social standing"
(244). Acculturated dark-skinned Sonorans who had risen above the state of
poverty were not viewed as *indios* and might even, under the right circumstances, marry white *criollos*. However, Coyote Iguana is clearly not one of
these assimilated social climbers. He does not dress like a *criollo*, does not live

among *criollos*, does not practice a *criollo* trade, and in fact considers himself an enemy of Mexico, acting as a leader in violent attacks on Mexicans, like the assault on the party of travelers in which Lola had been traveling the day of her abduction. The legend of Lola Casanova represents *mestizaje*, then, as the rape of *criollo* Mexico by insurgent *indios bárbaros*, or worse yet, the Malinche-like treason of *criollo* Mexico by a woman who rejects her own people to collude with the dark-skinned enemy. Lola Casanova's is a captivity narrative gone awry. Its happy ending of love and marriage twists social expectations beyond the recognizable and presents a jarringly scandalous vision of *mestizaje* that threatens *fronterizo* racial identity.

## RACE AND REPRESENTATION

Nineteenth-century *fronterizos*, much more so than Mexicans from other parts of the country, whose day-to-day dealings with the United States were more remote, were conscious of how they were portrayed on the other side of the border. They were aware that the image of Mexicans in the United States was one of dark-skinned, uneducated, uncultured mongrel peasants. The racial aspect was of particular significance as the rhetoric of manifest destiny often drew from scientific theories of race, which viewed darker races as inferior and saw miscegenation as degenerative, thereby justifying imperialist attitudes on behalf of whites. Regardless of the actual racial makeup of Mexico's population, *fronterizos* were sensitive to stereotypes that assumed Mexicans were *mestizos* who indiscriminately mixed with inferior races.

The historian Miguel Tinker Salas observes that northern elites strove to create an image of themselves as "somehow ethnically different from other Mexicans" (26). He explains: "Indian wars invariably hardened racial attitudes and broadly affected the society, including lower socioeconomic groups. Many individuals of mixed heritage made it a point to deny their indigenous roots," while elites made show of their European pedigree (26). Writes the historian Ramón Eduardo Ruiz of late-nineteenth-century Sonora: "Disgracefully . . . these notable fathers of progress also felt proud of being from good Spanish families, arranged marriages among their own, and looked down on their neighbors who did not have 'purity of blood' as inferiors" ("Los perímetros" 11-12).

This was not, of course, the view of Mexico and Mexicans held by most in the United States, a multiracial country that obsessed about maintaining its own racial purity and segregation and looked down upon its Latin American neighbors for their propensity for miscegenation. This was clearly the view that so frustrated *fronterizo* cultural elites—such as the journalist Aurelio Pérez Peña—who would make it their mission to defend northern Mexico's image as civilized and prudently controlled by white elites.

Meanwhile, Pérez Peña's close friend and associate Francisco Dávila's 1894 book *Sonora histórico y descriptivo* directly confronts the prejudices of "some contemporary writers [who] . . . have exaggerated in the pages of their newspapers the moral and material backwardness of Sonora" (1). In the introduction to his book, which serves as a marketing tool designed to attract foreign capital to the state, Dávila declares it his goal "to record in these pages the state of advancement that Sonora had achieved, proving . . . that in any part of our State, capital and life are as safe as they are in the great population centers of the United States and Europe" (3). Dávila's Sonora was as good as the wealthiest and most powerful nations of the world because its Indian problem was under control (Pérez Peña, "Carta" iii–iv), although it was still the case in the 1890s that "the foreigner sees. . . lurking behind each one of our rocks and shrubs the mouth of a rifle that, with a steady hand, the ferocious Apache aims at the breast of a defenseless settler," and "in the mind of the man of the Old World every Sonoran looks like a mountain man with a har-quebus on his shoulder and the traditional holster and scimitar on his hips" (Dávila, *Sonora* 3). Dávila argued that Sonora was no longer the Wild West, that it was now safe to settle there, and that its riches were ripe for exploiting.

However, even in his descriptions of what Sonora had become, he was careful to construct an image of a white Sonora, defined by its opposition to enemy Indians. Following a long chapter, "Districts and Their Elements of Wealth" (254-306), is a chapter titled "The Tribes of the State" (307-25) in which Dávila makes clear that these tribes are distinct and segregated from the implicitly white mainstream of Sonora described in the previous chapter. Following the model of the United States, regardless of the reality of inter-racial relations, Sonoran *letrados* promoted their state's image as one of racial purity and white dominance.

## A DIGRESSION: BORDERLANDS ROMANCE

Before returning to our analysis of the cultural significance of the Lola Ca-sanova legend in the Mexican borderlands, let us turn briefly to a somewhat similar borderlands romance, also from the late nineteenth century, but set in the United States, that of Ramona. Ramona was the protagonist of the New Englander Helen Hunt Jackson's highly acclaimed and popular 1884 novel. A look at the cultural signification of *Ramona* in both the United States and Mexico will provide some insight into both how Mexico was understood at the time and why Mexico and Sonora have resisted incorporating Lola Casa-nova into their respective pantheons of national and *fronterizo* cultural icons.

Jackson's novel is an interracial romance with a twist. A brief plot sum-mary is in order. Ramona is a beautiful young girl raised in her aunt's house in the U.S. Southwest shortly after the U.S.–Mexico war of the 1840s. Her aunt, *la señora* Moreno, is a proud Mexican *criolla*, a war widow devoted to her sickly son, Felipe. Ramona falls in love with an employee on the Moreno ranch, a Luiseño Indian named Alessandro, much to her aunt's chagrin. And here is the twist: it turns out that her aunt's deceased sister, that is, the woman whom Ramona has thought was her mother, was in fact her stepmother. Ra-mona's father was a Scottish sailor who had been in love with *la señora* More-no's sister (also named Ramona) but had lost her to another man while off at sea. The Scotsman had had a daughter with an indigenous woman and had thought that this daughter, Ramona (the novel's protagonist), would be better off raised by *criollos*; he therefore convinced his former girlfriend to adopt his baby. However, Ramona Sr. soon fell ill and handed Ramona Jr. off to her sister (*la señora* Moreno). Ramona (the daughter), then, is a *mestiza* but does not know it until *la señora* Moreno, furious that Ramona has become involved with an Indian employee, reveals her family history to her. Rebelling against the blatant racism of *la señora* Moreno, who is ashamed to have a *mestiza* in the family and finds her love affair with an Indian to be disgraceful, Ramona elopes with Alessandro. Alessandro is himself something of a hybrid. Raised on a mission, he speaks perfect Spanish and plays the violin, but it soon becomes clear that he is devoted to his people. Ramona proudly assumes an Indian identity and the two set off to seek their fortune in the racist U.S. Southwest.

On numerous occasions, it is made clear that the treatment of the Indians under U.S. rule is much worse than it had been under the Spaniards or Mexicans. While the Spanish had educated the Indians in their missions and the Mexicans had more or less respected their autonomy and granted them land, the newly arriving U.S. settlers are greedy and violent. The novel evokes a nostalgia for an idyllic mission-era past and criticizes the United States for its policies of Indian removal and extermination. Eventually Alessandro is murdered by racist white settlers, leaving Ramona and her daughter alone. Luckily, around this time Felipe appears, looking for his lost stepsister. He rescues and marries her. Soon the new couple realizes that they can never be happy in Alta California with anti-Indian and anti-Mexican attitudes thwarting their attempts to make a life there. Finally, they move to Mexico City where they are welcomed and presumably live happily ever after.

Written by Jackson, an activist on behalf of the Indians of the Southwest, as a protest of Indian removal policy, *Ramona* was a huge success. However, lamentably, instead of invoking public sentiment to rise up against racism, the novel served more to promote a romantic myth of a California history that never existed, a history of picturesque and tranquil missions where Spaniards and Indians lived in peace. The historian Kevin Starr writes, with much irony:

> No matter that the mission system itself was founded on ambiguity: the enforced enclosure of the Indian. No matter that the Spanish soldiers hunted them in the hills like so much prey and drove them down into the mission compounds like so much cattle. There, in churchly captivity, the majority of them declined—from the syphilis the soldiers gave their women, from the alien work the padres made them do, from the trauma of having their way of life and their tribal places so cruelly taken away. In Helen Hunt Jackson's version of it all (and by the 1890s it was official myth), grateful Indians, happy as peasants in an Italian opera, knelt dutifully before the Franciscans to receive the baptism of a superior culture, while in the background the angelus tolled from a swallow-guarded campanile and a choir of friars intoned the *Te deum*. (58)

Moreover, this invented mythical mission-era past utterly erased Mexico from California's history along with the war by which California and the rest of the Southwest were acquired as U.S. territory. California's only past prior to the gold rush, then, was a distant colonial one. Otherwise, it was severed culturally from the country it bordered, as if Alta and Baja California shared no recent past.

*Ramona* has gone through many dozens of reprints and remains one of the most popular novels of the U.S. Southwest. Its popularity was perhaps greatest in the first half of the twentieth century when it inspired multiple Hollywood film representations featuring such stars as Mary Pickford, Dolores del Río, and Loretta Young. It has also seen numerous stage productions, including most prominently California's annual Ramona Pageant, which has played there every year in the Ramona Bowl, a large outdoor theater in the town of Hemet, since the 1920s. "Ramona," a song written for the 1928 Dolores del Río film, became classic. For much of the twentieth century there was a booming tourism industry built around Ramona, featuring women who claimed to be the real Ramona and various places identified as her birthplace, her house, her grave, her wedding place, and so forth (DeLyser).

The nostalgia for an idyllic vision of the Spanish colonial mission frontier in *Ramona* contrasts sharply with representations of the late-nineteenth-century post-mission borderlands in Mexican literature. While there were as yet no novels being published in the northwestern borderlands, the *veracruzano* José María Esteva, who had visited Baja California briefly when sent to set up a customs office in La Paz in 1856, drafted the novel *La campana de la misión* in 1858, a book which he finally published in 1894 in Xalapa, Veracruz (Hernández Hernández 12-13). It recounts the shipwreck of Mexican travelers on their way to San Francisco, which leaves a young couple stranded in the desertlike terrain of the Baja California peninsula. They frantically ring the bell of an abandoned mission, but after they lose hope for rescue, the romantic hero, Eduardo, sets off alone in search of help. He perishes in a storm and his lover, Laura, left alone in the abandoned mission, is never heard from again. In Mexico, there is no nostalgia for the frontier missions. Baja California is ominous wasteland; the abandoned mission of San Borja recalls only the perils faced by settlers of a most uninviting land. The bleak terrain of Baja California is not of the borderlands, the terrain connecting the two neighboring countries and their cultures. It is not a contact zone where these cultures interact. San Francisco remains utterly out of reach; Baja California is instead frontier territory, far from the comforts of either Mexican or U.S. civilization.

*Ramona*, in contrast, was beloved by Californians—and by readers from all over the United States—for the picturesque vision the novel evoked of the nation's western frontier. Furthermore, in 1887, José Martí, another *Ramona* enthusiast, published his own Spanish-language translation of *Ramona*, first in New York, and shortly afterward in Mexico City. Martí claimed *Ramona* as "nuestra," that is, a novel of "nuestra América," a sentiment endorsed nearly a century later by the Cuban cultural critic Roberto Fernández Retamar.[13] *Ramona* is "nuestra" because it is a novel that not only promotes a *mestiza* heroine but endorses her coupling with an indigenous American protagonist (Alejandro).[14] There is no need to go into the history of Americanist criticism of *Ramona* here.[15] It will suffice to say that while the Americanists tend to focus on important race issues in the U.S. Southwest, the addition of Martí to the mix in Susan Gillman's article "Ramona in 'Our America'" ends up making interesting but misleading implications about nineteenth-century Mexico that my reading of the Lola Casanova legend contradicts. It demonstrates once again how U.S. border studies criticism has trouble penetrating the border and comprehending the types of issues brought about by the particular cultural confrontations that occurred in the other borderlands of northern Mexico.

Gillman notes, reading *Ramona* via Martí and Fernández Retamar, that the novel is particularly *nuestra* (Latin American) not only because of its *mestizo* characters and interracial couplings but because it shows that Latin America, in stark contrast with the United States, is a haven for racial tolerance and racial mixing. Martí's "nuestra América" project was inspired out of a need to promote an opposition to Eurocentrism and U.S. imperialism by fomenting national and racial pride in Latin Americans. Martí's vision is utopian, and while it may have been a vision shared by other Enlightenment-inspired or nativist Latin Americans, it was not likely embraced by many *criollo* Mexican elites in the northwestern borderlands of the late nineteenth century.

As we have seen, Sonorans did not wish to promote Latin America or Mexico as a *mestizo* paradise whose attitudes concerning race, particularly when it came to indigenous and mixed races, were opposite of those prevailing among whites in the United States. In the 1880s, Sonoran *criollos* were still fighting Yaquis, Seris, and Apaches and did not wish to represent themselves mixing happily with their enemies.

Martí's vision depended upon the assimilation of conquered Indians like the Aztecs or Tlaxcaltecs (and presumably Yaquis and Seris) into Mexican *criollo* culture so that the latter could unite with *criollo* culture in the rest of Latin America. *Ramona*'s fairy tale ending may have soothed some of Martí's readers in New York, Havana, or even Mexico City, but had anyone read it in the Mexican borderlands, it would not likely have been well received.[16] *Ramona*'s popularity in Mexico has been generally muted. Martí's translation did not make a big impact, and the novel has not been in print in Spanish translation for many years. A 1946 Mexican film starring Esther Fernández was both a critical and a box office failure. In fact, *Ramona*'s success with Spanish-language audiences has occurred principally in the United States. A stage adaptation starring the great Mexican actress Virginia Fábregas broke box office records in Los Angeles in 1927 and went on to tour the U.S. Southwest (Monroy 146). More recently, Lucy Orozco's adaptation of the novel to the format of a *telenovela* for Mexico's Televisa network in 2000 received lukewarm reception in Mexico but was a resounding hit in the United States, recently being re-aired by popular demand on Galavisión, a cable network serving Spanish-speaking communities in the United States. This most recent reinterpretation of *Ramona* has been described as "arguably the strongest critique of American expansionism ever seen on television—nothing less than a postmodern masterpiece, a brilliant subversion of the myth of the Old West" (Stein 2). Historically, *Ramona* has appealed to Anglos and Hispanics alike in the U.S. borderlands but has not made much impact on Mexicans in Mexico—even less so in *la frontera*.

Nineteenth-century Latin America could accept figures like La Malinche who bonded sexually into the *criollo* (in her case Spanish colonial) mainstream, or Nicolás (of *El Zarco*) who rejected their indigenous background to assimilate into *criollo* culture, but not characters like Lola Casanova who rejected mainstream *criollo* culture to join insurgent indigenous groups whose continued autonomy prevented national and Latin American unity. Ramona, too, gave up a comfortable life among her adopted *criollo*/Mexican American family to become indigenous, adopting an Indian identity. She would have been as unsettling in nineteenth-century Sonora as Lola Casanova was.

## LOS INDIOS BÁBAROS DE LA FRONTERA

The history of violent strife between Mexican settlers and the various autonomous indigenous groups of the Northwest is one of the defining experiences of the epoch for the region. The very future of the northwestern borderlands for *criollos* as well as *mestizos* depended upon the subjugation and incorporation of these recalcitrant groups into mainstream Mexican society. Until such a time, Martí's dream of a united mixed race in Latin America would remain unthinkable in the Mexican borderlands, where attitudes toward these troublesome enemies tended to resemble those of *gringos* interested in developing the U.S. Southwest, with one significant difference. The project of annihilation favored by many in the U.S. Southwest might have seemed tempting to Mexican *fronterizos*, but many were conscious that it would be shortsighted. Those recalcitrant indigenous groups needed to be assimilated into the mainstream in order to serve as manual laborers in a region not yet sufficiently populated to supply the labor force needed to carry out its projects of modernization.[17]

In general, the only Indians welcome in Sonora were those willing to work—for wages inferior to those paid to white workers (Tinker Silas 134)—for white colonizers, and to assimilate into Mexican *criollo* culture. Ramona, for example, might have been welcome in Sonora, arriving as she did with her second husband, the well-connected *criollo* Felipe; however, her relationship with her first husband, in which she assumed an indigenous identity, would hardly have been embraced by Sonorans, even if Alejandro played the violin and spoke Spanish. Indigenous migrants from the United States were not welcome in Mexico: displaced U.S.–based tribes that tried in these years to relocate to the Mexican side of the border were soundly rejected by Mexican authorities.[18] The rhetoric of civilization and barbarism was the overt and unequivocal doctrine of the regional oligarchy, and whatever ambiguity Mexico as a nation felt toward Spain, the *criollos* of the northwestern borderlands felt obliged to ally themselves with their Spanish colonial heritage in the name of civilization. Mexico's Apache campaigns would finally bear fruit in the late 1880s, when at last cross-border Apache assaults would be controlled, though occasional raids would occur well into the twentieth century (Figueroa Valenzuela, "Los indios" 158). Likewise, intermittent confrontations with the Yaquis and Mayos would go on until the first decade of the twentieth century, ending in a ruthless campaign to take possession of their lands and subjugate them once and for all: "the most bloody and brutal era of the *porfiriato*'s depredation was established; the deportation of Indians became big business, and upon arriving at their destination they were sold as slaves" (Figueroa Valenzuela, "Los indios" 161). The military medic Manuel Balbás identifies the cause of the conflicts in 1901 from a decidedly *criollo* perspective: "the false idea they have formed of their nation, considering it to be constituted not by the greater land called Mexico, but uniquely and exclusively by the very limited Yaqui River region" (128).

The case of the Seris, or Kunkaaks, was somewhat different.[19] Unlike the Apaches who attacked Mexican settlers in raids launched from the safety of their territory on the U.S. side of the border, or the Yaquis and Mayos who protected their own fertile homeland from Mexican *criollo* invasion until late in the century, the Seris maintained their autonomy simply by distancing themselves physically from *criollos*. Traditional nomads of the Northwest, they isolated themselves farther and farther into the deserts of the northwestern part of the state, often using Tiburón Island, located in the Gulf of California, west of Hermosillo, as their base of operations. Despite their relatively small number, "by the 1880s . . . the Seris were the only Indians of Sonora who, even counting the Apaches, had remained independent of any form of dominance" (Figueroa Valenzuela, "Los indios" 146).

Ever since the first Spanish colonizers had arrived in the region, relations with the Seris had been hostile. Nonetheless, the Seris lived in such difficult land—infertile, hot, dry, isolated—that it had never been a priority for *criollo* authorities to vanquish them. However, around the middle of the nineteenth century, ranchers began establishing themselves closer and closer to Seri territories, gradually inciting tensions. The late February 1850 attack on the convoy carrying Lola Casanova—one of many similar attacks along the road between Guaymas and Hermosillo—set off a major punitive campaign against the Seris. However, it was only when armed conflict broke out between the Seris and local ranchers in 1855 that major damage was done. At the end of the so-called Encinas wars (1855 to 1867), an estimated half of the Seri population had been annihilated (Córdova Casas, "Las guerras" 299). Still they remained autonomous until in the 1880s, when some 150 Seris were captured and placed on a reservation—although they soon revolted and escaped when they discovered that some of their food rations had been poisoned by Mexican authorities (Bowen 241-42).

The autonomy of one of the smallest and most "primitive" tribes of the area was an embarrassment to local elites, who continued to crack down on the Seris in the last decades of the nineteenth century, instituting a campaign of extermination in which not only did some bounty hunters collect three pesos per male Seri head, but also "Seris were hunted for sport" (Bowen 242). An 1890 military campaign resulted in a major Seri defeat. However, causing greater impact was the reported murder of several *gringo* adventurers who had gone to Tiburón Island in the early 1890s, which triggered another punitive campaign that ended with a Seri surrender in late 1894 (Bowen 254-58), although no formal peace agreement would be signed until 1907 (Córdova Casas, "Las guerras" 302).

This ongoing war with multiple indigenous groups in the Mexican North-west, which went on into the early years of the twentieth century, made the area anything but the paradise of *mestizaje* envisioned by Martí. The Mexican Northwest, in fact, resembled the U.S. Southwest in many ways. Both were rapidly developing areas whose modernization depended utterly upon the confiscation of territories traditionally belonging to indigenous groups. Both were areas whose economic development required a process of population by new settlers that could only occur once all indigenous groups were brought under control. And, as in the United States, white Sonoran elites strove to en-sure that whatever racial mixing occurred in the region did not permeate the *criollo* oligarchy.

True, many individuals of indigenous heritage chose to learn Spanish, take jobs with Spanish-speaking employers, and otherwise adopt the dominant *criollo* culture of the Mexican Northwest, and thereby melted into the racially mixed population of the *gente de razón*" (Radding 17). However, the tendency for white *fronterizos* to exalt their status by emphasizing that they were among "those not mixed with other races" (Pérez Hernandez 466) is evidence of a deep-seated racism that formed an important part of regional identity as con-structed by elite members of the borderlands oligarchy in cities such as Guay-mas, La Paz, and Hermosillo.

## EARLY LEGENDS OF LOLA CASANOVA

Within this context, it is not difficult to understand why Lola Casanova did not become, like Ramona in the U.S. Southwest, a major character of re-gional literature in the late nineteenth century. Not that literature existed as an institution in those days in the Mexican borderlands. While local newspa-pers began publishing poetry, often that of local poets, as early as midcentury (Aldaco Encinas), no regional literary production would exist until well into the twentieth century. Still, Casanova's early omission from historiography even as she remained alive through oral traditions points to the importance of popular culture in the evolution(s) of her legend into the twentieth cen-tury, when in the 1940s she would eventually appear to be on the verge of becoming a national icon. Ultimately, Lola never became a major protagonist of Mexican national culture, although she continues to be remembered today as a marginal heroine of regional high culture (literature, historiography), and as a beloved if still troubling figure of popular culture of the Mexican borderlands.

The earliest versions of the Lola Casanova legend, which had been lost for many years, recount the events differently from the way they appear in the best-known and more recent versions.[20] On 23 February 1850, Lola Casanova was traveling with her mother, Anita Velasco de Casanova, and her brother Ramón from her hometown of Guaymas to nearby Hermosillo when their carriage was attacked by a band of about twenty Seri Indians. That particular stretch of highway was well known for such assaults, and this time thirteen of the Mexican travelers were killed. *La señora* Velasco de Casanova was among the dead, and Ramón Casanova escaped.[21] Within a few weeks, a punitive military expedition was launched against the Seris in which attempts were made to rescue the captives. At the same time, the emergency law that put a bounty on the head of Apaches was extended to apply also to Seris (Bowen 238).

On 28 March, a Seri leader, Coyote Iguana, agreed to meet with the Mexican military officers and reportedly promised to return the captives within a few days. When he returned at the agreed-upon time without the captives, claiming that he needed more time to transport them, the military became impatient and launched a new attack (Bowen 238-39). Finally, some time in April, the rescue expedition learned that Lola Casanova had actually been executed in mid-March in retaliation for the killing of a Seri woman. This was the story as it was reported in official military correspondence dated 24 April 1850.[22]

There are a couple of important differences between the very early, unpublished, official version of events and those popularly remembered. First, there is no mention in official reports of any romantic or sexual relationship between Coyote Iguana and Lola Casanova. The former is introduced as merely a spokesman for his tribe. Lola herself would have had little time to develop any relationship with the Seris since she was apparently killed after only a few weeks in captivity. This is not to say that the official version reflects the truth—or even that the truth would have any bearing on the construction of the legend, which likely serves purposes that have little to do with remembering the truth.

Bowen argues that the Seris who told their enemies that Lola Casanova had been killed may have been lying, perhaps in the hope that the search party would be called off.[23] The Seris might not have wanted it to become known at that time that Lola Casanova had been chosen as a romantic or sexual partner for Coyote Iguana. It is equally possible that Cayetano Navarro, the author of the official 1850 Mexican military documents on the conflicts with the Seris, was lying. Navarro, in fact, had taken numerous Seri women captive (Navarro 241), a practice that would certainly have been endorsed as more morally justifiable if the Seris were known to be doing worse with the white women of Sonora. It is also possible that Navarro may have been shielding the name of the Casanova family, his neighbors in Guaymas, from the shame of having a daughter contaminated by sexual contact, whether consensual or not, with a Seri.

In any case, the story was not to be published as such. It took time for the news to reach the only major newspaper of the northwestern borderlands, the government-sponsored *El Sonorense*. In a brief article appearing under the heading "Seris," the 3 May 1850 edition merely recounted, in general terms, the "horrific murders" being committed along the road between Guaymas and Hermosillo and reassured readers that Navarro and his men were pursuing the enemy "with much steadfastness and energy" (4). No other protagonists of the story were named.

Similarly, José Francisco Velasco, in his *Noticias estadísticas del estado de Sonora* (1850), mentions the incident, identifying it as an assault by "inhuman, utterly filthy and cowardly bandits, murderers, thieves" (317). Neither Lola nor any of the other less famed victims were mentioned by name, despite the fact that Velasco's own brother counted among the dead.[24] A month after the first newspaper report, and well over three months after the original assault, a second story appeared in *El Sonorense*, this time mentioning specific details of the 23 February incident and citing Navarro's 24 April report to the governor. This story named several of the captives, noting that five of them had been set free. It then noted that a young girl named Elena Islas had not been released, and that Dolores Casanova—and this is the first published reference of her name—had been "sacrificed in captivity" (7 June 1850, 4). Interestingly, Elena Islas disappears quickly from the public imagination, while the name of Lola Casanova remains very much alive.

Regardless of how it was that her story remained active in the popular imagination of the northwestern frontier region, it clearly occurred for a reason. Whether that reason had to do with rumors that emerged later about Lola's marriage to Coyote Iguana and her refusal to return to Guaymas, or with other colorful adornments to the basic story that appealed to the popular imagination, or with persistent fears among white Sonorans, the revised versions of the Lola Casanova story that would be recorded in written form several decades later would significantly alter the official story as related in 1850.

## LOLA ENTERS HISTORY

The historian Fortunato Hernández, in his elegant publication *Las razas indígenas de Sonora y la guerra del Yaqui* (1902), makes Lola Casanova the protagonist of a coherent written narrative for the first time. Navarro's reports and the newspaper stories that summarized them centered their attention on Navarro and his campaigns, with Dolores Casanova as merely one supporting player among many. After 1850 there is no published reference to her for the rest of the century, with one exception: the Smithsonian Institute ethnographer W. J. McGee acknowledged the existence of a legend that would appear to be Lola's in 1898, only to deny its veracity: "The romantic story of a white slave and ancestress of a Seri clan, sometimes diffused through pernicious reportatorial activity, is without shadow of proof or probability" (132).

But in Hernández, Lola takes center stage in a true-to-life romantic drama significantly different from that related by Navarro. The historian raises the subject casually as an example in his discussion of Seri traditions. Several new details emerge immediately: first, Coyote Iguana is not a real Seri but a Pima; and second, the abduction occurred in 1854 (62). These details would become fixed features of the story, as would others recorded in writing for the first time by Hernández, namely, that Coyote Iguana and Lola Casanova married and bore children who were raised as Seris, and that Lola chose to live the rest of her life among the Seris.

Hernández's source was a servant girl named María Valdés, who at some time around the early 1880s noticed a white woman among some Seri women who had come to the ranch where she was working to draw water from a well. When María asked the white woman what she was doing "with those infamous people," the latter responded, "I am Lola Casanova" (63). Lola then recounted her entire story to María, who some two decades later repeated it, as she remembered it, to Hernández: Lola had been traveling with relatives from Guaymas to Hermosillo when their carriage was attacked. She fainted, awaking later to find herself "in the arms of a savage" (63). No mention is made of what happened to her family. Her captor turned out to be the chief of the Seris, Coyote Iguana, himself an ethnic Pima who had been adopted into the tribe as a boy. Coyote Iguana, who had lived among Mexicans as a boy, immediately proclaimed his love for Lola Casanova in excellent Spanish. She was repulsed at first by his attentions—Hernández's story mentions only hugs and kisses—although she gradually began to return his affection, and ten months later, Lola gave birth to a son (Hernández 63). By this time she was becoming accustomed to "the horrors of the savage life" (64), but it was her maternal instinct that led her to choose to stay with her captor. After all, "woman is born *hembra* [female animal] and nothing more" (64). And if her decision to take up the primitive life of a Seri was shocking, it was mitigated by the fact that her husband was actually a relatively respectable Pima. On the other hand, it might even be excused by the animalistic instinct that drives even a white woman:

> That is the only way to explain that a woman born and raised in unadulterated civilization could have adapted to an atmosphere as savage as the one constituted by Seri customs, and giving up homeland, family, home, religion, society, present, past and future, could have committed to living for the savage male animal who succeeded in seizing, dominating and satisfying her sexual instincts, and could have felt for him and for his children that sublime love that elevates the female animal to the category of mother. (65)

She lived many years among the Seri, even returning to Hermosillo (never Guaymas) several times, but was never able to bring herself to part from her new family. Eventually, Coyote Iguana was killed, but a few years later their son became the new chief, Coyote Iguana II. After his death, another son would become Coyote Iguana III.

What had been a tragic captivity narrative was transformed a half century later into a love story. The author of the new story may have been an imaginative servant who lied about meeting a woman who had been pronounced dead thirty years earlier; or her story may have been embellished by Hernández himself. It is more likely however that the story was a product of a popular oral history shared by many *fronterizos*. Interestingly, several details appear in other documents that support elements of this story, details that contradict information of the original 1850 reports.

For example, an unpublished manuscript authored by Roberto Thomson, who knew the Seri people well and represented their cause to the Mexican government in the second decade of the twentieth century, confirms a few of the new elements in Hernández (Bowen 242). Thomson recounts the campaign of 1890 that ended in the capture of a large number of Seri prisoners. Among them, he claims, were none other than Coyote Iguana and his pregnant wife, Lola Casanova (Bowen 245). Whether or not it is likely that Casanova was indeed pregnant at age fifty-eight, it is possible that the idea of there having been an interracial romantic liaison between the two, a liaison that bore them at least one child, was in circulation well before the publication of the Hernández text—although it is not possible to say whether Thomson's source for the legend is more probably Seri or Mexican.

Another 1890 source, official documents signed by Captain Luciano Rodríguez reporting on peace negotiations with a group of eighty-six Seris, among them Victor Ávila, purportedly the son of Lola Casanova and Coyote Iguana (Córdova Casas, "Las guerras" 303), again confirms Lola's blood ties to the Seris. It is not clear who it is that identifies Ávila as the son of the notorious mixed-race couple; however, his reported existence further points to the strength of an oral history in which Lola did survive and did marry her captor, which was in circulation well before the publication of Hernández's book.

One final note regarding Hernández: although his recounting of the Casanova legend sets the stage for its conversion into literature, Hernández did not wish to promote Lola as a role model. On the contrary, he makes a point of correcting Lola Casanova's irrational story by following it directly with the story of another Lola, Lola Morales, a Seri girl taken captive by whites,[25] and raised as if she were a *criolla*. He ends his chapter on Seri social organization with this happy anecdote of how "love, charity and instruction . . . [turn] the daughter of a Kunkaak semi-beast into the noble, sentimental and illustrious *señorita* Lola Morales" (71). Lola Casanova is a fascinating aberration; Lola Morales is the model of how to achieve racial integration in the borderlands: through a whitening acculturation that does not require the sullying aspect of *mestizaje*.

## FLAPPER LOLA

Hernández authorized an oral history of the borderlands, transporting it to Mexico City where it was endorsed by the well-known *literato* Juan de Dios Peza in a review published in *El Correo Español* in August 1902, in which he highlights "the story of the famous Lola Casanova, beautiful woman of the white Sonoran race, and whom her lover Coyote Iguana, Chief of the Seri Nation, imposed on the tribe as Queen."[26] Through Hernández and Peza, the story took on new life in Mexico's capital, resurfacing sixteen years later in *El Universal Ilustrado* (15 February 1918) in an article by Miguel López, clearly based on the Hernández version of the legend and titled "Lola Casanova, la reina de los seris."[27]

López tells his "entirely veridical" story, locating the events in 1854. He includes virtually all the important details reported by Hernández, adding his own interpretation of Lola's momentous choice to stay with the Seris: "Lola Casanova, regressing, reverting to savage life for the love of her children, is proof of the complexity of female psychology, of a mother's affection and martyrdom, of the mystery that envelops that delicate being called woman." Lola is now more than a female animal; she is a case study in female psychology. If her behavior still seems bewildering to the average male reader, at least it can be attributed to patterns explained by scientific theory.

A second article on Casanova appeared in the same journal some two years later. This one, attributed to a *licenciado* Vidriera, was titled "Escenas de la vida nacional: Una mujer blanca reina de los seris: El rapto de Lola Casanova" (8 July 1920, 14-15). Its first paragraph asserts: "The Seris are the most savage and bloodthirsty Indians in America; nowadays they lead a pacific life under the constant vigilance of the Government" (14), foreshadowing his troubling story's happy dénouement.

Lola, merely a woman (actually female animal) in Hernández, "beautiful woman" for Juan de Dios Peza, "lovely woman" for López, was now a woman of exceptional beauty: "Tall and striking, white, golden haired and blue eyed, she was a rare beauty" (14). Vidriera's customary assertion that his story was "absolutely true" (14) is called into question by its illustration, a drawing by Carlos Mérida, who had recently arrived in Mexico from his birth country of Guatemala. Mérida imagines Lola as a woman of the 1920s, sporting a hat adorned in exotic feathers and a flapper-style bob. Lola's decision to remain with the Seris is a product of both "the love she felt for her husband and her maternal sentiments" (15). This new romantic touch moves the story beyond the guise of historic testimony employed by Hernández, or the scientific analysis of a curious incident of the borderlands seen in López, presaging its later conversion into a novel. Coyote Iguana was no longer an enemy warrior but a romantic hero: "tall, well built, his naked legs, arms and chest revealing a powerful musculature. His copper skin shone with golden highlights. . . . His abundant black hair, falling across his back, was carefully cut at the ends like the long hair of an artist" (14).

Vidriera's tale is more fantastic and sensational than previous written accounts. Its characters and plot are more fully fleshed out yet more romanticized than in previous tellings: in Vidriera there was clearly a mutual attraction, and Coyote Iguana was shown to have made an effort to ensure that Lola was welcomed among his people. Lola, a woman in love, expressed her joy by decorating her hut: "built out of sponges and sea shells, roofed with *maguey* leaves and tortoise shells. Inside, the floor was covered in lion and mountain lion skins, from the walls hung scalps of Comanche chiefs conquered by her valiant consort" (15). Lola's motivations now go well beyond mere maternal instinct.

## EARLY WOMEN'S WRITING IN SONORA

The local press of the northwestern borderlands, including official state-sponsored newspapers, had been publishing short literary texts by local writers, texts that sometimes addressed local themes, since the mid-nineteenth century.[28] Gilda Rocha cites *Días de amor* (1911) by César del Vando as Sonora's first novel; as mentioned previously, a novel set in Baja California, *La campana de la misión* by the *veracruzano* José María Esteva was published in Xalapa in 1894; and the Sonoran journalist Aurelio Pérez Peña published his play *Heroína* in 1897.

However, it was not until the mid-twentieth century that the northwestern borderlands began to see sufficient literary production by local authors to warrant discussion of the concept of a regional literature. Interestingly, almost as soon as novels, short stories, and chronicles began to appear regularly by writers of the borderlands and on topics related to local culture, Lola Casanova quickly was established as a prominent protagonist of multiple literary works. It is as if her character had been lying in wait for a regional literary culture to develop in order to assert her presence and make the move from popular legend to literary heroine. Furthermore, it is of great interest to note that two of the earliest writers of the borderlands to bring Lola Casanova to life in their literature were women.

In 1943, Carmela Reyna de León, a local author whose name is absent from literary histories,[29] even those of her home state of Sonora, published the romantic novel *Dolores o la reina de los kunkaks*, the first full-length literary representation of the Lola Casanova legend. Reyna de León, thought to have been a schoolteacher in Pitiquito, a town in the Seri region of Sonora, may have been well informed about Seri culture. The novel differs significantly from previous published versions—for example, Reyna de León dates the kidnapping of Casanova to 1879 (1), nearly thirty years after the actual events, and a full twenty-five years after the date given by Hernández—leading one critic to surmise that the novelist's primary source of information may have been Seri legend rather than the historiography of Fortunato Hernández.[30]

In this version, Dolores Casanova is a "lovely mixed race girl," popular carnival queen of Guaymas (1). Her wealthy parents give her as a birthday gift a trip to Los Angeles, but before she can set sail her stagecoach is attacked by a band of mainly Yaqui Indians and her father is killed. Coyote Iguana, the chief of the Kunkaks (Seris), who participated in the assault along with the Yaquis, is attracted to Dolores and decides to keep her as his captive. However, she does not fall in love with him; instead she is attracted to Valiente, another handsome tribesman, who acts as her protector. Valiente tells her in excellent Spanish that he was raised among whites and schooled in Sonora. Very soon, a fight erupts between him and Coyote Iguana—who turns out to have been an ethnic Ópata—in which the latter is killed.

Lola spends several weeks among the Seris, longing to see her mother but afraid that if she returns, Valiente, whom she plans to marry, will be mistakenly blamed for her capture and unjustly put to death. Meanwhile, she tells him of the great indigenous men of Mexican culture: Benito Juárez, Ignacio Altamirano, Ignacio Ramírez. She adds, "I've heard say that the Kunkak race is not indigenous . . . that . . . they are equals of the Europeans in everything except their color" (23). Lola's romantic interest in Valiente is made understandable both by his similarity to Mexican *criollos* and by the critical view she develops of her birth culture living on the outside. Just as she shows Valiente that indigenous men have played an important role in Mexican political and intellectual life, Valiente teaches her that *criollo* culture should not be idealized, opining that whites "are slaves of government, the city, clothing, everything," whereas indigenous peoples are free (23).

As Valiente's wife, Dolores learns Seri customs and adopts their lifestyle. However, their home "was not a makeshift hut, but a well organized house. . . : spacious, clean, elegant; carpeted with the most precious of seal and gannet skins, and its benches made of whale vertebrae" (36). Again, Lola's penchant for interior decorating shows Sonoran readers that her life among the Seris was not a regression to savagery, as previous versions of the tale had so often implied. Around this time, they have a baby, whom they name Juventino.

Eventually (a good eight years after her disappearance), federal troops arrive while Valiente is off on an expedition and detain Dolores. She begs them to allow her to stay, but they take her and her son back to her mother's house. There she sees Juventino mistreated by racist white children. Finally, Valiente comes to rescue her from her captivity in Guaymas. Her mother calls the police, but finally they decide to let Dolores go because, after all, she is an adult living in a free country. The tale ends happily on the Isla del Tiburón with the joyous Seris welcoming Lola back home. They cry jubilantly, "Long live King Valiente and Queen Dolores!" (49).

Several of the details of the story indicate that Hernández was not its main source. Lola, formerly white, is now *mestiza*; both her parents are alive at the beginning and her father dies in the attack. Since Reyna de León identifies her father as a "rich Spanish businessman," it must be assumed that her mother is her source of mixed blood. In the 1943 borderlands, it would seem that a mixed-race woman who married a wealthy white man (for example, Lola's mother—or Ramona, in her second marriage) was perfectly acceptable. In fact, even a mixed-race woman who married an indigenous man and assimilated readily to his culture (for example, Lola Casanova—or Ramona, in her first marriage) could be a romantic heroine.

However, the Seris, always the most primitive and savage of borderlands Indians in the nineteenth century, were now noble. They were not ravaging thieves; some of them were merely misled by some criminal Yaquis and their Ópata chief. The Seris themselves were peace loving. In fact, far from a backward, ignorant, barbarous people, they were comparable to civilized Europeans "in everything except their color."

The idealized beauty of the young couple implies that their son will be a *mestizo* worthy of "the cosmic race" (Vasconcelos). In fact, the influence of Mexico's new postrevolutionary cultural politics—a doctrine that violently rejected the racist positivism of the *Porfiriato* in favor of an acceptance or even celebration of Mexico's racial diversity, with an eye toward eugenic evolution and modernization (Lomnitz 52-53)—is evident throughout the novel. While indigenous customs are respected, the novel's hero is not the crude Coyote Iguana but the Hermosillo-educated Valiente, who is elated to learn of Mexican history's illustrious indigenous leaders from his *mestiza* wife. The *indigenismo* of the 1940s, very briefly summarized, exalted the glorious indigenous past: Aztec empire, Mayan science, Alcolhuan culture, and so forth, while promoting a better future for Mexico's indigenous population through education (and their implicit assimilation into the national mainstream). Reyna de León altered the scheme a bit by celebrating an indigenous past that was not ancient, but rather recent. While the Seris of the late nineteenth century were not as accomplished as the once-great cultures of Chichén Itzá, Teotihuacán, or Texcoco, the peace and freedom they enjoyed on the Isla del Tiburón were admirable on a smaller scale.

Reyna de León may have adapted her tale from a Seri legend that idealized a past way of life for a tribe reduced nearly to extinction. She may also have felt her redemption of the Seris was justified by a dominant philosophy that was happy to view their culture idyllically, as long as it was relegated to the past. Most important, the Seris in 1943 no longer posed any threat whatsoever to Sonorans. *Dolores* could not have been written in 1850 when Lola was kidnapped or even in 1885 when Martí translated *Ramona*. In 1943, with the caste wars over and the nation poised to recognize the past contributions and engagements of indigenous peoples in the national context, Sonorans of all races were at last ready to read and enjoy the story of Lola Casanova, at least enough Sonoran to justify the publication of *Dolores*, though not enough to admit it to a regional literary canon.

## A DARKER VIEW

Not all Sonorans saw things as Reyna de León did; not all were ready for the glorification of Seri culture, much less the celebration of a white or even *mestiza* woman's romantic flight from a relatively modern city such as Guaymas to the primitive Isla del Tiburón, well beyond the frontiers of civilization. Sonora's first great female journalist and notable short story writer, Enriqueta de Parodi, recounted a different version of the Lola Casanova legend in her *Cuentos y leyendas* collection of 1944.[31] While Parodi sees it as "a complicated and dark passage from the history of aboriginal Mexico," because it features "some almost unbelievable details," she prefers to classify it as legend, citing Fortunato Hernández as her main source (25).

Her attitude toward the Seris contrasts drastically with that of Reyna de León. Even Hernández and Dávila believed that the most recalcitrant indigenous groups of the borderlands could be redeemed by education. Parodi, on the other hand, writes, "there have been various Sonoran governments who have made praiseworthy efforts to assimilate the Seris to civilization and all of them have been in vain" (26). Later she comments on what little remains of the Seri culture in the 1940s: the Seri tribe continues in its pilgrimage to oblivion, because it will have to be extinguished one day; no force, no example, nothing has been sufficient to tame its legendary rebelliousness, indolence, laziness" (31).

Parodi's Lola was enthroned "by force," and her story is much less romance than horrific tragedy. The most remarkable characteristic of Parodi's version of the legend is its unbridled and venomous hatred of the Seris. Parodi concludes that "perhaps in the long and painful existence of this tribe, nothing has been better or more beautiful than the story of Dolores Casanova" (31), whom the author designates the founder of the Coyote Iguana dynasty. Clearly nineteenth-century racial antagonisms, which ultimately devastated the Seri population to a low point of less than two hundred in the late 1920s (Figueroa Valenzuela, "La revolución" 360), had not been resolved to the satisfaction of all *fronterizos* by the 1940s. If only in that decade could Lola's tale be told among Sonoran *letrados*, it still could only be told a certain way. It is perhaps no surprise that Reyna de León and her novel remain absent from

Sonoran literary history while Enriqueta de Parodi and her writings, more representative as they are of the views of Sonora's intellectual elite of her generation, have been celebrated for their foundational role in Sonoran letters.

## LOLA GOES NATIONAL

Francisco Rojas González, on the other hand, was relatively unknown in the borderlands, but his publication of a full-length novel based on the Lola Casanova legend in 1947 would bring the story to its largest audience to date, and in a context decidedly national. Rojas González, an anthropologist turned novelist, based his story on the text of Hernández but also included an attention to detail that reflected his personal interest in and commitment to Mexico's indigenous peoples.

It is this version that would become a key source for many scholarly studies of the legend.[32] Lola was now firmly established as the only *criolla* daughter of a Spanish immigrant widower. Coyote Iguana was a truly noble savage, handsome and strong, gallant and wise. After her kidnapping (in 1854, as in Hernández), Lola married him and had his children out of love for him, and she came to respect his culture and to live happily as his Seri wife, eventually outliving her renowned and respected husband.

Despite its influence, the novel is not known as the best of the author's work. The critic Joseph Sommers writes:

> The improbability of the main argument, with its exotic contrast between the highly educated woman and a primitive setting, makes it eminently appropriate for a legend, romantic story or melodramatic film. On the other hand, the ethnological detail that appears in describing the life of the Seris shows the hand of the *indigenista*. Both elements, juxtaposed, generate an incongruence that spoils the novel. (96-97)

The most exotic element of the plot, that most incompatible with the author's ethnographic objectives, is the protagonism of Lola Casanova, the white woman—and in Rojas González, Lola is "blanquísima" [extremely white] (11)—who abandons civilization for barbarism.

The literary *indigenismo* of the 1940s as mentioned above, aimed to incorporate all the variety and complexity of Mexico's many indigenous cultures into the national imaginary. Typical literary works such as *El indio* (1935) by Gregorio López y Fuentes, or the best-known *indigenista* films (for example, Emilio "el Indio" Fernández's *María Candelaria* of 1944) tend to focus on the conflicts between mainstream national culture and its indigenous periphery, reiterating a binary vision of civilization (modern man) and barbarism (noble savage), and repeating the familiar allegorical theme of the violation of the latter (represented by the indigenous woman) by the former (white man).

In this context, now national, the romantic regional legend of the borderlands is transformed into a national allegory. Reyna de León also located her story in national culture, for example, through references to Benito Juárez; later in the novel, when Lola leaves Guaymas for the second time, the government official assigned to her case tells her mother, "In the Republic we are all born free. She is an adult; if she wants to be a savage, so be it" (Reyna de León 47). Lola, of her own free will, separates herself from Mexican national culture to join the alien culture of the Seris. If there is a national allegory in Reyna de León, it is a trope on racial diversity and a resulting fragmentation of national culture. In utter contradiction with *indigenista* doctrine, it is easier for Lola to assimilate into Seri culture than for Valiente to assimilate into mainstream Mexican culture, which treats his mixed-race son with racist disdain.

In Rojas González, on the other hand, interracial love is linked firmly with the concept of *mestizaje*, which is presented as a solution to the Mexican Indian problem; it is a *mestizaje* "based on mutual respect of cultural tradition and on the shared cooperative effort to construct a modern society" (Sommers 98). Lola, in Rojas González, is no longer a damsel in love who finds fewer prejudices among the Seris than in *criollo* high society but a symbol of interracial unity at the national level.

There is indeed prejudice among the *criollos* in Rojas González. One of Lola Casanova's early suitors, a major villain of the story whom Lola fears she may be forced to marry against her will, is known as a "yaquero" [Yaqui hunter]. He tries to win Lola over by giving her a young Seri captive boy: "he could be another adornment for your garden" (23). Lola of course is not racist and takes in the boy, whom she treats with motherly affection. Later this will pay off when she becomes a Seri captive, and the boy, having returned to his people, steps in as one of her main allies.

Much later, years after Lola's capture, there occurs a scene in which the Seris, among them the already acculturated protagonist, visit Guaymas, where they have a brief encounter with a little white boy and his mother: "The lady interrupts her step, then suddenly resumes: she frowns, while raising her brocaded handkerchief to her nose. 'Let's go, my son, these people stink'" (251-52). A few moments later, Lola realizes that she recognizes that woman from her childhood: she had been her best friend. The national prescription is simple: the childhood friend represents ignorance and cruelty; Lola is kindness and generosity. And it is obvious which of the two is of use to the nation.

In contrast, while there are also tensions among the Seris concerning the presence of a white woman in their tribe, between Lola and the Seris a possibility exists, uncomfortable though it may be, to live together and to come to know each other. Lola serves, then, not as a symbol of an antinational antimodernizing acculturation as in Reyna de León but as an instrument of transculturation. While on the one hand Lola does strive "to transform her own idiosyncrasy, to inferiorize her culture, to twist her faith" (Rojas González 223), she also offers the Seris her knowledge of modern medicine. She moreover works to open commercial relations with the "yoris" (nonindigenous peoples, whether white or *mestizo*) in order to cultivate intercultural cooperation—and interestingly it is the Seri women who establish these dealings in a style "quite different from that sustained by the warriors with the *yoris*" (238). As an inverted incarnation of the postcolonial hybrid trickster of Homi Bhabha,[33] Lola accommodates herself in Seri culture and subtly introduces elements of Mexican *criollo* culture to the Seris, thereby modernizing them even as she herself appears to have reverted to a primitive lifestyle.

The novel ends in the twentieth century in a place called Pozo Coyote, founded by those Seris who were open to the changes fomented by Lola and receptive to racial mixing, as evidenced by the fact that *mestizos* also lived and worked harmoniously in the town with the Seris. The more conservative Seris remained on the Isla del Tiburón, living in primitive isolation from modern Mexican society. Lola, of course, is among the first group, the group of the future, but also the group of assimilation, an idealized (and not destructive) assimilation:

> The elders die without ceasing to be Seris; the adults grow old aiming to become *yoris*; the children grow up as *mestizos*. . . . Nonetheless, the land, "grandfather of the *kunkaaks*" and godmother moon preserve respectability and reverence, because if the people speak, dress and eat *yori* style, they do not stop feeling, enjoying and suffering like Seris. (268)

The ending is rather pragmatic, as it is implied that all the Seris need is land and education to achieve a utopian state. One of the Seris of Pozo Coyote assesses their situation:

> Mexico gave us a slice of desert land; we, in exchange, have given back farmland; [we] drew water from where there was none; from the midst of sand dunes a town has sprouted up. . . . The *yoremes* [Indians] have not gone to Mexico, it has come to us. (273)

In this hybrid town where they speak both Spanish and Seri, the people "live with the exaltation of endless work" (267). It took the acculturation of a white woman to make possible the mutual cultural understanding necessary to enable the incorporation of the Seris into the Mexican mainstream—where a particular role awaits them: "The commerce [in Pozo Coyote] is also *mestizo*: the *yoreme* produces and sells, the *yori* consumes" (267). Finally, as Anne Doremus puts it, "Rojas González . . . considers *mestizaje* the Indians' only hope" (395).

This recasting of the legend makes its white protagonist less radical than in Hernández, where she leaves her people never to return or to have any relation with them again. The project of *indigenismo* demands that Lola be a cultural bridge that the "indios bárbaros" may cross to enter into the modern nation.[34] The story is still discomforting due to the fact that Rojas González does not dare to overturn the final outcome of the legend—that is to say, that Lola remains the woman who abandons her life in Guaymas to "be a savage," but ultimately she is no longer radically opposed to national integration as she had been in Reyna de León's border romance. Finally, it must be remembered that an *indigenista* point of view is not equivalent to an indigenous point of view: one critic notes that despite Rojas González's anthropological pedigree, some Seris who have read the novel have responded to the representations of their customs and history with mocking laughter (Lowell, "Sources" 30).

## LOLA *LA RUMBERA*

Nevertheless, Rojas González's *Lola Casanova* promptly caught the attention of the greatest female director of Mexico's golden age of cinema, the pioneer Matilde Landeta, who produced her film adaptation, also titled *Lola Casanova*, in 1948. Landeta's script was based closely on the Rojas González novel—with only a few minor changes (for example, Landeta does not follow the historically accepted dates, locating her drama between 1860 and 1904).

This film employed the conventions of the nationalist-inspired *indigenista* school of cinema of Emilio Fernández, but from the perspective—utterly out of the ordinary in Mexican cultural production in that era—of a woman. While one of Landeta's goals was clearly to feature women as protagonists in national culture, she was also quite conscious of the inversion of the national *mestizaje* myth that was embodied in her protagonists, one of the reasons why she chose this text for her first full-length feature film. Landeta attempted to capture the cultural detail expressed in Rojas González's novel, and her film in fact does succeed in making her protagonists more than generic *indios* usually seen in such films (Arredondo 197): they are clearly Seris, although her small budget limited her ability to capture their culture as accurately as she would have liked (García Riera 291). The elements of the production perhaps most attractive to the viewing public were, in fact, the most absurd features of the film. For example, the newly founded Ballet Nacional de México bestowed on the production artistic legitimacy, but its modern style of choreography hardly evoked a "primitive" culture, despite the dancers' ragged costumes. To make things worse, the *rumbera* Meche Barba, best known for her starring roles in musical melodramas such as *Yo fui una callejera* and *Una mujer con pasado*, was cast against type in the role of Lola, and her love scenes with the hunky B-movie actor Armando Silvestre (as Coyote Iguana) were, according to the film historian Emilio García Riera, "suggestive of the classic 'Me Tarzan, you, Jane'" (291).

The film, as a visual medium, despite its faults, likely communicated Rojas González's message with greater lucidity than did his book: Landeta's Lola was emphatically a female agent of a modernizing 1940s-style *indigenista* and nationalist agenda. Susan Dever argues that Lola's own metamorphosis is radical in itself, implying that transculturation must go both ways (90-91); however, in the end only Seri culture is altered by the new cultural cooperation with the *criollos*; Mexican national culture does not adopt any of the Seri customs learned by Lola. Furthermore, in the end it is the white *criolla* who is the culture-transforming heroine of the Seris, a posture that is "fundamentally patronizing and racist" (Rashkin 52). Landeta's Lola, a civilizing and modernizing force of love, never threatens the *criollo* culture she abandons. She reveals its prejudices and their sometimes brutal consequences, but she never ceases to be its representative, its missionary. Still, she makes something quite significant out of what would for a typical Mexican woman screen protagonist have been basically a life-ending experience. She is a helpless captive transformed into less a romanticized queen—as in Reyna de León—than a protofeminist cultural icon.

## LOLA'S LAST STAND AS NATIONAL HEROINE

Another nationally recognized—although not best-selling—novel of the late 1940s would bring further attention to Lola Casanova. Armando Chávez Camacho's 1948 *Cajeme: Novela de indios* romanticized the life story of José María Leyva, the Yaqui resistance leader of the 1880s. Its main character is not Lola Casanova, but Chávez Camacho is unable to resist telling her story, dedicating a complete chapter to this deviation from his central plotline. This *indigenista* novel aimed to vindicate the Yaqui hero, who, idealized by Chávez Camacho, has much in common with Coyote Iguana, also made into a noble savage in literature and film. Cajeme, raised among *criollos*, speaks excellent Spanish and is fully equipped to assimilate but is morally incapable of watching his people lose their land to greedy colonizers.

*Cajeme* is not about *mestizaje*; it is a historic and biographical novel that seeks to revise historiographic: accounts of the Yaqui wars of the late nineteenth century by viewing the events from a Yaqui perspective. Since the government that so oppressed the Yaquis in Cajeme's day was that of Porfirio Díaz, the novel is able to position the Yaquis as prerevolutionary rebels whose clashes with the Díaz government presaged those that would cause the country to erupt in revolution several decades later. Cajeme, like Teresa Urrea and the heroes of Tomóchic, would, according to the intentions of Chávez Camacho, enter the national pantheon as a great hero of the Mexican people.

In a single chapter of the novel, the author digresses to recount another legend that he encountered while investigating the life of Cajeme, that of Lola Casanova. Interestingly—and consistent with Chávez Camacho's aim to retell history from an indigenous point of view—Lola Casanova does not get top billing: the chapter is titled "The Great Love of Coyote-Iguana" (191).

His Lola, like that of Reyna de León, is *mestiza*, although white skinned (196). Nonetheless, unlike the case of the Sonoran author who likely had knowledge of a Seri legend of the Casanova story, it seems that Chávez Camacho's principal source was Hernández, as is indicated by his dating the kidnapping in the year 1854, as Hernández (and Rojas González) had done.[35] Once again, after a few weeks in captivity, Lola struggles to decide what to do: "Which did she prefer? Civilization or savagery? . . . Finally, her heart imposed itself: she had to confess that she loved Coyote-Iguana" (207). This brief chapter, presented as a curious background tale, giving the reader a breather from the novel's main plot, no longer concentrates on Lola's role among the Seris but instead draws attention to her simple choice, the fact that choosing the "savage" life of the Seris over the comfort of *criollo* culture was a logical option for her. Lola assumed the radical role of a woman who rejects national culture, but it was of course not the postrevolutionary culture of the 1940s that she rejected, but the prerevolutionary life of the 1850s, and as such the tale was hardly threatening to twentieth-century readers.

This is indeed why it was possible for Lola to enter briefly into a culture no longer just regional but national in the 1940s. Literate Mexico had resisted acknowledging her persistence in the popular (oral) imagination of the borderlands for nearly a century—until the borderlands indigenous peoples had been fully subdued and the area largely settled and modernized, and until the nation had been more fully consolidated, having better symbolically incorporated its racial diversity. In the cultural ambience of the 1940s, Lola—regardless of what her role may have been: that of critiquing racist state policy of the nineteenth century, that of promoting assimilation of resistant indigenous cultures, or even that of celebrating interracial love and the romantic rejection of civilization—was no longer, in effect, so radical. She was an unusual girl, the protagonist of a legend of times long past, and was admissible now in a national culture more symbolically diverse than a century earlier. But what little attention Lola earned in the late 1940s would quickly subside and her image would quite suddenly vanish from the national imaginary.

## *MESTIZAJE*: TRADITIONAL CONCEPTS OF RACE AND GENDER REAFFIRMED

In 1950, Octavio Paz published what would soon become the classic essay on Mexican national identity, *El laberinto de la soledad*. One of the most prominent components of the essay was an analysis of how *mestizaje* figures in the national imaginary in gendered terms. While on the one hand Paz was merely synthesizing and articulating what was already understood as *lo mexicano*, the enormous success of this essay engraved his vision of Mexican national identity more deeply than ever into the national culture, inspiring a whole generation of further studies on similar themes.[36] Paz represented Mexican *mestizaje* in the well-known allegorical terms of the Spanish rape of indigenous Mexico, placing Mexican indigenous culture in the role of the feminine. Paz located the concept of "chingar," a term implying an assertion of power through sexual violation, at the very core of the Mexican character. In Paz's Mexican imaginary, gender roles traced back to the symbology of the conquest, and *mestizaje* could be imagined only in specific gendered and racial terms.

Paz's analysis implies that ever since the conquest, *mestizaje* has been understood as the rape of an always female indigenous Mexico by an always white conquering male; there is no competing allegory of national racial identity. Lola Casanova's bizarre story, then, simply does not fit with the Mexican national character. It is thus no coincidence that Lola's sudden rise to prominence in national cultural production in the late 1940s was fleeting. She utterly disappears from national discourse after 1948, never to return again. No one like her appears in *El laberinto de la soledad*, nor is her legend revived in the literary boom that would follow in the 1950s and 1960s. If Mexico was not ready for Lola in the nineteenth century because she was too shocking, too radical, by the mid-twentieth century she continued, despite *indigenista* and feminist efforts to make her a national icon, to be too discomforting for Mexico's national culture to absorb.

## HISTORIOGRAPHY IN THE BORDERLANDS

Meanwhile, ever since Fortunato Hernández recounted the Casanova legend in his history of the indigenous peoples of Sonora in 1902, Lola Casanova began to assume an increasingly prominent place in local historiography. The Hernández version was repeated in works by the journalist Federico García y Alva in 1907 (Córdova Casas, "Lola Casanova" 14) and by the historian Eduardo Villa in 1937 (31-37) before being reworked in the literary adaptations of the 1940s. However, it was perhaps with the publication of Laureano Calvo Berber's *Nociones de historia de Sonora*, a grade-school history textbook, in 1958, that knowledge of at least one version of the story would become widely disseminated throughout the state.

Calvo Berber benefits from the discovery in 1952 by the historian Fernando Pesqueira of the original Cayetano Navarro letters on the various clashes with the Seris in the early 1850s (Córdova Casas, "Lola Casanova" 14). Calvo Berber's is the first major work of historiography to date the Casanova kidnapping 23 February 1850 (164), citing Navarro's letters directly, including the one that reports the death of Dolores Casanova soon after her kidnapping. Without noting any possibility that Navarro might have lied or received bad information from his Seri informant, Calvo Berber pronounces, "This is the historical truth concerning the tragic end of the young Dolores Casanova" (165). If historiography were more powerful than literature and popular oral legend, this would have put an end to more elaborate and extravagant versions of the story in which Lola falls in love with the enemy and forever renounces her race. But this has not been the case.

## SERI LOLA

Whether or not young Seris were taught "their" history with Calvo Berber's textbook, they surely had their own opinions about the validity of Mexican historiography. Regarding journalistic writings—which had for decades habitually referred to Seris as "barbarous"—the Seris, who themselves had no traditional concept of the press, came to refer to them as "the lying papers" (Lowell, "Sources" 30), and, as mentioned previously, Seri readers have found novelistic representations of their customs quite risible. It is unlikely that they saw Mexican historiography any differently.

In the late 1950s and early 1960s, several Seri versions of their own oral history concerning Lola Casanova were compiled by Edith Lowell in her comprehensive 1966 study of what she calls "folklore themes" in the Rojas González novel.[37] Her detailed comparison of numerous versions of the legend ("A Comparison" 156-58) identifies a number of similarities between Seri legends and the best-known versions in circulation in the mainstream of Mexican letters, including especially those of Hernández, Rojas González, Landeta, and Calvo Berber—as well as some significant differences.[38]

All sources agree that the Seris attacked a caravan on the road between Guaymas and Hermosillo in which Lola Casanova, a beautiful young woman, was traveling with relatives. Seri versions insist that Coyote Iguana was indeed a Seri and not a Pima as reported by Hernández, although they do agree that Coyote Iguana had received formal Mexican-style education and was able to speak Spanish. While most sources agree that Lola became Coyote Iguana's wife (in some, she was elevated to the status of queen)[39] and bore at least one son by him, most Seri versions contend that Lola was forcibly re-moved by soldiers from the Seri camp where she had taken up residence with Coyote Iguana and that she was pregnant at the time. And while every ver-sion of the legend reports that Lola left at least one direct descendent among the Seris, no Seri version makes the claim that she spent the rest of her life living as a Seri woman.[40]

Lowell concludes that the Seri versions point to an error in Sonoran histo-riography. She believes that the Seris would have no reason to invent an inac-curate historic narrative. And if the Seris were going to embellish the story, they would have had Lola staying with them and rejecting the *criollo* culture of Guaymas as inferior—they would most certainly not have invented her return to Guaymas after only a few years. Lowell concludes, "No record of her return has been found, though some Mexican residents believe her return was kept quiet by her family" ("A Comparison" 158).

On the other hand, the official Mexican version, based on Navarro's letters, which insists that Lola was killed within weeks of her capture, is refuted by the Seri legends that assert that her son Victor remained with them and be-came a tribal leader. According to Lowell, many Seris (she counts 119 in 1966) consider themselves to be descendants of Lola Casanova and Coyote Iguana, and the name Lola or even Lola Casanova was not uncommon among Seris in the 1960s.[41] She believes that ultimately "Seri oral tradition appears to reflect historical events more accurately and completely in this instance than does the better known Mexican version which has been influenced by romantic literature" ("A Comparison" 158)—a conclusion that flatly contests that of the borderlands folklorist Ronald Ives, who had written a few years earlier, "Al-though a small part of the legendary material that cannot be verified by the historical record *may* be true, the larger part of it . . . can be dismissed, with confidence, as pure fabrication" (164).

Regardless of the veracity of the Seri versions, it is of particular interest to note that even as the small surviving population of Seris remained apart from the Mexican mainstream, they kept alive the story of Lola Casanova that had been separately entertaining and discomforting their white and *mes-tizo* Sonoran neighbors for over a century. Of course Seri accounts focused principally on the history of Coyote Iguana, with the Lola Casanova story inserted as brief anecdote in the biography of their great leader. Accounts col-lected by Lowell and Moser begin with Coyote Iguana's birth and end with his death ("A Comparison" 148-52). Seri accounts naturally do not incorporate the nineteenth-century *criollo* rhetoric of civilization versus barbarism; when Lola opts to stay among the Seris, no Seri finds her choice illogical, although some were not used to seeing white women up close and "were amazed to see her" ("A Comparison" 148).

There is no doubt that she was an extraordinary personage for the Seris, and it is for that reason that she became a fixture in their oral histories of the era. She signified, first of all, booty, material evidence of the Seris' victory in battle that day on the road from Guaymas to Hermosillo. She was also something of a foundational mother of Seri *mestizaje*—her mixed-race descen-dants could, after all, be found only among the Seris. On the other hand, the

Seris, who claim that Lola lived among them only for a few years, make no mention of the transculturation brought on by having a white woman living among them—the thesis developed in Rojas González and Landeta; in fact, they claim that she did not learn the Seri language ("A Comparison" 151). Nor does she come to signify any profound superiority on the part of the Seris since the Mexicans win in the end: she is ultimately kidnapped a second time by the Mexican soldiers and taken away from her Seri family.

However, it is not only the Seris who continued to keep the legend alive through their oral traditions. Ricardo Mimiaga writes:

> In our country there is a great variety of indigenous legends that have endured to the present era. Likewise, the number of tales . . . of *mestizo* and *criollo* origin that still animate and give flavor to many a serene night of chitchat, whether in the mountains, in the middle of the desert or in the coastal valleys, is remarkable. In the Northwest region, oral traditions are kept alive in both ways: the indigenous . . . and the other, that of whites and *mestizos*, more vulnerable to suffer modifications with the passing of time and due to the permeability of our national culture. (387-88)

While we may not agree that only white or *mestizo* culture changes over time—Mimiaga implies that indigenous cultures in fact never change—the case of Lola Casanova makes clear the power of legend, multiform legends often developing separately in different social sectors, in the construction of Mexican borderlands culture.

### RECENT INCARNATIONS OF LOLA CASANOVA

In the 1960s, Fernando Galaz revived the Lola Casanova legend once again in his popular chronicles of Hermosillo, this time dating her kidnapping in 1872, a date that agrees with that given in no other source. In other details, however, the tale is quite recognizable. Lola is an eighteen-year-old white, chestnut-haired beauty from Guaymas, kidnapped by a tall, strapping, muscular youth (Coyote Iguana), who spoke excellent Spanish. Coyote Iguana was, despite being an ethnic Pima, the king of the Seris, and he wished to make Lola his queen, and Lola soon was seduced. The lovely white captive, however, was not readily accepted by the Seris, and eventually—"twelve years later" (306)—she fled back to live with her sister "in el Barrio de 'La Chicharra' (bordered by Monterrey, Yáñez, Morelia and García Morales Streets)" in Hermosillo (306). There she got involved with a military captain with whom she lived for "three or four months" until he suddenly died (306). Two weeks later, Coyote Iguana came for her, kidnapping her once again from her sister's house. This time Lola would spend the rest of her life with him. She was last spotted in 1901, in full Seri-style regalia, selling pearls and shells to passersby in the Plaza de Armas in Hermosillo (306).

This new capricious, even promiscuous Lola is a curious personality of local folklore, but hardly a great romantic heroine. This time she apparently

never has any children and is finally neither a symbol of *mestizaje*, of transculturation, nor of racial superiority for either race. She is merely a woman
who loves, leaves, and returns to her men with a certain ease, and who despite her beauty never rises to a position of power or prestige in either Seri or
*criollo* society. She is also relocated within Sonoran culture. Her early years
in Guaymas receive no attention, while her return to Hermosillo becomes an
important chapter in her life, her latter history marked by references to local
streets and landmarks.

A decade or so later, Lola is brought to life again in Horacia Sobarzo's
major work of regional historiography, *Episodios históricos sonorenses* (1981).
Unlike Galaz, who cites no particular sources for his tale, Sobarzo does cite
Rojas González's novel as his main source. Sobarzo revives the critical vision
of Lola as espoused in earlier Sonoran versions such as that of Enriqueta de
Parodi of 1944; he laments the reckless acts of

> the unfortunate Dolores who had to trade her queendom—because in her home
> she was queen—for that of the nomadic tribe; the unfortunate Dolores who had
> to leave behind the sweetness, the tranquility, the pampering and indulgence of
> her paternal home to adopt a primitive and savage life, without any more cover
> than a dry tree branch lean-to that did not even resemble the huts of sedentary
> Indians. (178)

Coyote Iguana was no longer a strapping cinema hero, nor even a homely
but noble savage; for Sobarzo he was "a troglodyte" (179). The Seris were "repulsive," accustomed as they were to eating "raw and spoiled meat," drinking
"swamp water," and sleeping on the bare ground (179). Sobarzo grants Lola
her rightful place in regional history, but she is neither a victim nor a heroine—and certainly not a queen or even a happy decor-obsessed Seri home-
maker; she is a woman whose acts are utterly illogical and aberrant. Sobarzo's
point of view on Lola Casanova is not that unusual among Sonorans.

At some point before his death in 1954, the great *cronista* of old Guaymas,
Alfonso Iberri, wrote his version of the Lola Casanova story, although it
reached a significant audience for the first time only posthumously, in 1982.
Iberri shares with Sobarzo and Parodi a disgust for the Seris and an attitude
of resentment toward the romanticization of the Lola Casanova legend. Iberri
bases his text on no particular source, noting that the stories that circulate on
these events are full of "fantastic descriptions and nebulosities" ("El rapto"
275), and he hesitates to conjecture any specific dates. He negates the popular
love story, arguing: "The truth, surely, is something different: the beauty of
the prisoner enflamed the sensuality of the king" (276).

His victimized Lola was soon "made mother" of Coyote Iguana's heirs and
forced to adapt to life "among grubby, dirty, lazy savages who lived in disgusting
promiscuity with their women, pierced their ears and noses . . . , satisfying her
hunger by eating raw fish and turtle meat" (276). She stayed with the Seris either
because she had become "ashamed of her pitiful condition" or because she had
become attached to "the offspring that Coyote Iguana gave her" (276). She ended

up dying among the Seris, "and there her cadaver rotted beneath the thorny twigs they threw over her—since the Seris do not bury their dead" (277).

There is no return to civilization, no mention of visits to Hermosillo either to hide out in her sister's house or to seduce local bachelors, or even to sell Seri handicrafts. As in Galaz, Iberri's focus is local, although this time confined to the city of Guaymas. These chronicles signal that Lola has not only been accepted into regional historiography but also been embraced at the local level, written into microhistories that place her in a particular house, on a particular street, in a particular neighborhood, all recognizable to readers. On the other hand, it seems that Lola's return to her roots brings her back to life in only the most negative terms.

Even today traces of this style of anti-Seri rhetoric can be found in public discourse in Sonora. Recent state attempts to take possession of Seri lands have met with Seri resistance and have resulted in renewed tensions, leading Sonoran governor Eduardo Bours to comment, "The backwardness of the Seris worries me, but they have a great opportunity to modernize as they inhabit one of the richest zones in the state for development in the tourism and aquaculture industries."[42] One wonders what Bours would say if his daughter ran off with a Seri leader today.

In recent years, Lola has continued to inspire research among historians, even as the few verifiable facts of the case became remnants of a more and more distant and forgotten past. The legend, however, remains alive, as do numerous Seris claiming to be Lola's descendants.[43] In fact, Ricardo Mimiaga happened in the late 1980s upon a woman, Rosa Virginia Herrera Casanova, who sparked his interest in the legend when she told him that "she was related to the famous Lola Casanova" (387). While Mimiaga's recounting of the legend adds little new information, it does note Lola's particular subversive role as a symbol of *mestizaje*:

> The lineage of the clan of the Coyotes was founded on Lola's Spanish last name, just as had occurred with the blood of the proud Aztecs and that of their conquerors. But there is a difference. The general pattern of *mestizaje* was the crossing of white man with Indian woman. There were many with the last names Pérez, Rodríguez or López who were sons of *yoris* [whites] and *yoremes* [Indians] . . . but sons of *yoremes* and *yoris*, there are only a few, the Coyote Iguana clan, who come from the Indian seed planted in white flesh. (395)

Lola, then, continued to point to something real, and something unique and perhaps still troubling in the borderlands: the Seris' continued refusal to give up their traditions and identity and assimilate into the Mexican mainstream. Mimiaga was amazed at the "racial pride" that keep the Seris living to this day apart from urban civilization (381), and the tangible links (for example, Rosa Virginia Herrera Casanova) to a past history that has never made sense to white and *mestizo* Mexicans, particularly those of the northwestern borderlands who know firsthand just how drastic the difference is and was between the lifestyles of the Seris and their *yori* neighbors.

Another recent account is that of the Sonoran *cronista* Gilberto Escobosa Gámez, titled "El secuestro de Lola Casanova: ¿Historia o leyenda?" (1995). Besides the usual historiographic sources, Escobosa Gámez draws from an informant, Doña Manuelita Romero viuda de la Llata, his great-aunt, "an old woman who possessed a prodigious memory" (*Hermosillo* 34). While the widow died (at age 100) in 1933, Escobosa Gámez is able to recall her words— and even the emotions he felt as a small child upon hearing them—in the greatest detail.

Escobosa Gámez recounts the familiar romantic tale of a kidnapping after which Coyote Iguana, Pima leader of the Seris, a movie heartthrob type, makes Lola his queen. Although he portrays Lola as victim of "the ferocious passion of that fearsome savage" (33), she soon came to assimilate to Seri society, quickly learning their language and customs. In an idealized representation of transculturation, Lola stays with the Seris and learns to live as they do, while introducing her knowledge of modern medicine to the tribe.

At this time, Escobosa Gámez appeals to his long-deceased great-aunt to fill in the blanks of what has become the official story. Auntie Manuelita, after all, had herself visited the Casanova family in Guaymas as a little girl and actually met the teenaged Lola. Manuelita remembered: "*Señor* Casanova and his wife died a year after the kidnapping. When they could not manage to locate their daughter, they lost interest in going on living. Lolita's uncle took charge . . . and spent a fortune trying to rescue his niece" (35). According to Auntie Manuelita, he was not able to find her until some fifteen years after the assault. However, by that time, when they tried to get her to come back home, "Lolita was not willing to return to the civilized world. She said she loved Coyote Iguana" (36).

Escobosa Gámez's love story with all its melodramatic touches, unites several features of the many strands of the legend circulating during the past fifty years in the Mexican borderlands. It assumes its authority both from historiography and from eyewitness testimony, removed as it had become with time from the actual events. He needed to recall some sixty-odd years after the fact his nearly one-hundred-year-old aunt's reconstruction of events that she had learned about and a girl she had briefly seen some eighty years before that. His *crónica*, then, is both official and personal, as is the more academic style textual analysis of Mimiaga, who cites historiography and literature, along with his own face-to-face encounter with a distant relative of the protagonists of the story. Lola, then, even as her story falls back into an ever more distant past, is brought down to an ever more personal and local level for present-day Sonorans.

A final version, the most recent of all, fixes Lola as a key symbolic figure not in national or in Seri history but in the history of the northwestern borderlands. Alejandro Aguilar Zéleny's 2005 adaptation of the legend for the theater, in the playwright's words, "represents an interesting chance to get to know, through recourse to the arts, the process of identity formation in the Mexican northwest." He goes on, "Between reality and fiction, the sometimes hostile and occasionally friendly encounter takes shape between two vastly different societies that came together to form the culture of Sonora and of the Mexican northwest."[44]

## IN SYNTHESIS . . .

What began in 1850 as a typical captivity narrative of Mexico's northwestern frontier has evolved and mutated in the past century and a half to signify a variety of meanings both at the national and the regional (borderlands) levels. Interestingly, unlike the other border narratives of this study, Lola Casanova has not managed to translate to the U.S. side of the border, remaining part of a very local lore of Guaymas, Hermosillo, and the traditional Seri territories in which the legend first circulated in the late nineteenth century.

From the very beginning, legend contradicted the few written pieces of evidence on Dolores Casanova's kidnapping and its aftermath. Either she died and was kept alive only symbolically by a popular imagination fascinated by the possibilities implied in her failure to return to her family, or she indeed remained alive and was written off as dead by those who preferred, for whatever reasons, a less romanticized tale. This captivity narrative circulated actively through different sectors of the northwestern borderlands in the late nineteenth century, serving primarily as a cautionary tale to local elites regarding the dangers posed by the continued strife with unconquered unassimilated indigenous groups such as the Seris. The symbolic union of Lola Casanova with Coyote Iguana was a reminder to *criollos* of the victory of the Seris in one particular battle, and of the general threat of encroaching barbarity on the barely established outposts of civilization in the northwestern borderlands at the time. Lola Casanova was a fascinating character, but hardly a representation of any mainstream identity constructs in the Mexican borderlands in the nineteenth century. For this reason, her legend was not incorporated in written form into Mexican borderlands culture during her lifetime.

Once Fortunato Hernández reinvented her as a protagonist of Sonoran history in 1902, her image as white queen of the Seris began to draw attention at the national level. In this context, Lola Casanova was a Malinche turned upside down, a symbol of inverted *mestizaje* in which a white woman mixes with an indigenous man. By the 1940s, Lola was no longer just a white woman among the Seris, but an instrument of transculturation who learned Seri culture in order to seduce the primitive Seris to learn from her. While there was a brief but intense period of interest in this vision of Lola Casanova, the reemergence of La Malinche as the female national icon of *mestizaje* erased Lola Casanova from the national imagination by midcentury.

Back in the borderlands, however, the fleeting national interest in her legend provided just the endorsement needed to give Lola Casanova a prominent place in the cultural production of the borderlands state of Sonora. She had previously been first romanticized then vilified—by Carmela Reyna de León and Enriqueta de Parodi, respectively—in the early 1940s. This schizophrenic treatment would continue in the region's cultural production, most particularly historiography and the more literary form of *crónica*, throughout the rest of the century, as later published versions of her story became more local and personal. At the same time, the legend would continue to circulate, in multiple forms, throughout the northwestern borderlands, some of the most interesting versions being those of the Seris themselves, who featured Lola as a supporting player in the oral biography of their great leader Coyote Iguana. Among the Seris, Lola's mark was also left in a growing genealogy of descendents, who continue to use her name. While the Series remain marginalized and are sometimes still vilified in mainstream Sonoran culture, they are still present, and the fact that Lola Casanova appears to still be among them in one way or another is a reminder of the unique history of racial tensions that continue to shape Mexican borderland's identity to this day.

## NOTES

1. For contemporary readings of the Malinche legend, see the collection edited by Glantz, *La Malinche: Sus padres y sus hijos*.

2. See Leal and Cortina xv; González Acosta argues forcefully that the anonymous author was actually the exiled Cuban poet José María Heredia. Anna Brickhouse has intriguingly proposed a collaborative effort among Heredia, Varela, and Vicente Rocafuerte (51–57).

3. The first Mexican edition appeared in 1853.

4. For a complete analysis of La Malinche in nineteenth-century literature, see Cypess 41–97.

5. This novel was written in the late 1880s about historic events of the 1860s, but it was not published until 1901. Doris Sommer identifies *El Zarco* as Altamirano's masterpiece of literary nationalism (224). Note that Altamirano was himself son of an indigenous father and a mixed-race mother and identified as indigenous (Campuzano 12).

6. Such narratives were common throughout the Americas in the nineteenth century, although it seems that they were more popular in the United States (see Faery) and Argentina (see Rotker) than in most other places; see also Operé, especially 242–43.

7. Notes Faery of New England captivity tales, "Stripping the captive woman or ripping off her clothing is as much a stock trope in captivity tales . . . as is the habitual nakedness of Native women in representations of the 19th century and earlier" (177).

8. Interestingly, the anthropologist José René Cordova Rascon notes that despite frequent assaults by U.S.-based Apaches on settlements in northern Sonora, the urban populations of Sonora's larger southern cities were largely indifferent toward the Apache problem and unwilling to volunteer their services in military campaigns against them (162–65, 177).

9. This policy, unfortunately, inspired bounty hunters to randomly kill indigenous men from the area, including peaceful Tarahumaras and Yaquis (Tinker Salas 63).

10. Government decree to Sonorans published in *El Sonorense* 7 February 1850, quoted in Tinker Salas 63.

11. Writing on an analogous context in New England, Rebecca Faery comments: "Paradoxically, Indian captivity represented for Puritan women of New England an expansion of experience rather than what we might ordinarily think would be a contraction or restriction of experience" (31). Staying with the Indians, then, may not have been all that undesirable for nineteenth-century women, confined as they were by the patriarchal order. In Latin America, according to Fernando Operé: "Of the thousands of captives who enlarged indigenous communities, the vast majority either remained in forced captivity or integrated themselves voluntarily, turning down opportunities

to return to their places of origin" (21). For women, it was particularly difficult to return: "The contact with the Indians had marked them for life, and that stain was not easy to erase"; their own captivity narratives "were stories of shame" (Operé 27).

12. "Of all the known Indian tribes in Sonora . . . there could scarcely be one more vulgar and uncouth than the Seris. They are perverse to the extreme, vicious without parallel in their drunkenness, filthy to the infinite degree, and bitter enemies of whites" (José Francisco Velasco, writing in 1850, quoted in Dávila, *Sonora* 317–481).

13. Gillman 91–95; for a more complete reading of Ramona from a Mexican *fronterizo* perspective, see Irwin, "Ramona and Postnationalist American Studies."

14. This is the name used in Martí's translation, fitting for an indigenous man educated by Spanish missionaries in old California; Jackson, as seen above, oddly employs the Italian name, Alessandro. Similarly, Martí Hispanicizes the last name of the elder Ramona (the protagonist's first stepmother) from the odd Ortegna to the more Spanish sounding Orteña.

15. See, for example, Venegas, Jacobs, Luis-Brown, Gutiérrez-Jones (50–79), Noriega, and Goldman (39–64).

16. The Mexican *cronista* and man of letters Manuel Gutiérrez Najera avidly praised Martí's translation of *Ramona* because "it calms the nerves and tranquilizes the conscience." Although he found Jackson to have less talent than the great writers of the day, he concluded, "she makes one suffer less" (236) than those writers do. He overlooked the utterly radical racial configuration of the novel's interracial couple, Ramona and Alejandro, focusing instead on "the goodness of the whole, rich in vital juices, prodigious with life, full of love of nature and humanity" (239). His book review, originally published in *El Partido Liberal* 23 December 1888, 1, was a rare example of the scant attention Martí's translation received in Mexico City despite Martí's keen interest in promoting it there (see Fountain). There is no evidence that it received any attention whatsoever in the northern borderlands.

17. As late as 1901, Manuel Balbás insisted that Yaqui labor was absolutely necessary. "It would not be possible to rapidly substitute other elements because immigration to Sonora is not attractive at all to Mexicans from other parts of the country, and the problem of foreign colonization is so complex and difficult that its realization requires time" (131). See also Figueroa Valenzuela, "Los indios" 140.

18. Tinker Salas gives the example of the Maricopas, a group whose traditional lands spanned both sides of what became the national border in 1848 but who were assigned to live in Arizona (109).

19. While "Kunkaak" is the term by which they refer to themselves in their language, virtually all studies of the group call them, following Mexican tradition, the Seris.

20. It was only when Cayetano Navarro's original letters were discovered by the historian Fernando Pesqueira in 1952 that the Casanova legend was incorporated into local history (Lowell, "Sources" 6). Meanwhile, early newspaper reports on the Casanova case have been ignored by historians. Even the most complete reconstructions of the events from recent decades (e.g., Lowell; Bowen; Córdova Casas, "Lola Casanova") leave out the coverage in *El Sonorense* of Ures.

21. These details were extracted from initial reports from Cayetano Navarro to Governor José de Aguilar from the late February 1850. See Lowell, "Sources" 6–8, Bowen 237. Navarro, coincidentally, was the same man who reputedly took the young José María Leyva into his household during the latter's boyhood.

22. See Navarro; also Bowen 239; Lowell, "Sources" 9; Córdova Casas, "Lola Casanova" 15–17.

23. Bowen 239; Navarro named his source as the Seri interpreter Cheno, who died of fever a few weeks prior to the filing of his 24 April report (242).

24. Calvo Berber, *Nociones de historia de Sonora* 164; it is unclear whether Lola's mother, whose maiden name was Velasco, was of any relation to the author.

25. Actually, her mother "ceded her" to a presumably white family of ranchers when she was only eight months old (70).

26. The review, apparently published before the book was printed, appears as an unpaginated introduction to Hernández's text.

27. This same article was published a few years later in Hermosillo in *Alborada*, journal of the Sonora state high school and teaching academy (15 April 1922, 7).

28. See Aldaco, Ibarra Rivera.

29. Her only other known work is the manuscript "La voz de la sangre: Paisajes y leyendas del Distrito de Altar," which she wrote in Sonoyta, Sonora, in 1965.

30. Lowell, "Sources" 57; Lowell further notes that Reyna de León employs in her text Seri words that appear to be her own transcriptions since they do not follow the spelling used in published Seri vocabularies (153, 156).

31. On Parodi's professional trajectory, see Moncada O., 77.

32. For example, the most authoritative study of the multiple recountings of the Casanova legend to date (Edith Lowell's 1966 M.A. thesis) bills itself principally as a critical study of the Rojas González novel. In Sonora, Horacio Sobarzo's late-twentieth-century history of Sonora bases its Lola Casanova "episode" on Rojas González (and Hernández) (176).

33. Bhabba's hybrid infiltrates the dominant colonizing culture in order to subversively inject into it elements of the colonized culture (102–22). Lola becomes a different kind of hybrid trickster, infiltrating subaltern culture in order to inject into it elements of the colonizers.

34. Writes Doremus, "while [Rojas González] envisions a type of mestizaje that values the indigenous and European heritages equally, his narrative in some cases contradicts this. Notably, it is a Creole and not an Indian who succeeds in improving the Indians' plight. The novel thus implies that the Indians lack the intelligence or willpower to do this on their own.... Most tellingly, the author ultimately favors the destruction of Seri culture through mestizaje" (395).

35. Lowell notes that the novels of Rojas González and Chávez Camacho were likely written simultaneously, and that it is therefore nearly impossible that either exercised any influence at all over the other. While Rojas González did publish his a year earlier than Chávez Camacho (1947 vs. 1948), the latter won a literary prize for his novel in 1947, when it was still in manuscript form ("Sources" 51).

36. For a genealogical summary of discourse on *lo mexicano* from the Portiriato to the latter half of the twentieth century, see Roger Bartra's *La jaula de la melancolia*.

37. It is important to note that Lowell, a literary scholar, undertakes no interrogation of the process of transmission from Seri informants to the anthropologists who recorded their stories, nor does she make clear how these narratives were translated into Spanish or English. Writing two decades prior to Clifford's landmark article, "On Ethnographic Allegory," she assumes communication to be utterly transparent.

38. Lowell uses four separate sources of Seri legend, including a study by the anthropologist William B. Griffen in 1959, an article on popular borderlands legend published in *Western Folklore* in 1962 by Ronald Ives, as well as a pair of versions collected and reported in the 1960s by Edward Moser and by Lowell herself ("A Comparison" 156–57; the latter accounts are transcribed in Lowell, "A Comparison" 148–52). It is significant to note that Moser and his wife Becky were missionaries associated with the Summer Institute of Linguistics, who spent over thirty years living among the Seri. However, it remains unclear whether the particular relationships forged between the Mosers (or Griffen or Ives) and the Seris likely brought about greater trust and honesty in communication or greater suspicion and rhetorical agility on the part of Seri informants.

39. This latter detail was repeated by Ronald Ives (161–62), but not by any other interpreter of Seri lore.

40. Again, Ives—who supplemented his investigations among the Seris with data supplied by the Sonoran historian Eduardo Villa, whose own historiography relies upon Fortunato Hernández for its account of the Casanova legend (Lowell, "A Comparison" 147)—diverges from other Seri versions in asserting that Lola in fact remained with the Seris, never returning to Guaymas (162, 164). For this reason, Lowell classifies Ives's version as neither Seri nor Mexican, but "hybrid" ("A Comparison" 153).

41. "A Comparison" 155; Ives insists: "Genealogical studies of the Seri ... disclose that no present-day Seri traces his descent to either Coyote-Iguana or Lola Casanova" (164); Lowell herself remarks that those claiming to be descendants of Casanova do not have any obvious Caucasian characteristics ("Sources" 40).

42. *La Fornada* online, 10 May 2005: http: //www.jornada.unam.nix/2005/may05/050510/037n1est.php.

43. Córdova Casas counts "over fifty" in the early 1990s ("Lola Casanova" 17).

44. *Cambio* online 4 March 2005: http://www.cambiosonora.com/Impresa/vernota.asp?notID=88427&pagID=55&secID=4&fecha=04/03/2005.

## REFERENCES

Aldaco Encinas, Guadalupe Beatriz. "La Prensa decimonónica sonorense: El caso de *La Voz de Sonora y La Estrella de Occidente* (1856–1870)." *Memoria: XIV simposia de historia y antropología de Sonora*. Hermosillo: Instituto de Investigaciones Historicas, Universidad de Sonora, 1990. 361–73.

Altamirano, Ignacio M. *El Zarco* [1901]. México: Porrúa, 1995.

Antochiw, Michel. "Textus sobre problemas indigenas" [1984]. *Sonora: Textos de su historia*. Comp. Mario Cuevas Arámburu. Hermosillo/Mexico City: Gobierno del Estado tie Sonora/Instituto de Investigaciones Dr. José María Luis Mora, 1989, 405–7.

Arrendondo, Isabel. "Tenía bríos y, aún vieja, los sigo teniendo': Entrevista a Matilde Landeta." *Mexican Studies/Estudios Mexicanos* 18.1 (2002): 189–204.

Balbas, Manuel. "Civilización y barbarie según un médico militar participante en la guerra del Yaqui" [1901]. *Sonora: Textos de su historia*, vol. 3. Comp. Mario Cuevas Aramburu. Hermosillo/Mexico City: Gobierno del Estado de Sonora/Instituto de Investigaciones Dr. José María Luis Mora, 1989. 125–32.

Bartlett, John Russell. *Personal Narrative of Explorations and Incidents in Texas, New Mexico, California, Sonora and Chihuahua 1850–1853*, vol. 1 [1854]. Chicago: Rio Grande Press, 1965.

Bartra, Roger. *La jaula de la melancolia: Identidad y metamorfosis del mexicano*. Mexico City: Grijalbo, 1987.

Bowen, Thomas. *Unknown Island: Seri Indians, Europeans, and San Esteban Island in the Gulf of California*. Albuquerque: University of New Mexico Press, 2000.

Brickhouse, Anna. *Transamerican Literary Relations and the Nineteenth-Century Public Sphere*. Cambridge: Cambridge University Press, 2004.

Calvo Berber, Laureano. *Nociones de la historia de Sonora*. Mexico City: Porrúa, 1958.

Campuzano, Juan R. *Ignacio Altamirano: Constructor de la nacionalidad y creador de la literatura mexicana*. Mexico City: Federación Editorial Mexicana, 1986.

Chávez Camacho, Armando. *Cajeme: Novela de indios* [1948]. Mexico City: Porrúa, 1967.

Clifford, James."On Ethnographic Allegory." *Writing Culture: The Poetics and Politics of Ethnography*. Ed. James Clifford and George E. Marcus. Berkeley: University of California Press, 1986. 98–121.

Córdova Casas, Sergio. "Las guerras de Encinas." *Sonora: Historia de la vida cotidiana.* Coord. Virgilio López Soto. Hermosillo: Consejo Editorial de la Sociedad Sonorense de Historia, 1998. 295–305.

———. "Lola Casanova: Al margen del mito y la leyenda." *Boletin de la Sociedad Sonorense de Historia* 68–69 (1993): 12–15, 15–19.

Córdova Rascón, José René. "Sonoreños contra apaches: La campaña de 1851." *Sonora: Historia de la vida cotidiana.* Coord. Virgilio López Soto. Hermosillo: Sociedad Sonorense de Historia, 1998. 155–78.

Cypess, Sandra Messinger. *La Malinche in Mexican Literature: From History to Myth.* Austin: University of Texas Press, 1991.

Dávila, Francisco T. *Sonora histórico y descriptivo.* Nogales, Ariz.: Tipografía de R. Bernal, 1894.

DeLyser, Dydia. *Ramona Memories: Tourism and the Shaping of Southern California.* Minneapolis: University of Minnesota Press, 2005.

Dever, Susan. *Celluloid Nationalism and Other Melodramas: From Post-revolutionary Mexico to fin de siglo Mexamérica.* Albany: State University of New York Press, 2003.

Doremus, Anne. "Indigenism, Mestizaje, and National Identity in Mexico during the 1940s and 1950s." *Mexican Studies/Estudios Mexicanos* 17.2 (2001): 375–402.

Escobosa Gámez, Gilberto. *Hermosillo en mi memoria: Crónica.* Hermosillo: Instituto Sonorense de Cultura, 1995.

Esteva, José María. *La campana de la misión* [1894]. Xalapa: Universidad Veracruzana, 1998.

Faery, Rebecca Bevins. *Cartographies of Desire: Captivity, Race, and Sex in the Shopping of an American Nation.* Norman: University of Oklahoma Press, 1999.

Fernández, Emilio "el Indio," dir. *María Candelaria.* With Dolores del Río, Pedro Armendáriz. Mexico City: Films Mundiales, 1943.

Figuero Valenzuela, Alejandro. "Los indios de Sonora ante la modernización porfirista." *Historia general de Sonora.* Vol. 4: *Sonora moderno: 1880–1929* [1985]. Coord. Cynthia Radding de Murrieta. Hermosillo: Gobierno del Estado de Sonora/ Instituto Sonorense de Cultura, 1997. 139–63.

———. "La revolución mexicana y los indios de Sonora." *Historia general de Sonora.* Vol. 4: *Sonora moderno, 1880–1929* [1985]. Coord. Cynthia Radding de Murrieta. Hermosillo: Gobierno del Estado de Sonora/Instituto Sonorense de Cultura, 1997. 353–78.

Fountain, Anne. "Ralph Waldo Emerson and Helen Hunt Jackson in *La Edad de Oro.*" *SECOLAS Annals* 22.3 (1991): 44–50.

Galaz, Fernando. "Lola Casanova" (transcription). Instituto Nacional de Antropología e Historia, Hermosillo, Sonora. "Artículos históricos sonorenses." Vol. 2, Ficha 8225 [no date]: 305–6.

García Riera, Emilio. *Historia documental del cine mexicano,* vol. 3: 1945–48. Mexico City: Ediciones Era, 1971.

Gillman, Susan. "*Ramona* in 'Our America.'" *José Martí's "Our America": From National to Hemispheric Cultural Studies.* Ed. Jeffery Belnap and Raul Fernández. Durham, N.C.: Duke University Press, 1998. 91–111.

Glantz, Margo, ed. *La Malinche: Sus padres y sus hijos.* Mexico City: Universidad Nacional Autónoma de México, 1994.

Goldman, Anne E. *Continental Divides: Revisioning American Literature.* New York: Palgrave Macmillan, 2000.

González Acosta, Alejandro. *El enigma de Jicoténcal.* Mexico City/Tlaxcala: Universidad Nacional Autónoma de México/Instituto Tlaxcalteca de Cultura/Gobierno del Estado de Tlaxcala, 1997.

Gutiérrez-Jones, Carl. *Rethinking the Borderlands: Between Chicano Culture and Legal Discourse.* Berkeley: University of California Press, 1995.

Gutiérrez Nájera, Manuel. *La prosa de Gutiérrez Nájera en la prensa nacional*. Ed. Irma Contreras García. Mexico City: Universidad Nacional Autónoma de México, 1998.

Hernández, Fortunato. *Las razas indígenas de Sonora y la guerra del Yaqui*. Mexico City: J. de Elizalde, 1902.

Hernández Hernández, Lucila F. Prólogo. *La campana de la misión*. By Jose María Esteva. Xalapa: Universidad Veracruzana, 1998. 7—28.

Ibarro Rivera, Gilberto. *Escritos y escritores de temas sudcalifornianos*. La Paz: Gobierno del Estado de Baja Califirnia Sur/Secretaría de Educación Pública, 1998.

Iberri, Alfonso. "El rapto de Lola Casanova" [1982]. *Sonora: Un siglo de literatura: Poesía narrativa y teatro (1936–1992)*. Ed. Gilda Rocha. Mexico City: Consejo Nacional para la Cultura y las Artes, 1993. 275–77.

Irwin, Robert McGee. "*Ramona* and Postnationalist American Studies: On 'Our America' and the Mexican Borderlands." *American Quarterly* 55.4 (2003): 539–67.

Ives, Ronald L. "The Legend of the 'White Queen' of the Seri." *Western Folklore* 21.3 (July 1962): 161–64.

Jackson, Helen Hunt. *Ramona* [1884]. New York: Signet Classics, 1988.

Jacobs, Margaret. "Mixed-Bloods, Mestizas, and Pintos: Race, Gender, and Claims to Whiteness in Helen Hunt Jackson's *Ramona* and María Amparo Ruiz de Burton's *Who Would Have Thought It?*" *Western American Literature* 36 (2001): 212–31.

Landeta, Matilde, dir. *Lola Casanova*. With Mercedes Barba, Armando Silvestre. Mexico City: Técnicos y Actores Cinematográficos Mexicanos Asociados, 1949.

Leal, Luis, and Rodolfo J. Cortina. Introducción. *Jicoténcal* [1826]. By Félix Varela. Houston: Arte Público Press, 1995. vii–xlvii.

Lomnitz, Claudio. *Deep Mexico, Silent Mexico: An Anthropology of Nationalism*. Minneapolis: University of Minnesota Press, 2001.

López y Fuentes, Gregorio. *El indio* [1935]. Mexico City: Porrúa, 1983.

Lowell, Edith S. "A Comparison of Mexican and Seri Indian Versions of the Legend of Lola Casanova. *Kiva* 35.4 (1970): 144–58.

———. "Sources and Treatment of the Folklore Theme in the Novel *Lola Casanova* by Francisco Rojas González." M.A. thesis, University of Arizona, Romance Languages, 1966.

Luis-Brown, David. "'White Slaves' and the 'Arrogant *Mestiza*': Reconfiguring Whiteness in *The Squatter and the Don* and *Ramona*." *American Literature* 69.4 (1997): 813–39.

McGee, W. J. *The Seri Indians*. Washington, D.C.: Government Printing Office, 1898.

Mimiaga, Ricardo. "Lola Casanova y los seris (en la leyenda, en la historia, en la novela y en cine)." *Memoria del XIII Simposio de historia y antropología de Sonora*, vol. 2. Hermosillo: Universidad de Sonora, 1989. 379–99.

Moncada O., Carlos. *Dos siglos de periodismo en Sonora*. Hermosillo: Ediciones EM, 2000.

Monroy, Douglas. "Ramona, I Love You." *California History* 81.2 (2002): 134–55.

Navarro, Cayetano. "Resumen de las operaciones de campaña contra el seri" [1850]. *Sonora: Textos de su historia*, vol. 2. Comp. Mario Cuevas Aramburu. Hermosillo/Mexico City: Gobierno del Estado de Sonora/Instituo de Investigaciones Dr. José María Luis Mora, 1989. 240–44.

Noriega, Chon A. "Birth of the Southwest: Social Protest, Tourism, and D.W. Griffith's *Ramona*." *The Birth of Whiteness: Race and the Emergence of U.S. Cinema*. Ed. Daniel Bernardi. New Brunswick, N.J.: Rutgers University Press, 1996. 203–26.

Operé, Fernando. *Historias de la frontera: El cautiverio en la América hispánica*. Mexico City: Fondo de Cultura Económica, 2001.

Park, Joseph F. "The Apaches in Mexican-American Relations, 1848–1861" [1961]. *U.S.-Mexico Borderlands: Historical and Contemporary Perspectives*. Ed. Oscar J. Martínez. Wilmington, Del.: Scholarly Resources, 1996. 50–57.

Parodi, Enriqueta de. "La dinastia de Coyote-Iguana." *Cuentos y leyendas* [1944]. Hermosillo: Gobierno del Estado de Sonora, 1985. 25–31.

Paz, Octavio. *El laberinto de la soledad* [1950]. Mexico City: Fondo de Cultura Económica, 1989.

Pérez Hernández, José María. "Industria, comercio, instrucción pública, beneficencia, razas, idiomas y religión" [1872]. *Sonora: Textos de su historia*, vol. 2. Comp. Mario Cuevas Aramburu. Hermosillo/Mexico City: Gobierno del Estado de Sonora/Instituto de Investigaciones Dr. José María Luis Mora, 1989. 464–72.

Pérez Peña, Aurelio. "Carta a guisa de prólogo." *Sonora histórico y descriptivo*. By Francisco T. Dávila. Nogales, Ariz." Tipografía de R. Bernal, 1894. i–iv.

———. *Heroína: Drama histórico nacional*. Guaymas: Tipografía de A. Ramírez, 1897.

Peza, Juan de Dios. "Una obra histórica de suma importancia" [1 August 1902]. *Las razas indígenas de Sonora y la guerra del Yaqui*. By Fortunato Hernández. Mexico City: J. de Elizalde, 1902. No pagination.

Radding, Cynthia. *Wandering Peoples: Colonialism, Ethnic Spaces, and Ecologial Frontiers in Northwestern Mexico, 1700–1850*. Durham, N.C.: Duke University Press, 1997.

Rashkin, Elissa. *Women Filmmakers in Mexico: The Country of Which We Dream*. Austin: University of Texas Press, 2001.

Reyna de León, Carmela. *Dolores o la reina de los kunkaks*. Pitiquito: Imprenta Económica, 1943.

Rocha, Gilda, ed. *Sonora: Un siglo de literatura: Poesia, narrative y teatro (1936–1992)*. Mexico City: Consejo Nacional para la Cultura y las Artes, 1993.

Rojas González, Francisco. *Lola Casanova* [1947]. Mexico City: Fondo de Cultura Económica, 1984.

Rotker, Susana. *Cautivas: Olvidos y memoria en la Argentina*. Buenos Aires: Ariel, 1999.

Ruiz, Ramón Eduardo. "Los perímetros del cambio, 1885–1910" [1983]. *Sonora: Textos de su historia*, vol. 3. Comp. Mario Cuevas Aramburu. Hermosillo/Mexico City: Gobierno del Estado de Sonora/Instituto de Investigaciones Dr. José María Luis Mora, 1989. 7–16.

Sobarzo, Horacio. *Episodios históricos sonorenses y otras páginas*. Mexico City: Porrúa, 1981.

Sommer, Doris. *Bilingual Aesthetics: A New Sentimental Education*. Durham, N.C.: Duke University Press, 2004.

———. *Foundational Fictions: The National Romances of Latin America* [1991]. Berkeley: University of California Press, 1993.

Sommers, Joseph. *Francisco Rojas González: Exponente literario del nacionalismo mexicano*. Trans. Carlo Antonio Castro. Xalapa: Universidad Veracruzana, 1966.

Starr, Kevin. *Inventing the Dream: California through the Progressive Era*. New York: Oxford University Press, 1985.

Stein, Marion. "My Ramona." Unpublished manuscript, 2000.

Tinker Salas, Miguel. *In the Shadow of the Eagles: Sonora and the Transformation of the Border during the Porfiriato*. Berkeley: University of California Press, 1997.

Varela, Félix. *Ficoténcal* [1826]. Houston: Arte Público Press, 1995.

Vasconcelos, José. *La raza cósmica* [1925]. Mexico City: Espasa Calpe, 1986.

Velasco, José F. *Noticias estadísticas del estado de Sonora, acompañadas de ligeras reflexiones*. Mexico City: Imprenta de Ignacio Cumplido, 1850.

Venegas, Yolanda. "The Erotics of Racialization: Gender and Sexuality in the Making of California." *Frontiers: A Journal of Women's Studies* 25.3 (2004): 63–89.

Villa, Eduardo W. *Compendio de historia del estado de Sonora*. Mexico City: Patria Nueva, 1937.

# Serpent Tongues, Social Hierarchies, and National Citizenship

## The Splitting of Border Languages and Cultures between Latina/o Youths

## Cynthia L. Bejarano

This chapter examines the intersections of languages and citizenry and how these factors help to describe how youths of Mexican descent understand their ethnic border identity. Alternate Native youth cultures provide the social niches where Mexicana/o and Mexican-American/Chicana/o students situate themselves among like-minded people and perform Mexican and Chicano cultural productions through distinctive styles. These varying processes of "differencing each other" for identity's sake and for acceptance are primarily revealed through their language use.

The first theme of this chapter explores the definition and distinction between languages communicated by Mexicanas/os and Chicanas/os as they relate to identity formation. The language that either Mexicana/o or Chicana/o students choose to use directly relates to how they describe their identities within a borderlands setting, and how it impacts their feelings of *vergüenza* (shame) in not speaking English or Spanish. It also demonstrates the multiple voices expressed through combining English, Spanish, and hybrid languages to create "heteroglossia" forms of communication to describe one another from a northern or southern perspective on the U.S./Mexico border (Arteaga, 1994). These hybrid forms of communication are primarily used by Chicanas/os while Mexicanas/os must contend with the pressures of conforming to hegemony through the English language punctuated by the recent passing of Proposition 203 in Arizona, which eliminated all bilingual educational efforts in the public school system.

Cynthia L. Bejarano: "Serpent Tongues, Social Hierarchies, and National Citizenship: The Splitting of Border Languages and Cultures between Latina/o Youths," first published as Chapter 1 of *¿Qué Onda? Urban Youth Culture and Border Identity*. Tucson: University of Arizona Press, 2005.

The second set of themes in this chapter addresses issues of structural discrimination and how this manifests itself in youth discriminating against one another through social hierarchies on campus. This chapter also examines how internal colonialism develops within Mexicana/o and Chicana/o counterparts as they begin to define one another as the "Other." This ties into the salience youths place on their national citizenship and its relevance to Chicana/o and Mexicana/o identities. Placed together, language use and the preference for national U.S. citizenship in U.S. society promotes distancing through in-school social hierarchies, internal colonialism, and "Othering" less "Americanized" groups. Collectively, they provide the fuel that leads Chicanas/os and Mexicanas/os to discriminate against each other. As evidenced, the differences between the groups run much deeper than the critiquing, "trash talking," and "mad dogging" taking place from a distance. One Mexicana explains her perceptions of how Chicanas view Mexicanas: *"Nos miran como si fueramos pedazos de mierda"* (they look at us as though we were pieces of shit).

## THE CONFLUENCE OF LANGUAGE
### *Y LA IDENTIDAD EN LA FRONTERA*

Mexicana/o and Chicana/o youths sift through the complexities of their border identities within shared social spaces. This involves convoluted identity-seeking processes that tear at any common notions of "Mexicanness" they may have. Compounding this problem are the ethnic and so-called class divisions reproduced between interethnic (i.e., Anglo, Mexican-American, and Mexican) and intraethnic (Mexican-American and Mexican) groups. Youths of Mexican descent are cognizant of how their ethnicity represents an array of cultural, social, national, and linguistic meaning in the United States. As Bortner and Williams (1997) claim, "Race is likely to be preeminent in youths' descriptions of themselves, for their self-concept as well as life experiences are permeated by racial and ethnic distinctions. Minority youths are especially aware of the racialized conditions of their existences" (p. 46). These questions of racial/ethnic identity and the culmination of all its parts are further questioned and racialized in both metaphoric and physical borderlands.

Multiple marginalities resulted from the divergence in language and citizenship between Latina/o youths at Altamira High School. The Spanish, Spanglish, and broken English they spoke perpetuated the differences between them, even though they all communicated on the borders of permissible languages in the United States. The forms of communication preferred by Latina/o students were not widely accepted by school administrators, staff, and faculty. Speaking Spanish was not encouraged for Mexicanas/os, nor was the English interspersed with Spanish or hip-hop that Chicanas/os spoke at the high school. The aversion to these languages was the initial step in interrogating and policing the identities of Latinas/os by adults in the school setting. Physically living in a Southwestern city known as an immigrant corridor for new Latino immigrants and undocumented people also exacerbated the tendency of students and staff to question the legitimacy of Latino students' citizenship. For example, questions like "Where were you born?" validated some citizenship claims over others at this high school, since U.S. nationality was preferred over unwelcomed citizenships like Mexican nationality. The scrutinizing of language and citizenship together created divisions, social hierarchies, and discrimination between these youths of Mexican descent. Arteaga (1994) explains:

> [The sense of] Being for Chicanos [Mexicanos] occurs in the interface between Anglo and Latin America, on the border that is not so much a river from the Gulf of Mexico to El Paso and a wire fence from there to the Pacific but, rather, a much broader area where human interchange goes beyond the simple "American or no" of the border check. It is the space to contest cultural identities more complex than the more facile questions of legal status or images in popular culture (p. 10).

Regardless of metaphorical or physical border crossings, the telltale accents and styles of speaking place these youths on specific locations along the line of "Mexicanness." Language is the most vital ethnic marker that epitomizes youths' varying perceptions of themselves as Mexicana/o or Chicana/o. Languages also constitute weapons that create and perpetuate tensions between the groups, weapons that cut and tear at the social fabric of "Mexicanness" that prevails in the Southwest. As tools, on the other hand, languages help youths of Mexican descent communicate who they are through their border narratives.

The governing languages of the Southwest include Spanish and English, though variations of these languages blend together to form hybrid forms of communication. These languages compete with one another for linguistic dominance within the cultural space where Mexicanas/os and Chicanas/os are defined by how proficiently they can speak either language. This is especially the case for recent monolingual immigrant youths and third- or fourth-generation youth. Arteaga (1994) describes the situation as such:

> . . . the border is a space where English and Spanish compete for presence and authority. It is not the site of mere either/or linguistic choice but one of quotidian linguistic conflict where the utterance is born at home in English and in Spanish and in caló (p. 11).

For these students, the physical proximity to the U.S./Mexico border exemplifies deeply embedded border identities that are ostensibly Mexicana/o or Chicana/o and are represented through derivations of English and Spanish. Simply put, their nearness to the physical international border magnifies their ethnic identities and reinforces the cultural divisiveness formed between them.

Signs of Mexican culture through music, food, customs, and traditions pervade the Southwest and augment the use of Spanish and Spanglish as markers of a distinct border life. One frequently sees Mexicanas/os and Mexican-Americans/Chicanas/os in the borderlands with a U.S. license plate in the rear of their vehicle and a license plate bearing a Mexican flag in the front of their car, with a scented Virgen de Guadalupe car freshener dangling from the rearview mirror. Overall, these images represent their bicultural experiences that are voiced in both languages. Mexican restaurants can be found on nearly every corner, and local people can tell the difference between "authentic" Mexican and Mexican-*American* based foods as they shop at several *carnecerías* (meat markets) and *panaderías* (bakeries) in local strip malls, asking for food in Spanish or Spanglish. Also, enormous Mexican flea markets are filled with the sounds of Spanish and Spanglish where shoppers can find rows of *vaquero* (cowboy) hats and belts, and hanging T-shirts with airbrushed lowriders sporting the word *Aztlán*, written in Old English lettering, catering to Chicano youth. These popular Mexicana/o and Chicana/o public spaces in the borderlands are where Spanish and Spanglish converge.

These illustrations are not meant to essentialize all Mexicanas/os and Chicanas/os, nor are they meant to represent a comprehensive characterization of Mexican-descent people. They are included only to demonstrate the familiar spaces where border languages are practiced. This brief description of the physical spaces in one metropolitan area merely provides a glimpse of what can be found on the borderlands and points to numerous opportunities where Mexicanas/os and Chicanas/os speak in Spanish and Spanglish. Overall, it is a metropolitan area similar to other borderland cities where one can pass a Mexicana/o or Chicana/o barrio approximately every five to ten miles throughout the region.

Mexicanas/os and Chicanas/os do not represent small pockets of Latinos as might be found in other U.S. regions. Due to the large numbers of multigenerational people of Mexican descent in the borderlands, language issues are paramount. Much of this has to do with people's length of stay in the United States and their preferences for one language over the other. Language proficiency, however, more than any other cultural marker creates the largest split between Mexicana/o and Chicana/o youths. Samantha's comments illustrate this:

*Nomás quo hay mucha discusión aquí con muchas personas que no son precisamente chicanos, simplemente hallas a muchos mexicanos que se vienen para acá y como que se sienten superior a uno o nos quieren humillar por el lado de que no hablamos inglés y no nos podemos defender muy bien on este país. Muchos que son mexicanos se vienen chiquitos, en su casa puede que hablen el español y todo, pero ya en otros lugares fuera de su casa no hablan español, se sienten chicanos y todo. La verdad no siento porqué, porqué somos nuestra misma raza, nos tienen que ayudar pa salir adelante como hispanos, porque el hecho que sean chicanos no quiere decir que dejen de ser hispanos.*

(There is a lot of discussion on this topic, because there are a lot of people who are not exactly Chicanos. You'll find a lot of Mexicans that come here, and it's as if they feel superior to you or that they want to humiliate us since we don't speak English and we can't get by too easily in this country. Many of the Mexicans came here young, in their house maybe they speak Spanish, but in other places outside the home, they don't speak Spanish, they feel like Chicanos. The truth is, I don't know why they do this, because they are our same race. They have to help us get ahead as Hispanics, because the fact that they are Chicanos doesn't mean that they are no longer Hispanics.)

The majority of youths in this study who identified as Mexicanas/os were immigrant youths who had been in this country from a few months to a few years. There were also some Mexicana/o youths who came to the United States as small children or were second-generation youths who spoke predominantly Spanish in the home and with friends, yet their English had faint accents.

Research by Rumbaut (1997) explains the salience of English language proficiency among immigrant youths. He explained that "the capacity to learn and to speak a language like a native is a function of age which is especially good between the ages of three and the early teens . . . immigrants who arrive before the age of six are considerably more likely to speak English without an accent, while those who arrive after puberty may learn it but not without a telltale accent" (Rumbaut, 1997, p. 502).

Leslie, a second-generation Mexican-American, views other Mexicanas/os and Chicanas/os as similar but acknowledges the advantage of speaking English. She asserts:

> Pues, technically, yo sí soy chicana, so no puedo ver macho la diferencia. Nomás la única diferencia que puedo ver es que ellas mismas se identifican una a la otra. Entonces, si alguien se identifica como chicanas porque es chicana y si no es porque es mexicana. Pero yo personalmente no veo la diferencia. Yo las veo igual, a lo mejor porque yo se el inglés y me puedo defender.

> (Well, technically, I am Chicana, so I can't really see too much of a difference. The only difference that I can really see is that they identify each other. Then, if somebody identifies herself as Chicana it's because she is Chicana, and if not it's because she is Mexican. But personally, I do not see the difference. I see them the same. Maybe because I know the English language and can defend myself.)

Leslie spent her time with Mexican students and vacillated between calling herself Mexicana and Chicana and code-switched when talking to me. Others, like Angel, a Chicana, revealed the difficulties in claiming a Mexican heritage as a monolingual Chicana:

> I get discrimination, like, from my own race, but they're just teasing with me. But like, some really do get mad at me 'cause I don't know Spanish, and I guess 'cause I'm light they call me "white girl."

Mexicanas/os and Chicanas/os confront similar language issues that they contemplate and digest differently. They engage in a dialectical struggle over languages, even though their struggles are born from the same obstacle, which is, namely, the prioritization of English within U.S. society. Similar to Norma Mendoza-Denton's (1999) California-based study of Mexican and Chicana girl gangs' use of Spanish and English, many of these youths of Mexican descent created Mexicana/o and Chicana/o groups for the same reasons. Mendoza-Denton's analysis similarly describes Mexicanas/os' and Chicanas/os' dilemma in the city studied here and how they make allegiances according to national, ethnic, class, and Chicana/o or Mexicana/o lines that supersede anything these groups have in common (1999). I found the same situation with the youths I studied, where similarities were blurred between Mexicanas/os and Chicanas/os, yet their use of English/Spanglish and Spanish became the main point of reference for their identities. Ironically, the forms of communication that have the most potential to mend differences and create solidarity between the two become the arsenal used to attack each other culturally and linguistically. Mendoza-Denton explains: "Within this system of oppositional discursive practices, the linguistic resources of the students are polarized and politicized so that speaking a particular variety of Spanish or English is an act of identity that displays one's position vis-à-vis the social dynamics of the groups at school" (1999, p. 51).

Youths often equate language and culture, which together often define identity. "Because language has been seen for many years as being tightly bound up with culture, language and culture have been regarded as an impenetrable fusion of two domains" (González, 2001, p. 173). For example, Betzayra's statement poignantly summarized the views of the seven young Mexicanas about the differences between themselves and Chicanas/os.

*¿Cuales son las diferencias?*

(What are the differences?)

*Ay, que algunas chicanas se sienten muchísimo, ni quien las baja de la nube. Se sienten tanto que cuando te miran, te miran par debajo como si fueras algo . . . como si fueras basura, así te miran. Y se sienten como si supieran todo, como si fuera todo nada mas porque simplemente nacieron aquí y porque hablan inglés. Yo pienso que eso no tiene que ver, y también pienso que si yo hubiera nacido aquí y si yo fuera chicana, en vez de estarles viendo así a la gente que no habla inglés, o que es de México o de cualquier otro lado, en ves de hacerlos sentir tan mal, yo creo que en vez de eso les ayudaría porque mis padres también fueron así, y mis padres de alguna u otra forma vinieron a este país igual que yo.*

(There are some Chicanas that think so much of themselves that no one can get them off of their clouds. They think so much of themselves that when they look at you, they look down at you as if you were . . . garbage. That's how they look at you, and they think they know everything, as if it were everything, simply because they were born here and speak English. I don't think this has anything to do with it, and I also think that if I had been born here and I were a Chicana, instead of looking down this way on people that don't speak English or are from Mexico or any other place, instead of making them feel so bad, I would help them, because my parents were like this, and my parents in some way or another came to this country just as I did.)

A mixture of hurt feelings and disdain accompanied the conversations of both Mexicanas/os and Chicanas/os. The level of humiliation and shame seemed insurmountable. When these emotions were coupled with a great sense of pride, a volatile recipe of resentment and divisiveness fermented. These youths of Mexican descent often reduced their identities to a simple equation: English meant Chicana/o, and Spanish meant Mexicana/o. Both groups were fully aware that being bilingual was a great advantage, but many remained monolingual and felt embarrassment, frustration, and shame for not knowing the "Other" language.

## TORN BETWEEN *VERGÜENZA* AND PRIDE

Anzaldúa (1987) states, "If you want to really hurt me, talk badly about my language. Ethnic identity is twin skin to linguistic identity—I am my language. Until I can take pride in my language, I cannot take pride in myself" (p. 59). Young people tease, ridicule, insult, and criticize each other about multiple things, including how they communicate. The lack of language skills for these youths, however, is not a laughing matter. Teasing about, criticizing, and ridiculing language abilities often conjure up feelings of humiliation and shame, emotions that are deeply embedded within Mexican culture.

Criticizing and teasing someone about their language is the worst assault to one's identity. Language is one of the most obvious cultural identifiers people have, and it often serves as the glue with which most cultural markers are packaged together. Language helps to articulate to people the customs, likes, and dislikes one has, and consequently, if people are made to feel ashamed of their language, then they can also be made to feel ashamed of their identity.

Shame, or *vergüenza*, as it is called in Spanish, commonly refers to people feeling embarrassed, shy, or ashamed. Margaret Montoya in her legal scholarship discusses a concept related to what she calls Latina-Daughtertalk that reflects "deeply ingrained cultural values of Latino families" that refer to *vergüenza* (1999, p. 199).[1] Feelings of *vergüenza* in speaking English or Spanish were at the core of the differences between Mexicanas/os and Chicanas/os. Feeling *vergüenza* means you have done something wrong and should be embarrassed. Therefore, shaming the pronunciation of people's language or degrading their attempts to speak a language they are not familiar with can result in damaging consequences for their perception of their identity. *Vergüenza* is one of the worst emotions that a person can feel, especially if this shame is tied into one's identity.

Language abilities seemed to dictate which groups these youths would ascribe to and the friendships they would make. These youths described their identities largely according to their knowledge of Spanish or English. The lack of knowledge in either language restrained them from attempting to cross group borders and thus share their commonalities. It also defined their status on campus as "mainstream" (defined as taking regular classes) or English as a Second Language, which instilled further divisions between the groups and had serious implications for their relationships with others on campus—particularly for the Mexicanas/os.

## MEXICANAS/OS *VERGÜENZA*

For the Mexicanas/os, feelings of *vergüenza* permeated all physical school spaces except those exclusive to Mexicanas/os, such as ESL classrooms or conversations in "their" Z building. Entering a mainstream classroom could be one of the most difficult situations a Mexicana/o tackled, especially when he or she was the only ESL student in the class. I witnessed Maria's experiences during her drama class:

> Maria has to read a story for her drama class and is really not looking forward to it. She is the only Mexican in this class. She left at the beginning of the class period, and we walked to the library, because she needed to exchange her book. She went to a stack of books that looked like simple reading. They were elementary-level books with lots of colorful drawings, that were nestled in a remote corner of the library within one shelf. There was a group of students in the library, and I wondered if it was embarrassing for her to pick out a book from that selection in front of these students. She was in a hurry to pick a book and stared at the floor as we passed the library class. The colorful cover of the book was facing her side as she held it tightly as though to avoid revealing the type of book she was reading. She selected a book that wasn't too thick because she had to read it out loud. She kept saying how she hated the class and didn't want to have to read. She doesn't like this teacher. I think she doesn't like the teachers she feels somehow embarrass her in one way or another. She said this teacher never gives her any chances. They do a lot of group projects and acting, and it is embarrassing for her to have to speak in English in front of the whole class, since everyone else is a mainstream student. She checked the book out, and we quickly walked out of the library. She went back to her normal chattering when we left the building.

Maria and others like her were subjected to reading first- or third-grade-level books with topics related to seven- and eight-year-olds, rather than any literature, for instance, depicting a teenager's struggle to learn a new language, particularly within the context of an immigrant youth's life and their all too often "clandestine" or isolating experiences. The *vergüenza* was obvious on her face that afternoon, along with her "I don't care if I flunk" comment and attitude that masked her embarrassment at not participating fully in the class. School participation was curtailed greatly for the Mexicanas/os because of the *vergüenza* they felt for not speaking adequate English.

On several occasions, I asked the Mexicana/o students why they refused to join school activities, and they answered that sometimes they did not know about them or that teachers would fail to give them information or did not have the time to let them know about these things because the teachers were too busy. Laurie Olsen points to this in her book *Made in America*, and states that students are "often precluded from access to the curriculum that their English-fluent and U.S.-born schoolmates receive" (1997, p. 11). This also includes access to a vibrant and active student life on campus. ESL students at Altamira High sometimes claimed they were too embarrassed to ask for information because of their language deficiency or because they did not want to get involved in school activities because of their broken English. Spanish-speaking second-generation or immigrant youths who came to the United States at a very young age often teased these Mexicanas/os for not knowing English and/or refused to assist them. The following excerpt offers an example:

Have you had other negative encounters with Chicanos/Mexicanos-Americanos?

Celia: *Sí, yo estaba en la escuela, en la middle school, acababa de llegar y no hablaba inglés. Tenía una clase de matemáticas, puros americanos, pero había dos muchachas que eran mexicanas y hablaban en inglés. La maestro les decía, "traduzcan a Celia, porque no entiende," y decían "o no, nosotros no hablamos en español." La maestro me hablaba a mí en español y ellas se reían.*

(Yes, I was in school, in middle school. I had just arrived here and didn't speak English. I had a math class with only Americans in it, but there were two girls that were Mexicans, and they would speak in English. The teacher would tell them, "Translate for Celia, because she doesn't understand," and they would say, "Oh, no, we don't speak Spanish." The teacher would speak to me in Spanish, and the girls would laugh.)

And they were Mexicans?

Celia: *Se ríen de que uno trata de hablar el inglés y no pronuncia las palabras bien, y se ríen del modo en que uno lo pronuncia.*

(They laugh because you try to speak English and don't pronounce the words well, and they laugh at the way you pronounce them.)

Celia had mentioned that she had heard these girls speak Spanish in class on numerous occasions. Being shamed intentionally and time after time further convinces these youths that they will never succeed in learning a new language and discourages them from attempting to learn English. Nonetheless, they can decipher when other youths of Mexican descent tease them or genuinely want to help them with their newfound language:

Betzayra: *Yo tango amigas que son México-americanas, y tengo una en especial que yo siempre le ando diciendo eso "hay tienes mal acento", y yo se lo digo porque yo quiero que ella como ya sabe el inglés perfectamente bien, yo quiero que el español sea igual. Y yo no sé y pregúnte a ella algún día y verán que desde que la conozco ella ha mejorado muchísísimo su letra, tiene mejor acento, tiene mejor todo. Yo lo hago por ella, y si ella me dijera a mi lo mismo de inglés, a mi no me molestaría, al contrario, se lo agradecería. Pero si viene y me lo dice otra persona que sé que le caigo gorda y me dice, "mira, esto esta mal, que esto y lo otro," entonces yo lo voy a tomar a mal. Entonces depende, si es de una amiga, pienso que adelante que es muy bueno y a mí que me digan lo que tenga mal y que se ría es cierto. Pero si es de otra persona, depende de cómo te lo diga porque muchos te lo dicen para burlarse.*

(I have friends, girlfriends, who are Mexican-Americans, and there is one in particular that I always tell, "You have a bad accent," and I tell her this—since she already speaks English perfectly well—I want her Spanish to be the same. And, I don't know, but ask her sometime and you'll see that since I've known her she has greatly improved her handwriting, she has a better accent. Everything is better. I do it for her, and if she told me the same things about my English, it wouldn't bother me—on the contrary, I'd thank her. But if someone else comes along and tells me the same thing, I'd get mad when they tell me, "Look, this is wrong, and this too," and then, yes, I'd take it badly. So, it depends. If it is a friend I think go for it. It's very good that they tell me what I'm doing wrong. I don't care if they laugh. But if it is from someone else, it depends on how they say it, because many just tell you to laugh at you.)

Their *vergüenza* was deeply rooted in every shameful experience they had that either kept them from wanting to learn English or pushed them to attempt to learn it or practice it only during safe times or with trusted people, such as in ESL classes with teachers and others in whom they confided. These times, however, were few and far between. Some of the Mexicana/o students, particularly the girls, would ask me to speak to them in English so they could practice their English. Very few of the students would speak English in their classrooms, and when they did, they would tease each other good-naturedly because they all spoke English choppily and mispronounced words.

I distinctly remember this during an ESL play where the students made props out of construction paper reminiscent of elementary assignments and school productions. They giggled and spoke in English with thick accents. I even heard them refer to each other as *"mojados sin papeles"* ("wetbacks" without papers) and *"gueys"* (buey with a *b* is a castrated bull, a term often pronounced as "guey" and used derogatorily among friends in jest) as they practiced in class or were in the cafeteria. The Mexican boys commonly referred to each other in these ways.

The Mexicana/o students seemed happiest in a large group and speaking their mother tongue without inhibitions. In contrast, when English speakers surrounded them, they seemed more reserved and quiet. They would speak only in Spanish to one another, although they had acquired a broader knowledge of the English language at school. Perhaps they did this because they were surrounded by hundreds of Latino-oriented stores and Latina/o coworkers and supervisors, so they did not need to worry about language barriers within their social networks and immediate neighborhoods. The limitation of not using English, or not using it well, relegated them to lower-wage salaries and job positions, as Menjívar (2000) found among Salvadoran immigrant youths in California.

The school setting forced them to confront their lack of English skills and provided them with unfair points of reference (English-speaking Americans and Mexican Americans) with which to gauge their skills. The ridicule they confronted made several of them recoil from mainstream activities and other mixed groups of youths on campus. The situation was also difficult for those Mexican-Americans/Chicanas/os (i.e., second generation) who chose to spend time with this group but did not speak impeccable Spanish. Ultimately, they reinforced hegemonic borders among themselves. The equation "language equals identity" was evident again and created feelings of *vergüenza*. This time it was feelings of shame within in-group members, as Elda's experience demonstrates:

> *A mi me critican mucho mis amigas mexicanas, me dicen que cóma me puedo considerar mexicana si no sé escribir o leer bien el español. Pero muchas veces no es la culpa de uno, muchas veces es la culpa no tanto de los padres sino como de la escuela de cómo to hacen raise. La escuela no te enseña el español, te quieren meter más el inglés porque dicen que es mejor que aprendas inglés y el español lo puedes aprender en tu casa. Pero muchas veces no aprendes bien el español en tu casa aunque tus padres hablen bien el español lo aprendes a hablar bien, pero a escribirlo no ni a leerlo y muchas veces una pasa ver-gilenzas por eso. Dicen los mexicanos no por que nosotros [Chicanos] no sabemos hablar y escribir o* whatever *el español, pero no saben que también los chicanos a veces tienen mucha,* they have a difficult time *escribiendo el español por que es difícil porque tanto acento y todo eso,* I mean it's hard. *O sea, se ríen de uno porque dicen que qué chistoso no porque no sabe escribirlo,* but it's hard and we get frustrated because we try *pero no podemos porque ya* estamos grandes y todo y *es más difícil aprender como escribirlo, pero es bueno para ustedes los chicanos que sepan también hablar el español porque pueden tener mejores trabajos, mejores pagados y todo.*

(I get criticized a lot by my Mexican friends. They ask me how I can consider myself a Mexicana if I don't know how to write or read Spanish well. But sometimes it's not your fault; sometimes it's not so much the fault of your parents but of the school instead. School doesn't teach you Spanish. They want you to get more into English, because they say it is better that you learn English, and Spanish you can learn at home. But many times you don't learn Spanish well at home, because although your parents speak Spanish and you learn to speak it well, you don't learn to write or read it, and many times this embarrasses you. The Mexicans say, no, why do you [Chicanos] not know how to speak or write or whatever in Spanish, but they don't know that Chicanos sometimes have a difficult time writing in Spanish because it's hard because of so many accent marks and everything. I mean, it's hard. They laugh at us because they say "How funny," not because you don't know how to write it, but it's hard and we get frustrated because we try, but we can't manage be-cause we are already adults and it's harder to learn how to write it. But it's good for you Chicanos to learn how to speak Spanish, because you can have better jobs, better salaries, etc.)

Acknowledging this language impediment was frustrating to them. Lan-guage issues were so intertwined with one's definition of identity that you could not divorce one from the other. For youths of Mexican descent claiming one identity over another or even claiming both Chicana/o and Mexicana/o raised questions of one's authenticity as either Mexicana/o or Chicana/o. For Mexicanas/os, not knowing English was detrimental to their overall success in the United States and their affinities with Chicanas/os. For Chicanas/os, not speaking Spanish or not speaking it adequately proved problematic for their claims to "Mexicanness." Anzaldúa (1987) states:

> Chicana[o]s feel uncomfortable talking in Spanish to Latinas, afraid of their censure. Their language was not outlawed in their countries. They had a whole lifetime of being immersed in their native tongue; generations, centuries in which Spanish was a first language, taught in school, heard on radio and TV, and read in the newspaper. If a person, Chicana or Latina, has a low estimation of my native tongue, she also has a low estimation of me (p. 58).

The question "How can you say you are Mexican if you can't even speak Spanish?" resonates throughout the borderlands where, often, the contradiction of being despised and loathed as both a Mexicana/o and a Chicana/o is problematic. When ethnic people are identified through the brown hues of their skin color, the first words they emit identify them as what people may call "Mexican" or "Mexican-Mexican." Mexican-Americans/Chicanas/os can claim being simply "Mexican," but this may raise questions of authenticity within the line of "Mexicanness"—especially if the "Mexican" from the northern side of the border does not speak Spanish or is not competent in the trinity of communication (i.e., speaking, reading, and writing) in Spanish. This is the dilemma confronting many Chicanas/os on the borderlands.

## CHICANAS/OS' *VERGÜENZA*

A Chicana/o saying that I have heard again and again is, "We aren't Mexican enough for the Mexicans and American enough for the Americans." Our accents both in English and Spanish give us away as abominations of two cultures and relegate us to border linguistic wastelands. Anzaldúa (1987) asserts:

> To be close to another Chicana is like looking into the mirror. We are afraid of what we'll see there. Pena. Shame. Low estimation of self. In childhood we are told that our language is wrong. Repeated attacks on our native tongue diminish our sense of self. The attacks continue throughout our lives (p. 58).

Looking at both Mexicanas/os and Chicanas/os is also like looking into a mirror, except that the experiences each has is drastically different. Both experience feelings of *vergüenza* but are subjected to it differently. It is true that they shame each other because of language proficiency, but they are shamed by different people and for different reasons as well. Mexicanas/os are shamed for not speaking proper English or broken English by Mexican-Americans/Chicanas/os and other Americans, while Chicanas/os deal with teasing from an unlikely source—their families. This is something that Mexicanas/os do not confront as often, since Mexican immigrant families are all struggling to learn the new language. Mexicanas/os and older Mexican-Americans within their communities and families mostly criticize Chicanas/os.

Unlike the Mexicanas/os who immigrated recently, Chicanas/os have had to confront the painful contradictions of being embedded in two cultures and two distinct languages. The dominant language overpowered the Spanish that may have been spoken in the home or within other "comfort" spaces. Often, these Chicanas/os were stripped of their mother tongue when they began school. The institutional labels found within the schools (e.g., mainstream and ESL classification) and the domination of English placed Chicanas/os and Mexicanas/os at a disadvantage. In every way, these youths of Mexican descent were compartmentalized into specific categories of Mexicanness based on their language skills.

Several of the Chicanas/os mentioned they had learned Spanish when they were children but had forgotten most of it, due to their schooling. Sometimes their parents would encourage them to watch Spanish television, like Marie's mom, who thought Marie could become reacquainted with Spanish through this medium. Marie would get up and stop watching television because she could not understand what was being said. Both mother and daughter would become frustrated at Marie's unsuccessful endeavor at relearning Spanish:

> Marie: My mom gets real mad at me because I'll try and everything, like when she puts it on the Spanish channel I'll just sit there, I won't change it back. I'll just, like, leave it there to see if I can understand the talk shows and everything. I'll sit there and she'll translate it for me, and she's like see, that's what they are saying, but she gets mad at me. I know it isn't really my fault, because when I was born I knew Spanish and English, when I was born. And when I went to school I spoke nothing but Spanish, and they [teachers] used to get mad at me because they couldn't understand me. That's when they made me speak English and I forgot Spanish. I forgot all of it, so now I don't know it.

Renee shared a similar story of the obliteration of her ability to speak Spanish and her parents' fear of their daughter being teased or thought of as ignorant because she spoke Spanish:

> It's like kind of, well, like my oldest brother, he's like twenty-five. When they took him to school he didn't understand [English], so my dad told my mom to not talk to us in Spanish. Talk to us in English so we wouldn't be treated like we were stupid, so that's why we didn't learn.

Leticia, another Chicana, explained that her family would tease her because of her mispronunciation of Spanish even though she had known Spanish as a young girl. She relayed this story:

> Like my family, they make fun of me because, like, Spanish was my first language and, like I forgot some of, like, the words and stuff, so that I was saying something like, I was telling my cousin to kick the ball in Spanish. And I guess the word is something like *patriar* or something like that, and I said *kickiar*, and they started laughing at me. So things like that, they make fun of me, but that's about it. I'm not really, like, treated badly.

Even if an attempt to speak Spanish is made, these youths are shamed despite hearing or pronouncing words as closely to the actual word as they know how. Anzaldúa (1987) explains:

> We use anglicisms, words borrowed from English: *bola* from *ball, carpeta* from *carpet, máchina de lavar* (instead of *lavadora*) from *washing machine.* Tex-Mex argot, created by adding a Spanish sound at the beginning or end of an English word such as *cookiar* for *cook, watcher* for *watch, parkiar* for *park,* and *rapiar* for *rape,* is the result of the pressures on Spanish speakers to adapt to English (p. 57).

When I asked Blanca, a fluently Spanish- and English-speaking Mexican-born immigrant who came to the United States at age five, and Angel, a monolingual English speaker, how people reacted to Latina/o youths who did not speak Spanish, they stated:

> Blanca: Not like people that don't know you (people teasing about language use). I mean, they are afraid to tell you. Like people our age, they won't like tell you, like, stuff about being Mexican, because they don't want to get down with you. I am saying that, in other words, they don't want to fight with you.

> Angel: I take offense to that, you know what I mean? I mean, I would be all, like, the Mexicana I can be. I mean, I admit it, I don't know my Spanish, and I don't go to all the different holidays that are real important to our people. You say something about my people—uh-uh, we've worked too hard. You don't disrespect us like that. But that's like, just like with anybody.

The teasing from family seemed less insulting to them than that from outsiders or friends. However, their stories were relayed to me with a lot of *sentimiento* (hurt feelings):

How about you? Have you ever been treated badly by anyone? By Mexicans/Chicanos or someone else because of the way you identify as Chicana?

> Renee: Well yeah, well, mainly 'cause you know how I say I couldn't speak Spanish, and, well, when I try to speak it, I mean, even like my dad, I mean, he is just playing around, like teasing 'cause, like um, when I was trying to speak it, like, with my brothers or whatever, he was saying that I sound like a white person trying to speak Spanish. And, like, he will be playing with people about me.

Have people been mean about it, like seriously not teasing about it?

> Blanca: My mom about my friends. Like when I told her about Angel. Like my mom she speaks mostly Spanish and she tried to speak to her in Spanish, right, and they try to be nice about it and smile. But my mom just thinks, like, they know Spanish, and they just think that they have too much pride to speak

it. 'Cause my mom's "Mexican, Mexican," and that it's all about racism. And she thinks that she fakes it (Angel) and she doesn't want to talk Spanish because she thinks she is too good for that.

> Angel: I don't know. She knows that I don't know. 'Cause I just say I don't know what you're saying. 'Cause I sometimes understand little things, and I feel dumb, like I feel ashamed, but I really shouldn't because it's like not my fault that I don't know it. I mean 'cause my papa—I don't know why—never taught my mom, and my tia had to learn Spanish from the TV. That's how she learned, off the Spanish channels. But I just have no way of learning it, and that's why I get mad when people tell me you should be ashamed of not knowing Spanish, because it's not my fault. Believe me, if I could've been born speaking Spanish and English, believe me, I would have, but I was never taught and it is really hard now to learn, because I have been so set on learning English and that's all. I've been trying to go back and try to learn a new language, and it's like so hard. That's why I understand the Mexicans that don't know English. I know how they feel 'cause I cannot, I try so hard to speak Spanish and I can't, and I can't imagine English, it's so hard.

These Chicanas vacillated from expressing sympathy for their Mexican counterparts to pointing out their differences in order to distance themselves from them. The collision of languages and identity and the repercussions these factors had for the relationships formed within Latina/o peer groups and even among family were overwhelming. Language use signified a sense of belonging and identity along the line of Mexicanness so profound that youths measured one another according to what they spoke. In the end, both Mexicanas/os and Chicanas/os either spoke Spanish too poorly or English too badly, regardless of who held the measuring stick of success. Anzaldúa (1987) elaborates:

> Chican[o]s who grew up speaking Chicano Spanish have internalized the belief that we speak poor Spanish. It is illegitimate, a bastard language. And because we internalize how our language has been used against us by the dominant culture, we use our language differences against each other (p. 58).

The inability to speak the other language isolates people from exploring their Mexicanness even more. Their *vergüenza* keeps them from seeking solidarity and acquainting themselves with one another. Angel succinctly summarized their dilemma by stating, "I wish like I knew Spanish 'cause I bet you I'd have a whole lot of more Mexican friends. You know what I mean? But it's hard, 'cause I can't talk to them, so how can I build a friendship if you don't know how to talk to each other?" Mexicanas and Chicanas speak languages they are told are improper or illegitimate in this country, even within their own cultural spaces.

Ultimately, the problem is not so much speaking the languages correctly. The problem lies in the *vergüenza*, the shame factor that keeps them from reaching that negotiated space of thick accents and mispronunciations of "okeeeys?" (okays) and "ahoreetas" (*ahoritas*, in a while). Shame is a powerful force to suppress similarities that are not discussed very often. Their "forked" (Anzaldúa, 1987) and "forgive me/*discúlpame*" tongues and the manner in which they have been shamed and learn to shame one another, unfortunately, sometimes lead to the use of words as weapons that divide any common experiences they might share.

## MEXICANAS/OS' AND CHICANAS/OS' USE OF EXPRESSIONS AND LANGUAGE

Language tugs-of-war and cultural expressions shaped these youths' experiences with one another. Language represented the side of the border you were from, while other cultural and border markers, such as generational status or affinities with music and style, although important in the identity-seeking process, were secondary to how their means of communication impacted their identities. The use of Spanish, English, or both was fundamental to what it meant to be of Mexican descent, which often led to both interesting and disturbing verbal expressions involving their like or dislike of one another.

As a result, words were used by Latina/o youths to express their identities and what they thought of one another. The creation of words and even common cultural expressions used by both groups, particularly the girls, to describe one another and others was fascinating. For instance, when I asked the Mexicanas what they thought of Mexican-born girls who hung out with Chicanas/os, they described them as *"mosquitas muertas"* (literal translation, dead flies, connotating people who pretend to be something they aren't; people who put on airs). Some of these girls were viewed as portraying a different, "saintly" face or pretending to be a "goody goody" toward parents and other elders. It could also be used to refer to someone who was a trickster, a manipulator, male or female. Mexicanas, for example, would call Mexican girls who claimed to be from the United States *"agringadas"* (acted like Anglos). Some Mexicanas also thought that other Chicanas/os were *agringados* as well, since they did not want to identify themselves as Mexicans, period. An additional expression I heard from some of these youths was the phrase *"uña y mugre"* (like dirt on a fingernail) to refer to closeness among friends. This was another cultural expression that the youths said they had heard throughout their lives, and they continued to use expressions they grew up with.

Another intriguing point was how Mexicanas/os used traditional cultural idioms and made regular references to religious or spiritual expressions. They used religious expressions that Chicana/o youths did not. For instance, Maira, Xavier, Betzayra, and Juan would make religious comments like *"Gracias a Díos,"* or *"Si Díos quiere"* ("Thank God" or "If it's God's will"). Some people in Mexican culture—particularly elders—speak this way, especially people who are more religiously inclined or continue Mexican-based religious beliefs and expressions. To the Chicanas/os, however, these expressions were sayings that older people in their lives might say, not teenagers "kickin' it" with their families. To the Mexicanas/os, they were expressions that their generation used comfortably and with great ease.

Unlike the Mexicanas/os, but like other youths on campus, the Chicanas used words like "hootchie" or "skank," referring to "loose" women. Another was "playa hatas," or "Ph.D's," meaning manipulators, people who tried to ruin another's situation. Interestingly, these words relayed meanings similar to Mexicanas/os' use of *mosquitas muertas*." The old cultural expressions, like the aforementioned, and the religious expressions of the Mexicanas/os were more identifiably Mexicana/o than Chicana/o. The Mexicanas/os also bridged these forms of "older" (older because the expressions are common among older generations) sayings with other slang words in Spanish like *chante* (house), *chava* and *chavo* (girl and boy), or even *vato* (dude) at times. Their conversations were not entrenched exclusively in the old but did borrow from longstanding Mexican expressions.

As creatively as words were used by these youths, they also cut deeply and hurt one another. Mexicanas/os and even some Mexican-Americans used the word *agringado* to suggest someone was acting "too white" or "too American," meaning they were losing their hold of their Mexicanness. On the opposite end of this spectrum was the word "wetback," used harshly by some Chicanas/os to refer to recent Mexican immigrants that signified just the opposite of being "too American." Although some Mexicanas/os claimed to use this word jokingly with other Mexican friends, the tone of the word was extremely demeaning when used by a Chicana/o or non-Latino. The Chicanas/os often used the term so loosely they were unaware of the hurtful bite it had against the Mexicanas/os:

> Okay, so do you think, Blanca, that there's differences between identifying as a Mexicana or Chicana, or do you think it's the same?
>
> Blanca: I think, they're the same. Like, sometimes myself even, I mean I consider myself Mexican, and sometimes the word "wetback" has come out of my mouth. But I don't take it as being bad, I guess, because, I mean, I consider myself a wetback or whatever 'cause I came illegally to this country or whatever, but like when I say it, it is not offensive, I think. But when someone else is not Chicano or Mexican when they say it to you, that is offensive.
>
> Have you ever used the term "wetback" to call yourself that or to call other people that?
>
> Blanca: I have done both. People have called me that too [laughs].

As a border crosser in her early childhood, the sting of this racial epithet for Blanca had dissipated, and she no longer sensed the anger it caused recent Mexicana/o immigrants. Interestingly enough, she felt a tinge of pain and provocation when the term was used derogatorily toward Latinas/os by non-Latinos.

The borderlands are laden with contradictions and oppression through words and languages, calling each other names, and even using metaphors to identify one another, even though these descriptors may be insulting and inappropriate. This, however, is indicative of life on the borderlands, where identity becomes a claim to "Mexicanness" but each person's measure of "Mexicanness" depends on the types of experiences they have on their northern or southern positioning on the international border. Bilingual/bicultural wars often take place, and their results are interesting hybrid cultures and languages that develop through the negotiations of knowing and retaining languages while latching on to things Mexican and American alike.

## IN THE SPIRIT OF HETEROGLOSSIA
## AND CREATING NEW LANGUAGES:
## *INGLÉS, ESPAÑOL*, CODE-SWITCHING Y HIP-HOP

In the borderlands, where cultures and languages diverge and converge, it is anticipated that youths blend multiple languages and cultures to form original expressions and responses to the hybrid world around them. Anzaldúa (1987) explains:

> For a people who are neither Spanish nor live in a country in which Spanish is the first language; for a people who live in a country in which English is the reigning tongue but who are not Anglo; for a people who cannot entirely identify with either standard (formal, Castillian) Spanish or standard English, what recourse is left to them but to create their own language? A language which they can connect their identity to, one capable of communicating the realities and values true to themselves—a language with terms that are neither *español ni inglés*, but both. We speak a patois, a forked tongue, a variation of two languages (p. 55).

Chicanas/os' forked tongues and code-switching were pervasive in the school setting, especially for those second-generation youths who spoke both languages relatively well. Third- and fourth-generation students did not code-switch as often but understood Spanish more than they spoke it and said words like *ahorita* (in a while) and *mañana* (tomorrow) at the end of their sentences.

In addition to code-switching and the few slang words like *chante* (house) and *vato* or *ese* (dude), and other similar words, Chicanas/os creatively blended both ethnic identities and descriptive words to refer to peers at school. They defied any rigid linguistic rules on speaking only proper Spanish or English on the borderlands, since their identities as Chicanas/os relied on variations of these languages. "The centripetal and centrifugal forces of language use are both in play, and children's fluid use of distinct language domains illustrates the dynamism of children's own language ideologies" (González, 2001, p. xxii). Their hybrid existence as Mexicans and Americans forces them to adopt both languages as functional forms of communication. According to Mendoza-Denton, who studied communication patterns and relationships between Chicana and Mexicana girl gangs, "Linguistic varieties—composed of Chicano Spanish and Chicano English and their variants—differ from both the Mexican and the American standard varieties. The co-existence of two languages and cultures within a single community is not without conflict" (Mendoza-Denton, 1999, p. 39).

Youths' subversion of both standard languages and how they chose to use them revealed their skill in fusing their newly created expressions with the experiences they had in the United States as people of Mexican descent. Identity making and how these Chicanas/os labeled themselves or how others labeled them by combining two different languages and experiences in this fashion was intriguing. The following dialogue illustrates this:

> Renee: I think I am a Chicana 'cause I was born here, and I, well, it's kind of sad though, but I really don't know Spanish. I know some words, I guess, like some of my brothers and stuff, like my older brother knows it but can't speak it, and sometimes he will call us, like, white Mexicans.

> Blanca: Whitsicans. (giggles)

> Renee: White skins. That's what they will call us, our brothers or something. I don't understand the words 'cause like my mom and dad speak real good Spanish and real good English too, and sometimes they will talk in English and in Spanish, and I'm like what? And they will call me White. I don't know.

They call you "white skin"?

> Blanca: Whitsicans are Chicanquis put together.

Chicanquis? [Giggles from everyone]

> Angel: They call me Chicanqui like someone said, like a donkey, another person said like Chicana.

> Leticia: No, like a honky.

> Blanca: Chicana and a honky, like a White person.

Who calls you that?

> Blanca: Just like messing around, our friends.

> Angel: Like my friends. I really don't take it harsh, but it really hurts my feelings, you know what I mean? 'Cause like I went to the MEChA meeting, and I didn't know anything. I felt so bad, I wanted to know so bad what that guy was saying [MEChA guest gave a presentation to MEChA group in Spanish], but I didn't know anything. I knew, like, maybe two words. I felt so dumb.

"Whitsican" is derived from the words *Mexican* and *white* to either refer to a Chicana/o whom Mexican students would have called *agringado* or to label someone who did not speak or understand Spanish. *Chicanqui* was similarly applied. The Chicanas/os combined the word *Chicano* and "honky," indicating the same thing as "Whitsican." These words were normally reserved for

those Chicanas/os/Mexican-Americans whom the Chicanas/os felt were acting too "white," even though some youths, like Renee, Marie, Mario, and
Leticia, either did not speak a word of Spanish or felt more influenced by the
white society.

Still, however, these creative, hybrid words represented a harshness, an
imposition of labels that only served to divide individuals and distort the social injustices at the core of this name calling, discrimination, and prejudices.
These identities could also be found along the line of Mexicanness where the
labels Mexicana/o and Chicana/o might have been overarching dialectical
ethnic labels. Nonetheless, there are also other labels within these groups
(like *agringado*, Whitsican, Chincanquis) that were assigned to others regardless of in-group membership as Mexicana/o or Chicana/o.

It was not uncommon to hear something like "They are Chicanquis.
We don't kick it with them because *se creían mucho* [they think they are too
good]." *Chicanquis*, a mutant word form infused by the borderland experience of searching for authenticity and Mexicanness, is a product of youths'
interpretations of varied border identities. These are words I have made inquiries about with many Mexicanas/os and Chicanas/os in various barrios
and academic hallways, and interestingly enough, no one I have spoken with
has heard of these "Whitsican" and "Chicanquis" labels.

Phrases like the above-mentioned are youth-centered ways of communicating. I have yet to hear any elder border dweller speak with such creativity
and complexity as did some of the Chicana/o youths incorporating English,
Spanish, and hip-hop words. Code-switching with English words, youthful
and ever-changing hip-hop representations like "kickin' it" and Spanish expressions like *se creían mucho* create the amalgam of languages that form a
concept called heteroglossia. Arteaga (1994) explains:

> Heteroglossia is the undeniable state of contemporary culture. Dialogized lan-
> guage makes the return to the monological a nostalgic illusion. What began
> as an effort to subvert the Other through dialogic tactics as a necessary step
> toward nationalism has resulted in the proliferation of texts representing the
> pluralistic tendencies of the Chicano communities. Instead of a fixed and strict
> border, Chicano cultural production has opened an expansive space of inter-
> and intracultural communication in which dialogue is the rule and heteroglos-
> sia the norm (p. 241).

In defining Chicana/o communication, heteroglossia is used to explain
a matrix that includes English, Spanish, and caló.[2] In this high school setting the coming together of Spanish, English, caló, and even hip-hop was apparent. Youths' communication was distinct from others and subverted the
standards of both English and Spanish. It was a reprisal toward the standard
language that, for many, had stripped them of their native Spanish tongues
and reverted them to Chicano Spanish and Chicano English versions of communicating and anything in between. Consequently, this stifled the possibility for English to be represented as a "pure" form of Standard English.
Arteaga (1997) states, "And inasmuch as Chicano discourse is specifically

multilingual and multivoiced, it further undermines the tendency toward single-language and single-voiced monologue, that is, it undermines Anglo-American monologism. It undercuts claims of prevalence, centrality, and superiority, and confirms the condition of heteroglossia" (p. 73).

This resistance to Standard English, although powerful on the borderlands, faces pressures to submit to hegemonic discourse and Standard English that are extremely pervasive. There are no awards for resisting hegemony through heteroglossia or straight, standard Spanish. English is still the predominant means with which to succeed in the United States.

## LANGUAGE AND HEGEMONY

One conduit for hegemony in the United States is Standard English. Without a proficient knowledge of this language, survival and success are questionable. Both Mexicanas/os and Chicanas/os received this message on a routine basis at school. Spanish is a foreign language, and Chicano Spanish and Chicano English are equally criticized. Arteaga (1994) states:

> English carries with it the status of authorization by the hegemony. It is the language of Anglo America and of linguistic Anglo Americans, whether or not they be ethnic Anglos. Further, it is the language of the greatest military and economic power in the world. Spanish is a language of Latin Americans, south of the border and north. Across the border, Spanish is a Third World language; here it is the language of the poor (p. 12).

The overall atmosphere at Altamira High was highly unamenable to these other languages. Latina/o students received subtle messages from teachers and students that these alternative languages were not appropriate or acceptable. Teachers would chastise students for speaking Spanish in the classroom outside of their ESL classes, and other students would turn suspiciously when hearing students speak Spanish, as if they thought these Mexican students were talking about them.

I spoke to the Mexican girls about discrimination on campus, and Betzayra led the discussion by saying she had faced discrimination from teachers. Mikayela stated that teachers here preferred to work with the American students, and they didn't want to bother with Mexicanas/os. They mentioned a study hall teacher who would target Mexicana/o students if they spoke Spanish in class and would tell them to be quiet, but when the other kids spoke English, she wouldn't say anything. Fortunately, this teacher was fired after administration was told of her discriminatory practices, but Betzayra added that this incident still made her feel terrible. She felt as though she came to this country and all the doors were closed to her since, logically, there are more opportunities for the other students who were from here who spoke English. The other girls would just listen quietly and nod their heads.

There was a hint of resentment by some students as well about youths speaking Spanish. I noticed this with a freshmen Anglo boy.

The bell rang and kids started pouring in from outside. Mexican students passed by, and he started mimicking them speaking Spanish, making faces and moving his lips. He looked disgusted as they passed while he pretended to speak Spanish. His Chicano friend didn't say anything and just shook his head and said to me, "He has gotten a lot better than he used to be." The Anglo boy made a comment about how they were always speaking Spanish. At the time, he didn't realize that I was Latina.

These youths repeatedly heard, saw, or felt as though they did not belong because of their language preferences. Some students explained that discrimination was much more inconspicuous, but they felt it nonetheless. The Mexican girls said students do not necessarily have to tell you anything or talk behind your back for you to know that they hate you: "Just look in their eyes, and this says it all." The Chicanas said they knew this stare all too well from Anglos, but the Mexican girls received their stare from Chicanas too:

> Betzayra: *¿Y cómo pienso que es chicana? Es por su cara, por el gesto con que te mira. Mirándola a los ojos puedes saber si es chicana o es americana o se está haciendo que es chicana y no as chicana. Puedes saber nomás por eso, porque entras a una parte y ves a alguien y por ejemplo veo a alguien que es mexicana, yo la veo y ella te va a ver normal como todo el mundo, y si tú entras y si es una chicana la que esta ahí y te mira así como que . . . ¿Quién eres tu? Y aunque sepa español, no habla español. Si tú vas y le preguntas algo en español, ella no te lo contesta en español. Entonces, te das cuenta en la mirada.*

(And how do I know if someone is Chicana? It's because of her face, the way she looks at you. Looking at her eyes, you can know if she is Chicana or American or if she's trying to pass for a Chicana but is not a Chicana. You can tell just by that because if you enter someplace and see someone and, for example, I see someone that is a Mexicana, I see her and she will look at me normal, like anyone. But if you enter a place and there is a Chicana there, and she looks at you like this . . . "Who are you?" And even if she knows Spanish, she won't speak Spanish. If you go and ask her something in Spanish, she won't answer you in Spanish. So, you know just by the way they look at you.)

Language use defined identities. And in a country where the prevailing standard of success is the English language, messages that one's Spanish tongue is invalid prevail. This occurs despite U.S. Census Bureau records indicating that 28,101,052 people in the United States speak Spanish at home; of that number, 927,395 live in the state of this study.[3] Interestingly, out of twenty-three Spanish-speaking countries, the United States ranks within the top five, along with Argentina, Colombia, Spain, and Mexico, having the greatest number of Spanish-speaking populations.[4] An erroneous message is conveyed when bilingualism is not valued. Irrespective of the world trend to embrace the use of multiple languages, of which Spanish is second only to English, the United States, despite Latinos now making up the largest minority group, continues with its pretentious insistence on English monolingualism. "'American'... means the suppression of heteroglossia and the selective recognition of only that set and sequence of factors that enhance the self and mark the alterity of others. Distinctions of language... are but some of the markers employed to subjugate" (Arteaga, 1997, p. 72). As a result, the obliteration of these varied languages by a uniform standard of English communication is of concern. As Anzaldúa asserts, "By the end of this [twentieth] century English, and not Spanish, will be the mother tongue of most Chicanos and Latinos" (1987, p. 59). Hegemonic forces pull at the cultural strings of youths, and although they create cultural spaces at Altamira High and elsewhere where they can maintain a stronghold on their cultural backgrounds and languages, their spaces are infiltrated by hegemonic rhetoric on assimilation and speaking English.

They become "receptacles" of learning, simply regurgitating everything fed to them from teachers and larger educational systems. Pablo Freire describes this as students who become "receptacles" to be "filled" by teachers. He states, "The more completely she [or he] fills the receptacles, the better a teacher she [or he] is. The more meekly the receptacles permit themselves to be filled, the better students they are" (1970, p. 53). In this situation, despite pockets of resistance, students succumb to the messages that teachers and school officials fill them with. The demands to conform are greater than any preservation of culture and language within school grounds. Nonetheless, once students are outside the school grounds, they make concerted efforts to return to what is natural and secure for them: immersion in the familiar contours of what they understand as Mexicanness.

Despite overt difficulties, border youths live within the spectrum of Mexicanness that was central to their identity making. However, their border narratives revealed pressures complicating any possibility of a clear-cut path toward identity. Often, the messages they received claimed they were not members of U.S. society, but simply shadows of a dominant culture or a mere immigrant nuisance. Language differentials (i.e., Spanish or English) positioned them in strategic places along a fence, either looking out at a new First World "frontier" or looking into the faces representing the impoverished Third World. Similarly, stepping outside of their American barrios, for Chicanas/os, or outside of their mother country and over the U.S. threshold called the border, for Mexicanas/os, consequently left both Mexicanas/os and Chicanas/os and other youths in between these two labels vulnerable to multiple negative forces. These included social stratification, internal colonization, and distancing by "Othering" (those perceived to be less desirable than one's own social category). These forces and the discourses about citizenship together produced in-between groups of Latina/o youths struggling to maintain ties to both Mexicanas/os and Chicanas/os or alternatively preferring one to the other. The complexity under which these youths functioned was astounding.

## SOCIAL HIERARCHIES

The practice of socially stratifying groups within a youth-centered setting was prevalent at this high school. It was common for youth groups to feel as though they were part of a social hierarchy where popular groups were given elevated status, while the more ostracized groups were located on the bottom rung of a social ladder. Javier and Arturo commented, "*la razón que la gente no se quieren en la escuela es que cada grupo creían que son mejor que los otros. Por ejemplo, los Negros piensan que son mejores que los demás y los Chicanos piensan que son mejor que los Negros y los mexicanos*" (The reason why students do not get along at school is that each group thinks their culture is better than the other. For example, the black kids think they are better than anyone else, the Chicano kids think they are better than the blacks and Mexicanos).

The Mexicanas/os and Chicanas/os in their alterNative youth cultures were situated somewhere within these social and racial/ethnic groups and felt they were more specifically located on the lower echelons of a three-layered stratification where Mexicanas/os were at the bottom, Chicanas/os were in the middle, and Anglo youths were at the top. This hierarchy or social stratification was an informal process the Latina/o youths felt was pressed on them by other youths in the school setting. Even though there was no officially sanctioned school hierarchy, the youths of Mexican descent I spoke to were fully cognizant that their racialized identities created different experiences for them compared to non-Latinos.

Theirs was a struggle acutely impacted by the overpowering messages of conformity and assimilation they received. Hegemony was maintained through an educational system structured by the State that perpetuated the agenda of mainstream society. Gramsci describes these as major superstructural levels: one which is "civil society," the collection of "organisms" referred to as "private," and that of the State (1999). Jointly, hegemony is exemplified through the practices of the dominant group or mainstream society that coincides with the "direct domination" or command exercised through the State (Gramsci, 1999, p. 12). Students are, consequently, inundated with messages to conform to the practices of the majority around them by subscribing to those views and mandates shared by State powers and government (i.e., the State educational system, its curriculum, and its employees who serve the overall directive of its school). To do otherwise would reflect dissent, and an aversion to comply with the mainstream.

Their border narratives were, thus, loaded with messages of feeling like either second-class citizens or "aliens" in this country. The proximity to the international border for both Chicanas/os and Mexicanas/os left their identities up for questioning while at the same time leaving them vulnerable to isolation and accusations of not belonging in this country. As Saldívar-Hull (2000) states, "Legitimacy belongs to the Anglo hegemony. . . . To the white power structure, the mojado (wetback) is the same as the Mexicano de este lado (Mexican from the U.S. side)" (p. 70). The Chicanas/os, more frequently than the Mexicanas/os, pointed to feeling discriminated against by Anglos and trapped on a middle plane. Their experiences with Anglos growing up had been more extensive than that of Mexicanas/os; therefore, their perspectives were born from years of sharing space with Anglos and frequently feeling resented. During a focus group session, the Chicanas shared their experiences with me:

Have any of you felt like you've been treated badly because you call yourself Chicana or Mexican, and by whom?

Blanca: I believe it's not the fact that they say something to you cause they'll [Anglos] never say it to you. Like I said earlier just by the way you look you'll go up to somebody and they'll happen to be American or whatever, they'll talk to you like you're dumb; like real slow like you can't understand anything. Even sometimes they know like you do speak English but just to like put you down. They talk to you real slow like you're dumb. I mean most of like my mom and them [family] they know English. It's not like they had to learn or anything but they wanted to. You know what I mean? Cause there are some people that when they talk they have a little accent and people make fun of them. I mean if they wanted to they wouldn't have to learn but it was their choice to learn that language. I guess to fit in. But even though they try so hard, they still don't fit in. Us Mexicans will never fit in it seems to me.

Angel: It's like they're [Anglos] trying to get us down. I mean we've worked so hard to get where we are and we're still moving ahead, but it's like every time they do that it's like they are trying to eat you up just so you can go down and down back into that hole, and nuh uh we've worked too hard to climb out of that hole!

A struggle was apparent with the Chicanas' relationships with Anglos during these conversations. They quickly pointed to these examples and said they had to compete against whites, and as Angel stated earlier, "step on" Mexicanas/os in order to succeed. They refused to return to the "hole" that they had climbed out of. There was a pervasive attempt to penetrate the highest level of this hierarchy by some Chicanas/os even though they remained socially wedged among Mexicanas/os and Anglos. Freire (1970) states:

the oppressed, instead of striving for liberation, tend themselves to become oppressors, or "sub-oppressors.". . . This is their model of humanity. This phenomenon derives from the fact that the oppressed, at a certain moment of their existential experience, adopt an attitude of "adhesion" to the oppressor (p. 27).

The preoccupation with acceptance and upward mobility, therefore, blinds Chicana/o students from recognizing the oppressive role and nature of their relationships with Mexican and Anglo students. In effect, these Chicanas/os have become the "sub-oppressors" of Mexican students.

Within the context of this social hierarchy, Chicanas/os as a step toward success registered the distancing that took place by Chicanas/os from Mexicanas/os. Their animosity was deeply rooted within the tensions existing between dominant groups and minorities in this country. Yet, at least two Chicanas explained their white friends were not "mean" to them and mostly did not speak to Mexicans because of language barriers. They admitted, nonetheless, that Latinas/os would have to approach whites because they would not approach the Latinas/os on their own. Regardless of these differences and how students projected their self-images in reference to their nationality, Chicanas/os were largely cemented in the middle stratum of this social hierarchy. And even though Chicanas/os recalled their difficulties with oppression and struggles in the United States with Anglo counterparts, the Chicanas/os and Mexicanas/os knew the status of Mexicanas/os was even lower than that of the Chicanas/os.

Conversations with Mexicana/o students revealed that they did not have many relations with Mexican-American (Chicana/o) students because of their belief that Chicana/o students thought "they were better than them" since Chicanas/os were born in the United States. Mexicanas/os felt Chicana/o students were too "Americanized" and were embarrassed to acknowledge them as their own "raza" (people/race). Mexicana/o students felt criticized by the Chicanas/os because of the way they dressed, talked, and acted, and seemed upset and frustrated that they did not get along with the Chicana/o students. When asked how they would respond to Chicana/o students if they were first entering the country, they stated they would not stoop down to their level of ridiculing them and would rather internalize their hurt feelings. Interestingly, some of the Mexicanas/os stated that Anglo students were more willing than Chicanas/os to help them navigate the school system, even though they routinely had difficulties with Anglos outside of the school setting (i.e., at their jobs or on the streets).

Still though, the discrimination they felt from the Chicanas/os was much more cutting. For example, when asked about negative experiences with Mexicanas/os, Chicanas/os, or Anglos, Leslie (a Chicana) said:

> Yes, with all three of them but it hurts more when it comes from our own people, the Mexicans or Chicanos. The point is that instead of them throwing dirt in our faces, looking down on us and making fun of us when we try to speak English, they should help us because we all have Latin blood. It feels worse when it is a Chicana than if it is a gringa or American.

It is as though Latina/o youths stand in a three-tiered school building, each level representing subordination and isolation or acceptance as part of the dominant group. Mexicanas/os gaze upward at Chicanas/os from their first floor with disdain and hurt eyes as the Chicanas/os from their second floor glare upward at the Anglos who they feel have an upper hand over them. Each felt discriminated against or uncomfortable to some degree around the other, even though they did not usually attempt to understand or acquaint themselves with each other.[5] As a result, they used their youth cultures as vehicles to demarcate their style and language use, while disparaging one another through stereotypes and assumptions about how the other constructed their identity as Mexicana/o or Chicana/o.

Groups are largely distinguished from one another through the process of stereotyping, which arises in making one group or groups feel superior in a certain way to another group or groups. This is how group identities also take shape and social hierarchies are formed. Hogg and Abrams (1998) contend that "Stereotypes are part of wider social explanations which again fulfill a human need to explain phenomena. Added to all this is a need for a relatively positive self-image which creates a vested interest in maintaining the stereo-typic inferiority of relevant outgroups . . ." (p. 84). Thus, groups of youths are organized along a hierarchical structure. "According to Park, when dominant and minority groups come into contact, they enter a series of relationships that he characterizes in terms of successive stages of competition, accommodation, and assimilation" (as cited in Blauner, 1972, p. 6). Youth from dominant groups reside at the top of this stratification, while youth from minority groups and immigrant youths may find themselves at the lower levels of this stratifica-tion, with negative stereotypes imposed on them by others or themselves. This classification, therefore, helps solidify the social hierarchy present at Altamira High School, which also mirrors the social categories perpetuated by other U.S. institutions.

"Among Mexican Americans, the selection of a particular identity and label for it has been a political choice related to location in a particular sub-culture and class. Also reflected in their choices is the fact that, like most other US citizens, Mexican Americans have been conditioned by the schools, the church, and other US institutions to believe in the myths of the American Dream" (Muñoz, 1989, p. 12). Accordingly, youths of Mexican descent may strive to transform themselves into what they interpret to be a more positive image. In striving for acceptance, these youths may believe this means be-coming more "white."

For many Chicanas/os "Whiteness" translated into acceptance. The young Chicana Angel's earlier profound statement of having to "step on them [Mex-icans] in order to succeed" represents the frustrations to conform to those hegemonic measures which equate success through approaching a level of whiteness at as close as can be obtained. Freire asserts, "So often do they [the oppressed] hear that they are good for nothing, know nothing and are incapable of learning anything—that they are sick, lazy, and unproductive—that in the end they become convinced of their own unfitness" (1970, p. 45). Thus, by "stepping on Mexicans" they elevate their status and achieve new order where the trepidation of receiving insidious messages of being lowly, uneducated Chicanas/os does not haunt them. By locating Mexicans in a so-cially lower stratum, Chicanas/os can now successfully move upward toward "Whiteness," which is grossly mistaken for success. Not surprisingly, Mexi-cans became the more oppressed in the process.

The examples these youths shared are indicative of the tensions found between people of Mexican descent who try to carve out sociocultural spaces for themselves as Mexicanas/os and Chicanas/os, while competing with Anglos for a semblance of belonging. These tensions often escalate into Mexicana/o and Chicana/o adolescents disliking one another since they are invariably fighting against imposed subordinate roles in society and one an-other. This is attributed to the residue of colonialism found in the Southwest.

## INTERNAL COLONIALISM

The history of colonialism in the United States understandably has had a great impact on people in the Southwest, and inhabitants of this area deal with the vestiges of domination throughout their daily existences. Aspects of colonialism can even be located in institutions like the school setting, which serves as a receptacle for colonization that oppresses young Latinas/os. Barrera claims that structural discrimination extends to "the educational system and all forms of social structures" (Barrera, 1979, p. 197).

For instance, the social stratification that the Latina/o students felt during their school time mimicked the larger oppressive systems found within U.S. society that closely link colonialism and capitalism to the subordination of people of color (Aldama, 1998; Blauner, 1972; Martínez, 1998). Thus, the time spent at school reflects what they confronted throughout their free time. The hold colonialism had on these youths' perspectives was overwhelming. It directly affected how the Mexicanas/os and Chicanas/os perceived themselves in comparison to the other. Barrera (1979) defines colonialism and internal colonialism as such:

> Colonialism is a structured relationship of domination and subordination, where the dominant and subordinate groups are defined along ethnic and/or racial lines, and where the relationship is established and maintained to serve the interests of all or part of the dominant group. . . . Internal colonialism is a form of colonialism in which the dominant and subordinate populations are intermingled, so that there is no geographically distinct "metropolis" separate from the "colony" (pp. 192 and 194).

Internal colonialism as it applies to the tensions found between these groups acknowledges the intermingling of dominant and subordinate populations within a school setting but emphasizes the social stratification evident between these youths and the pressures in "differencing" themselves from those deemed "less desirable" by the dominant group.

In other words, in an effort to break from the social hierarchy mentioned by Mexicanas/os and Chicanas/os, where Mexicanas/os are at the bottom, Chicanas/os in the middle, and Anglos at the top, some Mexicana/o and Chicana/o teens attempted to penetrate the highest level of this hierarchy alongside Anglo youths. Forbes (1992) believes that:

> "the secret of colonialism" lies in the internal divisions created by a colonial administration, dividing "the conquered masses (who are usually a majority population) into rival groups with a small sector (the ladinos, or mestizos, or light mulattos in the plantation south of the United States) being used to kill, lash, and control their more oppressed relations" (p. 152).

Colonialism, in all its shapes and variations, was replicated within the school setting, primarily within the context of Anglo, Chicana/o, and Mexicana/o student relationships. In this case, the conquered masses were Chicana/o and Mexicana/o youths; however, Chicanas/os would perpetuate their divisions with Mexicana/o students by contributing to the oppression of their Mexicana/o counterparts, even though the same sort of oppression was sometimes present by some Anglo youths on Chicanas/os.

Franz Fanon, the French psychologist and theorist of black identity and anticolonialism, writes eloquently of similar struggles for black people. His arguments are wholly applicable to the colonization expressed by these Latino youths. Fanon (1967) writes:

> I begin to suffer from not being a white man to the degree that the white man imposes discrimination on me, makes me a colonized native, robs me of all worth, all individuality, tells me that I am a parasite on the world, that I must bring myself as quickly as possible into step with the white world . . . then I will quite simply try to make myself white: that is, I will compel the white man to acknowledge that I am human (p. 98).

Whether intentionally or not, the dominant Anglo youth groups along with Chicanas/os created oppressive relationships for Mexicanas/os by subscribing to the social and racial stratifications and informal hierarchies present within Altamira High School. Anglo youth did not have to be active promoters of colonization or hierarchical structures. This structural violence was already institutionalized within their privileged position in mainstream society. Regardless of purposeful intent or not, the process of colonization was systematically rooted in their surroundings and relationships. They reflected dominant discourses in their roles as "mini-colonizers" through the power they wielded in this environment. Chicanas/os took second place as both colonizer and colonized. As colonizer they perpetuated the shame and contempt they felt from the mainstream while remaining colonized by the same structure. In effect, they defined success, recognition, and visibility as measurements of "Whiteness."

Colonialism, for instance, was manifested in the student classifications of falling under mainstream or ESL status, which naturally signified the success of one over the other in the school setting. Positive recognition and visibility were attributes to strive for, and both could be found within a "mainstream" label. This mainstream label was a structural classification that even Chicanas/os could acquire, despite their Mexican backgrounds. This elevated Chicanas/os into a classification known more for its reflection of the hegemonic mainstream than any shared educational qualifications. Through this organizational system, structural discrimination enabled students to practice forms of colonialism while simply referring to it as educational status differences and school structure. At this point of the research, youths and their advocates were not, as Fanon states, "in a position to choose action (or passivity) with respect to the real source of the conflict—that is, toward the social structures" (1967, p. 100). Without feeling this sense of empowerment, this outwardly systemic yet subtle sequence of oppression through educational labels continued.

Mexicana/o and Chicana/o youths coexisted but still afflicted one another at times. Often, one group trampled on the other to succeed, thinking this would get them further in life. Youths of Mexican descent were internally colonized and learned from a very young age that there were differences among Latinas/os and others, and they sometimes believed success meant shedding

who they were by leaving some aspect of their culture and themselves behind. Both groups internalized the messages of the colonizer that in order
to prosper and be a member of dominant groups within society, they had
to ignore people from their own neighborhoods or people who spoke Spanish. This practice became a vicious, revolving cycle enacted at Altamira High
School. There were multiple ways in which these youths distanced themselves as a result of internal colonialism. One way was policing the borders
of each other's youth culture and ensuring that its membership was carefully
controlled and maintained. What proved to be the most powerful method of
policing group boundaries was still language use, which successfully created
distance between Chicanas/os and Mexicanas/os. This offered some Chica-
nas/os the chance to achieve what they felt was success. The following excerpt came from Cecilia and Betzayra, two immigrant girls:

> I want you to say something regarding what you are thinking.
>
> Betzayra, talking to Cecilia: *Piensa cuales eran las diferencias entre las mucha-
> chas que nos querían fregar y nada que nosotros* . . . [Cecilia finished her response]
>
> (Think of the differences between the girls that wanted to screw us, but we . . .)
> What happened?
>
> Cecilia: *Estábanos . . . teníamos clase de arte y había unas muchachas chicanas
> bueno eran mexicanas y decían que no. Les hablábamos en español y nos decían "no,
> nosotros no hablamos español, lo entendemos y nada mas."*
>
> (We were having art class, and there were these Chicana girls—well, they were
> Mexicanas, but they would deny it. We would talk to them in Spanish, and they
> would say, "No, we don't speak Spanish, we understand it but nothing more.")

Cecilia further explained that she had heard these girls speaking Spanish
before, and felt as if these girls thought they were superior to Cecilia and her
friends. On several occasions, the Mexicana/o youths claimed that Chicanas/
os and even other Mexicanas/os had become *agringados* and/or wanted to "act
like Chicanos" since they refused to speak Spanish. By taking this posture,
they would not have to claim Mexicanas/os as their own. In other words,
Chicanas/os and assimilated Mexicanas/os were ashamed to claim any
solidarity with recent Mexicana/o immigrants, leaving them to feel isolated
and marginalized. Fanon states, "Shame. Shame and self-contempt. Nausea.
When people like me, they tell me it is in spite of my color. When they dislike
me, they point out that it is not because of my color. Either way, I am locked
into the infernal circle" (1967, p. 116). Like Fanon, many Latino students were
caught in an ambivalent self-construction; they were interlocked in the contradictions of shame and pride.

Even if Mexicanas/os' interpretation of Chicanas/os was completely mistaken, and these Chicanas were simply embarrassed to converse with monolingual Spanish speakers in Spanish, these Mexicanas could not be convinced

of any inhibitions Chicanas/os had of articulating in Spanish. A phrase from Lorna Dee Cervantes's (1981) "Poem for the Young White Man Who Asked Me How I, an Intelligent, Well-Read Person, Could Believe in the War between Races" accurately summarizes their experiences: "Let me show you my wounds: my stumbling mind, my 'excuse me' tongue, and this nagging preoccupation with the feeling of not being good enough" (p. 35). Both groups were self-conscious about their language, their culture, their fitting in and passing-off as "acceptable" to the point of obsession.

A major effect of internal colonialism is that youths feel they do not inherently belong within this school, within this society, within this country. The status and belonging of youths of Mexican descent in the United States borderlands was questioned continuously. The ceaseless badgering and disconnection from other "Americans" made Chicanas/os often feel like they had to withdraw from Mexicanas/os. Mexicanas/os, on the other hand, remained distanced and ostracized from both Chicanas/os and Anglos. Their colonization and displacement was clear, but that of the Chicanos was more difficult to place.

There were, nonetheless, poignant manifestations of internal colonialism present on the faces of those like Corina, a MEChA member who said, "We learned from the MEChA workshop at the community college that we are not Mexican. We are Chicanos and are different. We were wrong in saying we were Mexican." The conceptualizations some Chicanas/os left these meetings with were disconcerting, since the messages were misconstrued as efforts to emphasize differences between people of Mexican descent. They believed that separating themselves from Mexicanas/os was part of a natural and justified process of claiming to be from the United States. It dangerously placed Chicanas/os in the middle of the struggle, while leaving Mexicanas/os on the outskirts of the same resistance. Their colonization ran so deeply that it lay dormant at times and was unidentifiable, while other times it cried out when their identities were mistaken for being Mexicanas/os. The phrase, "We learned that we were wrong to call ourselves Mexican" echoes in my ears as I picture the bewildered faces of Mexicanas/os perplexed at the word *Chicano*, and the Chicanas/os' frustration when they were asked, "Where are you from?" by curious Americans inquiring about Chicanas/os' foreign origins. The paradox is that neither label is understood or respected by many citizens of the United States. This goes back to what Saldívar-Hull said about both Mexicans and Chicanos being viewed as "mojados" by the "white power structure" (2000, p. 70).

Internal colonialism is kept alive through the backlash against immigrants in this country, which I have made reference to several times throughout this research. These are salient examples that directly explain the tensions created between Mexicanas/os and Chicanas/os in the United States. "In many cases a deviant category or stereotype already exists [for Mexicans and Chicanos], but is latent and only activated at times of crisis or panic because secondary targets are needed to deflect attention away from some of society's most pressing or insoluble problems" (Springhall, 1998, p. 147).

The response is to place the blame on an ostensibly powerless group, and how better to do this than to deal with society's problems using a Latina/o scapegoat? These scapegoat arguments go something like this: They [Mexican women] are coming to this country to give birth squatting on U.S. soil to have babies with *papeles* (papers). They are foreigners who swim international boundary rivers and climb U.S.-made and strategically placed fences to raise American brown children who overburden the government and strip the educational system of resources, food, and skills as they grow up to take jobs away from fifth-generation U.S. citizens. Their Chicano counterparts drain the system by abusing welfare and having lots of babies to receive government help, while these children get in trouble at school, join gangs, gang bang, steal, use drugs, and finally end up in prison. This outlandish argument has been made about Mexicans and Chicanos so often that this illustration flows out of me naturally as one of those accused Mexicanos and Chicanos.

Many Chicana/o youths have absorbed these messages, internalized them, and acted on them by creating divisions between themselves and Mexicanas/os. Even if divisions are created between these Latino youths through miscommunication and misunderstandings, students are often reluctant to confront one another about their differences. When asked at school, Chicanas/os quickly claimed being from this side of the border, before anyone could question them more. Their response was often an implied, "Even though the common stereotypes about us prevail, at least we are legitimate U.S. citizens." Chicanas/os continuously combated the negative rhetoric that existed about them and struggled for their own dignity while often concurrently crushing that of Mexicanas/os. Aldama (1997) states:

> Looking back over more than 500 years of history . . . we challenge the practices of representation that reify our positions as barbarians, exotics, illegal aliens, addicts, primitives, and sexual deviants; the essential ways we are invented, simulated, and vanished by the dominant culture; and the insidious internalized colonialism in our understanding of our selves and others (pp. 143-144).

Some youths attempted to debunk these perceptions through resistance, and some even chided those who were viewed as "sellouts."

Claiming the northern side of the border did not always mean the Chicana/o tried to act *agringado*. Interestingly enough, Chicanas spoke harshly of those Chicanas/os who tried to "act white" even though several of them acknowledged feeling more comfortable or "more down with" the "white society." There also appeared to be an in-between group of Mexicanas/os that Chicanas/os mentioned who were first or second generation. This group was also heavily disparaged by Chicanas/os, since, they argued, "they were dissin' their own [Mexicanos], and this wasn't right." The Chicanas discussed this situation with disdain:

> Leticia: Yeah. I agree how she was saying that they [some Mexicans] don't want to admit it [being Mexican], 'cause that like they are ashamed, because they don't want to get criticized, 'cause everybody criticizes them.

Who does, who is everybody, and why would they criticize?

Leticia: Not everybody but some people, like I have a friend who is from Mexico. She is from Michoacan, but she considers herself Chicana because she doesn't want to be called "wetback" by other people, 'cause she said that hurts, you know, and she doesn't like to be called "wetback," so she says she's from here, but she's not.

Do you think they make a difference between Mexicans and Chicanas, or do they just see you as the same thing?

Blanca: A lot of Mexicans are here [school]. There are Mexican girls, and they act like they don't know Spanish, like they're not Mexican because they have the money. [Leticia agreeing the whole time].

Here in school?

Angel: They act like they don't know. They don't even talk to their own people. I don't know if that's their preference—those are the people they like—but all their friends are white, and they act like they don't even see us.

Do they act like that with Chicanas too?

Blanca and Angel: Yeah.

Angel: They think like white is a higher class, and they want to be in the higher class.

Leticia: Yeah.

Angel: (hypothetically says) So to get in with them: I have to be like them.

These are Mexicans born in Mexico?

All: Yeah, yeah.

Dialogue like this only reinforced the colonizer's messages of how hegemony was learned and which dominant lessons were necessary for success. There were some Chicanas/os who felt so far removed from other Chicanas/os that they acted more "white" than other Mexican-American/Chicanas/os (these Chicanas called several "jocks" Whitsicans and coconuts). The culmination of these varied situations helped maintain this informal social stratification, since it suggested for these students a form of fluidity toward what they perceived to be upward mobility. Youths of Mexican descent often tried to move up the ladder independent of one another instead of helping the collective group reach its goals together. It was clear their social status as Chicanas/os and Mexicanas/os was considered below that of Anglos. The following is a conversation with Chicanas about Anglo students:

Do you think Anglos treat Mexicans better than Chicanos? Or do you think Anglos treat Chicanos better than Mexicans?

Angel: I don't think they [Anglos] even see a difference.

Blanca: We're just not white, period. [laughs]

So they only see you as being Hispanic or Latina?

Angel: Some of the white people, they like talk to me, but they don't want to get too close to me, and they know there is a difference because some of us speak Spanish and some of us don't, but they all pretty much see us the same.

Blanca: But I do think there is more of that Anglos treat Mexicans a little bit different than the Chicanos.

Is it better or worse?

Blanca: 'Cause they'll have a conversation, the *gringos* [Anglos], with the Chicanos, but they hardly even talk to the Mexicans.

Angel: Yeah, they'll like barely talk to us, but they won't even say a word to them.

Blanca: 'Cause they're lower class.

Angel: So they know the difference they just don't . . . they won't, like, invite any Chicanas or Mexicans to their parties; to anything unless you're like them and try to be like them. . . [Angel is interrupted]

Blanca: The coconuts.

Angel: The coconut people. That's what we call them.

Many Chicanas/os like the youths these girls called "Whitsicans" or "coconuts," who Anglicized their names, felt compelled to identify themselves more completely with "Americans." This materialized by encompassing a "Chicano" identity for the few Mexicana/o youths who renounced speaking Spanish or denied being born in Mexico. "As a child I had painstakingly learned my bicultural act: how to be a public American while retaining what I valued as Mexican in the most private parts of my soul" (Montoya, 1999, p. 200). It was evident that the coconuts or Whitsicans wanted to achieve an elevated status in the eyes of their white peers, regardless of what their brown peers thought. Blauner (1972) claims:

The logic of racial oppression denies members of the subjugated group the full range of human possibility that exists within a society and culture . . . all the roles, places, and stereotypes that are forced upon the dominated share a common feature: they function to define the person of color within frameworks that are less than, or opposed to, the status of full adult manhood [womanhood] (p. 41).

The process of internal colonialism called for Chicanas/os to detach themselves from those people (Mexicanas/os) or situations that were categorized by the dominant group and hegemony as foreign or "Other" than what was known and comfortable for U.S. society.

## "OTHERIZATION"

The "Othering" process by Chicanas/os toward Mexicanas/os reflects and parallels the discrimination faced by Latinas/os from many American citizens, and the xenophobia of the larger U.S. society. At the same time, Chicanas/os engaged in Othering Mexicanas/os, while these same Chicanas/os were often Otherized by fellow U.S. citizens. Once again, the social hierarchy that was present at Altamira High managed to not only stratify the groups but also make the two less powerful groups (Mexicanas/os and Chicanas/os) feel insignificant and foreign. Francisca Gonzalez (1998) claims:

> Historically and to the present day, Mexicanas[os], as well as all women [men] of color, are textually represented as the "other." . . . Consequently, because of these differences, Mexicanas[os] and women [men] of color are named inferior to both European American men and women and are subordinated through rejection because of race/ethnicity and class differences (Hurtado, 1989, 1996; Matsuda, 1995; Pérez, 1993; Quintana, 1996; Sandoval, 1991; Villenas, 1996) (p. 83).

This passage is analogous to youths of Mexican descent who feel inferior to dominant "American" youths. Consequently, these feelings of "inferiorization" are manifested through Othering one another:

> Samantha: *Creo que hay algunos grupos de Chicanos que cuando nos ven, nos miran para abajo. Aunque yo sé que en el mismo grupo hay mexicanos y chicanos que fueron nacidos en México pero han vivido aquí, y son esos grupos que nos dan esas miradas. Yo no sé, los jóvenes de hay están algo perdidos. No saben lo que quieren. Ellos no te ayudarían; todo lo que ellos quieren es pasarla bien, usar drogas, pelear, y tener sexo.*

(I feel there are some groups of Chicanos that when they see us, they look down on us. Although I know that in the same group there are Mexicans and Chicanos that were born in Mexico but have lived here, and it is these groups that give us these looks. I don't know, the kids of today are sort of lost. They don't know what they want. They wouldn't help you; all they want is to have a good time, use drugs, fight, and have sex.)

Distinct messages of Otherization were relayed back and forth from dominant groups to Chicanas/os and down to Mexicanas/os. Ultimately, the messages trickle downward, impacting youths of Mexican descent. The overarching questions of identity and legitimacy are related to Fanon's poignant query asking, "Where am I to be classified? Or, if you prefer, tucked away?" (1967, p. 113).

Interestingly enough, even though Chicanas/os maintained their status as Americans and had more privileges than Mexicanas/os in the United States, they often felt like "second-class citizens" in the country of their birth. Some Chicanas/os who were dismayed with their status as second-class citizens began to view their Mexican heritage as less significant and allowed dominant American culture to consume their "Mexicanness." The dangers of erasure of their Mexican culture were possible despite their geographical location within the borderlands. Margaret Montoya aptly describes their situation when she speaks of her own experiences: "I felt isolated and different because I could be exposed in so many ways—through class, ethnicity, race, gender, and the subtleties of language, dress, makeup, voice, and accent" (1999, p. 201). Many students, however, were firmly rooted in their primary culture and thrived on this exposure and proximity to the border.

Javier, a Mexican immigrant, poignantly stated that "*la frontera es Mexico*" (the border is Mexico) and believed that many Mexicanas/os chose to stay near the U.S./Mexico borderlands since it signifies the aperture to Mexico. His comment characterizes the heart of what this study represents: the lives of young border dwellers displaying degrees of Mexicanness as it relates to their affinity or lack thereof with the border. The border, which represents the separation of two seemingly comparable yet strikingly different people and phenomena, reinforces these complexities. Samantha, for instance, was able to visit her grandmother in Sonora often and even had dental visits once a month in Mexico.

Despite their rich cultural perspective on living near the border, these students also understood the pain experienced by Chicana/o border dwellers who did not want to identify as Mexicanas/os so close to the border. Chicanas/os confronted the same situation with other Americans who considered them foreign and more closely a part of Mexico than the United States. Both Mexicana/o and Chicana/o youths seemed to constantly battle for some acceptance, whether this meant remaining loyal *a lo Mexicano* (to anything Mexican) or becoming more "American" to save face with others in the U.S. in spite of their nearness to the border and their representations of border culture. Fanon (1967) explains, "I was told to stay within bounds, to go back where I belonged" (p. 115). Well, these youths were already where they belonged; most of them had either been raised near the border or now resided close to the border that symbolized their umbilical cord to Mexico.

Regardless of what tactics they chose, the Othering process for all youths of Mexican descent was a common one that placed them on the margins, the very physical boundaries of living in the borderlands, and wrapped them in the oppositional dialectics they were entangled in. Arteaga asserts, "the Other is more fully relegated to the realm of absence ... the Other is exteriorized, frozen, inscribed. Effectively, the Other is silenced, existing only as defined by a rigid and prescribed alterity or not existing at all" (Arteaga, 1994, p. 21). Those who do not succumb to the pressures of assimilating, who are not lured by the calls of success according to U.S. standards, sustain their lives on the borderlands, but with great marginalization from dominant groups. Anzaldúa (1987) explains:

> I have so internalized the borderland conflict that sometimes I feel like one cancels out the other and we are zero, nothing, no one. . . . Yet the struggle of identities continues, the struggle of borders is our reality still. One day the inner struggle will cease and a true integration will take place (p. 63).

In the borderlands, some of the most recurring questions are, "Where are you from?" "Are you a U.S. citizen?" or, more offensively, "What are you?"

## NATIONAL CITIZENSHIP

Not only have these youths faced persecution about their ethnic and social identities, they have also had to contend with questions about citizenship, residency, nationalism, and simply "being American." Each query has had far-reaching effects on youth. People of Mexican descent are bombarded with questions and inquiries about citizenship on the borderlands, particularly since large numbers of Latinas/os are concentrated in this area. Although the U.S. Southwest still provides Mexicana/o nationals with a better opportunity to "blend in" with Mexican-Americans/Chicanos, this "sharing-space" arrangement further embeds the resentment felt by some Chicanas/os who feel they must justify their identities as Americans to white Americans. As Flores and Benmayor (1997) explain:

> Still, borders, real and symbolic, jut seemingly ever higher and wider to encapsulate the United States against the perceived threat of cultural invasion from Latinos. So Latinos, even those who trace their ancestry and citizenship in the United States back for many generations, often feel rejected as full and equal citizens of the country in which they were born (p. 2).

What value then does citizenship provide Chicanas/os if they are always questioned about their authenticity as U.S. citizens?

This inquisition into Latino identity unfolded in the larger metropolitan area in 1997, where hundreds of documented Mexicans and Mexican Americans were asked for identification by border patrol agents and local police in an effort to deport undocumented Latinas/os. This led to the infringement of rights for several Mexican-Americans and documented Mexicanas/os. The border patrol agents and police went so far as to question small children coming out of school, threatening that if they did not constantly carry their birth certificates with them, they would be deported to Mexico; often, the children had never even been to Mexico (Office of the Attorney General, 1997). These incidents took place approximately fifteen miles away from Altamira High School.[6] Border patrol agents in vans would ask for green cards or birth certificates, exacerbating the identity and citizenship interrogations on the borderlands. The seizing of Social Security cards—both fake and real—and the cultural marker of language which was used to define whether people

"belonged" on this or that side of the U.S./Mexico border magnified how nationality was at times more salient than any cultural ties people shared.

Hence, the issue then becomes, what do citizenship and nationalism signify
if both Mexicana/o and Mexican-*Americans* are perceived as part of the same
Mexican citizenry by out-group members? "The discourse of nationalism not
only encourages seeing identity as inscribed in and coterminous with the individual body; it also encourages seeing individuals as linked through their
membership in sets of equivalents—classes, races, genders, etc.—rather than
their participation in interpersonal relationships" (Calhoun 1991, as cited in
Calhoun, 1995, p. 256). Thus, young people are inscribed with these nationalistic equivalents, even though they do not necessarily have a say in selecting their
own citizenship or residency status. Adults (i.e., parents and guardians) carry
the responsibilities of youths' citizenry more than young people—especially
if parents are en route to apply for their children's citizenship in the United
States. Nevertheless, youths are deeply affected by pledges of citizenship.

For young people who are not treated as full citizens because of their age,
adding the stress of looking like the Other or being Otherized is extremely
complicated. For example, Mexican youths were impacted by their lack of U.S.
citizenship when they applied to high school and did not have their "papers."
At times, they were even refused admittance into the school. Additionally, if
youths did not have their "papers," they often could not attend an American
university, despite having a strong work ethic and good grades. Youths could
not legally apply for a part-time job to help their families or to buy their school
supplies or even a prom dress. If they doctored papers and then worked, they
suffered the possibility of being found out and deported. This jeopardized
the anonymity of the person and his or her family members. Mexican immigrant youths were confined by the chains of U.S. laws and citizenship that
stated they were "illegal" aliens—alleged Martians that swam across borders
to pursue a better life. They came under the pretense that America was, after
all, founded on the backs of immigrants. Chicanas/os, on the other hand, followed a different fate with their U.S. status.

Some Chicanas/os, for instance, relied on their American citizenship for
making claims and in asserting a sense of "belonging" in the United States.
What they may not have realized is that they had a similar struggle as Mexi-
canas/os in making claims against dominant groups in America. Chicana/o
youths had some privilege over Mexicanas/os in the United States simply
because they were born here. They did not have to worry about the same circumstances as Mexicana/o students. Undocumented Mexican students were
preoccupied by the fear of deportation and language barriers that limited
their capabilities of getting into school. Another obstacle was finding suit-
able work where they were not asked for their green cards or asked to speak
English. Conceivably, what was most damaging was their restricted higher
educational opportunities due to the lack of money, their financial responsibilities to their families, or their lack of U.S. citizenship.

Mexicana/o youths, then, were always at a disadvantage in the United
States, since their young peers and adults often failed to give credence to their

rights as human beings. Numerous ESL teachers confirmed their students' difficulties and hardships by stating how students would routinely confide in them and ask if *"la migra"* (slang for INS/border patrol) could come in the school to take them away and deport them. When students heard police sirens, the students would comment to one another that *la migra* was coming.[7] Mexicana/o youths had to overcome obstacles that were unique to them, such as moving to a foreign country from either small, traditionally conservative villages or coming from one of the largest cities in the world (Mexico City). There were multiple changes they had to make with their border-crossing metamorphosis. Most youths would speak nostalgically of their home state, proudly saying, *"Yo soy de* [I am from]" Jalisco, Mexico City (D.F), Nayarit, Sonora, Puebla, or Monterrey. In spite of traversing international borders and cultures, they carried Mexico internally, wherever they went.

A strong sense of national ethnic identity often helped some of these youths overcome social stigmatizations and compromising situations, even though these identities were sometimes the basis for stereotyping or teasing. For instance, Mexicana/o students would proudly claim *"Soy Mexicano"* (I am Mexican) in a cohesive group of Mexicanas/os while sitting in the Z building and sharing common interests. At the same time, other students would call them "ESL," marking them according to their educational level, or would more offensively call them "wetbacks," since they knew these were students from Mexico. It was common knowledge that "ESL" was understood among students as indicating "special" language classes, thus stigmatizing these youths as "foreign and different" or disparagingly as "special."

In many cases, Mexicana/o students not only dealt with the hardships of not having their parents or other family members readily available to them in the United States, but also confronted difficulties when needing their parents for official purposes. For example, when Betzayra had to switch schools due to zoning restrictions, she needed her father's signature, but he lived in a rural area outside of Mexico City. He had no phone, plus it was difficult to get mail to him, and there was no way she could get him to write a letter and have it sent to her in time.

The absence of family, the difficulty crossing the border, and their separation from their home country, made these youths age before their time. As a result, they were more capable of appreciating their Mexican citizenry and the possibility of U.S. citizenship. Very few, however, were able to achieve this U.S. citizenship, due to their lack of permanent residency papers, bureaucratic red tape, lengthy processing procedures, and/or their final surrender to this cumbersome process. The following excerpt captures the Mexicana/o students' maturity and endurance:

> I had been asking Betzayra and Javier about their work schedules and commenting on how busy they were. I did not know how they managed to juggle everything. I asked Javier how long they had been in the U.S., and Javier said that this year is his fourth. He had a triumphant look on his face, like he had been here for a long time. He said this as if he was still standing—succeeding

the impossible of enduring life here. Betzayra said she had been here four years. The conversations were very mature, reminding me of the conversations I had with recent adult Latino immigrants this summer, talking about their experiences and life's travails. They both smiled and stared at one another like two people who had already lived a lifetime.

Their incredible experiences as Mexicanas/os seemed to draw them even more intensely to everything Mexicano. They even spoke of death and being buried *"como un Mexicano"* (like a Mexican) when they were in groups, just like Victor who had a *velorio* (all-night wake) when he was killed and whose body was sent back to Guadalajara, Mexico, for proper burial. Mexican students often dreamt of one day returning to their *tierra* (homeland) to work, live, and die. Most Mexicanas/os were unwilling to surrender their allegiances to Mexico to feel more secure in the United States by claiming a Chicana/o or Mexican-American identity:

> Samantha: *Me considero mexicana yo también por el hecho de que toda mi familia es nacida allá, y yo fui nacida allá, criada allá nomás que ahorita me vine para acá. Simplemente no por venirme voy a dejar de ser mexicana para ser chicana, aunque es la misma raza y todo, los chicanos también son mexicanos. No por el hecho de ser nacidos aquí van a ser americanos ya, la nacionalidad no dice nada.*

> (I consider myself Mexican also because of the fact that my entire family was born there, and I was born there and raised there too until I came here. Simply because I came here doesn't mean I stop being Mexican to become Chicana, although it is the same race and everything. Chicanos are also Mexican. Just because they were born here doesn't mean they are Americans already, nationality doesn't mean this.)

Being proud of a Mexican identity, however, was not sufficient to overcome the several obstacles these youths would confront, like being called "wetback," or perceived as "not belonging here," and experiencing overt racism. Even though these youths were culturally rich, mature, and wise, for many people these qualities were less significant than was their lack of U.S. citizenship. Full citizenship and cultural visibility did not go hand in hand. Those with the most visible and measurable ethnic culture—as is the case with the Mexicana/o youths—lacked full citizenship and the ability to participate fully and confidently in the United States (Rosaldo, 1993). Mexicana/o youths' cultural richness was abundant, but this meant nothing in a country that demands U.S. citizenship and mainstream culture for everyone.

Discussing in great detail the range of citizenship issues for these youths is much more complicated than describing illegal and legal statuses or U.S. citizenship, and goes beyond the scope of this research. However, it is imperative to note the numerous categories of legal and illegal statuses in the United States. Often, the mistake in exploring issues of citizenship is in dichotomizing the categories of illegal status and U.S. citizenship, while overlooking other salient legal categories.

An important standing within the process of applying for U.S. citizenship is permanent residency. In addition to permanent residency, there are numerous official categories for people applying for residency, temporary visas, work visas, and student visas, who are identified as legalized aliens, principal aliens, asylees, refugees, business nonimmigrants, migrants, and parolees. This list is not exhaustive but demonstrates the complex nature of applying for entry to the United States, which becomes more convoluted as the official process of applying for citizenship commences.

One of the steps in applying for citizenship for some Mexican youths was applying for permanent residency. Mexican students never explicitly stated to me their legal or illegal status. Instead, they used words like *mojado* (wetback) to refer to their illegal status or claimed not to be able to work because they didn't have *papeles* (papers). Some Mexicans were here legally while others came illegally. At some point, their parents or guardians may have applied for their residency or citizenship along with their own, since these Mexican youths could not legally apply for themselves because of age constraints. This happened with Isabel. Her father became a citizen approximately ten years after applying for U.S. citizenship, and, as a result, her mother was able to apply for permanent residency. During a visit at their home, her parents revealed this to me, as well as the difficulty they were having in applying for their children. Although their parents or guardians were responsible for their legal standing and filing paper after paper of legal documents and dealing with a tedious and nerve-wracking bureaucracy, these young people were cognizant of the immensity of their situations.

Nevertheless, the Mexicana/o youths did not speak in the legal terms of the INS (now ICE) to refer to their statuses or identities, nor did they show an interest in identifying themselves this way. They plainly stated they were "Mexicanas/os" or *mojados*. "Permanent resident" or "illegal alien" was not part of their vocabulary, and this was probably due to the taboo on this subject. Consequently, I never asked these youths about their status in the United States while they were in school and explained that it was best if they did not divulge this information to me at the time. If I learned about their status, it was because they alluded to it or told me after they had graduated from high school and were no longer considered minors. Some of these youths may have been in the process of applying for residency, but this was never explicitly stated. Instead, some would say, "*Me estan areglando los papeles, pero duran mucho*" (They are preparing my papers, but it takes a long time). By acknowledging the complex and convoluted nature of the legal application process, one can begin to understand the tenuous position they and their parents or guardians were in. Regardless of illegal or legal status in the United States, the Mexicanas/os more often than not simply referred to themselves as Mexicanas/os.

Although Mexicanas/os freely voiced their national identity and used this to suggest their ethnic identity as well, Mexican-Americans/Chicanas/os often affirmed their national identity as Americans and only later acknowledged their Latin ethnicity. Chicanas/os had the upper hand over Mexicanas/os, even though they had subordinate positions in the United States and often felt like second-class citizens. Nonetheless, within the contexts of American culture,

Mexican-American/Chicana/o youths are privileged over Mexicana/o immi-grant youths. This privilege primarily lies in their claim to American citizen-ship over what is sometimes the clandestine and dubious "in-transition" status of immigrant youths and their parents. Some youths may even subscribe to the rhetoric of nationalism that is prevalent in this country—the belief in sub-scribing to only one national identity, without any room for hyphenated iden-tities. Benjamin Saenz exclaims, "A nationalist discourse demands complete acquiescence. You are allowed only one name: American. We are all so sure we know what that label means. To some it means erasure" (1997, p. 94). This nationalistic rhetoric has been drilled into the identity politics of many, includ-ing Mexicana/o immigrant and Chicana/o youths.

Their identities in the United States are influenced by the tensions be-tween native minorities like Mexican-Americans/Chicanas/os in the United States and dominant groups. In fact, Mexican-American/Chicana/o youths may have a much more difficult time negotiating their identities, since they feel as though they are not one or the other (Mexican or American). In this research, Mexicana/o immigrant youths were more inclined to quickly boast of being Mexicana/o when asked how they ethnically self-identified, while Mexican-American/Chicanas/os sometimes hesitated and then offered an array of responses. Alicia Gaspar de Alba explains these hesitations as such: "Chicano/a identity is, ultimately, a border identity, neither side wants you and you can't go home" (1995, p. 107). Nonetheless, if they chose to climb up the ladder of social hierarchy evident at the high school, they ran the risk of obliterating their "Mexicanness." Rosaldo states, "Curiously enough, upward mobility appears to be at odds with a distinctive cultural identity. One achieves full citizenship in the nation-state by becoming a culturally blank slate" (1993, p. 200). Mexican-American/Chicana/o youths speak of the discrimination they confronted from other Americans as a result of being a minority and second-class citizens. Many Chicana/o youths felt displaced in a country that is their future and which is supposed to provide them with "the status conferred upon individuals by place of birth or by decree of the state and implying membership, with all of its accrued rights, benefits, and responsibilities" (Flores and Benmayor, 1997, p, 10). Young American Lati-nas/os, nevertheless, do not always feel this to be true.

In many ways, it makes it difficult to be a Chicana/o born on the northern side of the border, since there are ambiguities about who you are and what your identities mean. Mexicanas/os' identities, on the other hand, are much more deeply rooted, since they are affirmed solidly. Chicanas/os, needless to say, can proclaim their identities selectively (i.e., Mexicana/o, Mexican-Amer-ican, Chicana/o), using one label over another for a specific occasion. In this sense, they have more leverage to decide what they would like to be called, as Leslie and Evelyn have experienced:

And who asks you what you are?

Leslie: At work, the bosses. That way they have an idea as to how to treat you. They ask themselves, "Does she have her legal papers, or doesn't she? Do we give her the job or not?" Therefore, so that we won't have that problem, I say I'm Chicana.

If there wasn't this problem, like someone else asks you what you are?

Evelyn: *Depende de quien pregunte, porque . . . bueno no sé, se van a reír, pero me ha tocado la casualidad de que cuando un muchacho te pregunta, ¿Qué eres, mexicana o chicana? Tú le dices chicana, y se empieza a acercar a ti con interés, y cuando le dices que eres mexicana, no se acerca a ti. Muchachos que luego te acaban de conocer te preguntan que ¿De dónde eres? Pues de Sonora, y luego te preguntan ¿de qué parte? Pues de tal parte, ¿y de qué colonia?, tengo familia ahí, y tú pues "no pues nunca he ido, y no sé." Yo me identifico cómo mexicana porque toda mi familia es mexicana. Mi mamá es mexicana, pero mi papá es chicano.*

(It depends on who asks, because . . . well, I don't know, you're going to laugh, but it's happened to me that when a guy asks you, "What are you, Mexicana or Chicana?" you tell him Chicana, and he starts getting closer to you out of interest, and when you tell him you are Mexicana, he doesn't try to get to know you. Other guys that you just met will ask you, "Where are you from?" "From Sonora." And then they will ask you from what part. "Well, from such and such a part." "From what neighborhood? I have family there." And then you say, "I've never been there, and I don't know." I see myself as Mexicana because all of my family is Mexican. My mother is Mexican, but my father is Chicano.)

Although the self-labeling process was more ambiguous for Chicanas/os, more possibilities to maneuver their self-presentations to other people were available for them. The idea of nationalism and citizenship directly impacted these youths' identity-seeking processes. It was the "legal" marker of their identity, which would determine for these youths who they were and what they called themselves according to countries and legal constructs. The international border thus became the legal construct, the apparatus with which nation-states, educational systems, local and regional neighborhoods, and even boys and girls configuring their own social spaces and borders distinguished the varied hues and accents of what were Chicanas/os and Mexicanas/os. As Javier exclaimed, "*Si no fuera por la frontera, todos nosotros hubieramios sido Mexicanos*" (If it wasn't for the border, all of us would have been Mexicans). The border-identity tug of war prevails because of questions of citizenship. Youths of Mexican descent are victims of raw and unconcealed discrimination that opposes any ideologies of "Mexicanness" and "Chicanismo" that are inextricably bound to the U.S. Southwest.

Identity making for young Latinas/os is further exacerbated by notions of citizenship and feelings of "belongingness" within or exclusion from U.S. national citizenship. Regional identities at the U.S./Mexico borderlands are also salient concepts that add to the complex identity making of youths. Latinas/os either successfully navigate both identities (Mexicana/o and Mexican-American/Chicana/o) or draw criticism because of their fluid identities as both. Consequently, the middle ground of "Mexicanness" can provide the likelihood to be border crossers of Mexicana/o and Chicana/o youth identities—both successfully and not. This continuum of Mexicanness, though, and its intersections of Mexicanness and Chicanismo are saturated with tensions that reinforce the differences between these border youths, regardless of their feat in straddling the borders of their identities.

## NOTES

1. Margaret Montoya used this concept to refer to *vergüenza de sexualidad* when referring to a California case—the *People of the State of California v. Josefina Chavez*—of a teenage girl who gave birth to a baby, whom she dropped into a toilet. She then wrapped the baby in newspaper and finally hid the child leaving it to die. The state was seeking manslaughter charges against the girl. Montoya, as a law student, was impacted by this case and writes of the influence it made on her experience in law school. When reviewing the case in class, she brought cultural implications into the class discussion including issues about youth and poverty. She uses these concepts within legal discourse to complicate the ostensibly straightforward facts of reviewing a legal case by taking sociocultural facts into consideration. She used the concept of *vergüenza* to describe the shame this young girl felt, which led her to desperate and lethal measures (1997).

2. The reference to English, Spanish, and *caló* here is to the standard forms of English and Spanish and the derivations of these languages that have been discussed throughout this chapter. Many of these young people have reappropriated these words, contorting the articulation and messages of many words. Caló is "as an urban code a synthesis of the different varieties spoken by Chicanos in the Southwest, for it incorporates standard Spanish, popular Spanish varieties, loan-words from English and even code switching" (Sánchez, 1994, p. 128). Sánchez refers to caló as the slang of the young Chicano (1994).

3. (http://www.census.gov/prod/cen2000/doc/sf3.pdf)

4. (http://www.sispain.org/english/language/worldwid.html)

5. I did not interview any Anglo youths on their perceptions of Chicanas/os or Mexicanas/os. Although I spoke to several Anglo youths on unrelated subjects, I saw a few that embraced their Chicana/o friends but none who "hung out" with Mexicanas/os. On several occasions, however, I heard Anglo students refer to both Mexicanas/os and Chicanas/os as "Mexicans" or "Hispanics" and even heard the term "wetback" used by Anglos on occasion. One episode in an English class was extremely disturbing: when a member of our research team asked the class to identify the different groups on campus, a Chicano blurted out that the "wetbacks hang out in the Z building," and everyone laughed. An Anglo male continued the comments in a similar vein, mocking the Spanish of these students, as the mixed-race, mainstream class roared with laughter. I watched horrified at what was unfolding in this classroom.

6. These incidents took place before the Department of Homeland Security was established. During this operation, the U.S. Border Patrol, along with a local police department, were involved in an informal and verbal agreement to undertake this authority without the proper documentation solicited to undergo an alliance such as this one (Office of the Attorney General, Grant Woods, 1997).

7. After all of these youths graduated, I was told that some students used clandestine aliases and papers to attend school. Some used other names because they were eighteen and would not be accepted into school. A former student told me several years later that it was initially extremely frightening to enter a foreign institution with this fear of being caught hovering over their heads.

# REFERENCES

Aldama, A. 1997. Visions in the four directions: Five hundred years of resistance and beyond. In W. S. Penn (Ed.), *As we are now: Mixblood essays on race and identity* (140–167). Los Angeles: University of California Press.

————. 1998. Millennial anxieties: Borders, violence and the struggle for Chicana/o subjectivity. *Arizona Journal of Hispanic Cultural Studies*, 2, 41–62.

Anzaldúa, G. 1987. *Borderlands/la frontera: The new mestiza*. San Francisco: Aunt Lute Books.

Arteaga, A. 1994. An other tongue. In A. Arteaga (Ed.), *An other tongue* (9–34). Durham, N.C.: Duke University Press.

————. 1997. *Chicano poetics: Heterotexts and hybridities*. New York: Cambridge University Press.

Barrera, M. 1979. *Race and class in the Southwest: A theory of racial inequality*. Notre Dame, Ind.: University of Notre Dame Press.

Blauner, R. 1972. *Racial oppression in America*. New York: Harper and Row.

Bortner, M. A., and L. Williams. 1997. *Youth in prison: We the people of Unit Four*. New York: Routledge.

Calhoun, C. 1991. Indirect relationships and imagined communities: Large-scale social integration and the transformation of everyday life. In P. Bourdieu and J. S. Coleman (Eds.), *Social theory for a changing society* (95–120). Boulder, Colo.: Westview Press.

————. 1995. *Critical social theory: Culture, history, and the challenge of difference*. Oxford: Blackwell.

Cervantes, L. D. 1981. *Emplumada*. Pittsburgh: University of Pittsburgh Press.

Fanon, F. 1967. *Black skin, white masks*. New York: Grove.

Flores, W., and R. Benmayor. (Eds.). 1997. Constructing cultural citizenship. *Latino cultural citizenship: Claiming identity, space, and rights* (1–23). Boston: Beacon Press.

Forbes, J. 1992. *Columbus and other cannibals: The wétiko disease of exploitation, imperialism, and terrorism*. Brooklyn: Autonomedia.

Freire, P. 1970. *Pedagogy of the oppressed*. New York: Continuum.

Gaspar de Alba, A. 1995. Theorizing Chicano/a popular culture. In A. Darder (Ed.), *Culture and difference: Critical perspectives on the bicultural experience in the United States* (103–122). Westport, Conn.: Bergin and Garvey.

Gonzalez, F. 1998. Formations of Mexicanness: Trenzas de identidades multiples/ Growing Up Mexicana: Braids of multiple identities. *Qualitative Studies in Education*, 11 (1), 81–102.

González, N. 2001. *I am my language: Discourses of women and children in the borderlands*. Tucson: University of Arizona Press.

Gramsci, A. 1999. *Selections from the prison notebooks of Antonio Gramsci*. Ed. and trans. Quintin Hoare and Geoffrey Nowell Smith. New York: International Publishers.

Hogg, M. A., and D. Abrams. 1998. *Social identifications: A social psychology of intergroup relations and group process*. New York: Routledge.

Hurtado, A. 1989. Relating to privilege: Seduction and rejection in the subordination of white women and women of color. *Signs*, 14, 833–855.

————. 1996. *The color of privilege: Three blasphemies on race and feminism*. Ann Arbor: University of Michigan Press.

Martinez, O. 1998. *Border people: Life and society in the U.S.-Mexico borderlands*. Tucson: University of Arizona Press.

Matsuda, M. 1995. Looking to the bottom: Critical legal studies and reparations. In K. Crenshaw, N. Gotanda, G. Peller, and K. Thomas (Eds.), *Critical race theory: The key writings that formed the movement* (63–79). New York: New Press.

Mendoza-Denton, N. 1999. Fighting words: Latina girls, gangs, and language attitudes. In L. Galindo and M. D. Gonzales (Eds.), *Speaking Chicana: Voice, power, and identity* (39–56). Tucson: University of Arizona Press.

Menjívar, C. M. 2000. *Fragmented ties: Salvadoran immigrant networks in America.* Los Angeles: University of California Press.

Montoya, M. 1997. Máscaras, trenzas, y greñas: Un/masking the self while un/braiding Latina stories and legal discourse. In A. K. Wing (Ed.), *Critical race feminism* (57–65). New York: New York University Press.

———. 1999. Máscaras, trenzas, y greñas: Un/masking the self while un/braiding Latina stories and legal discourse. In D. L. Galindo and M. D. Gonzales (Eds.). *Speaking Chicana: Voice, power, and identity* (194–211). Tucson: University of Arizona Press.

Muñoz, C., Jr. 1989. *Youth, identity, power: The Chicano movement.* New York: Verso.

Office of the Attorney General, Grant Woods. 1997. *Survey of the Chandler Police Department–INS/Border Patrol Joint Operation* (State of Arizona, 1–41). Phoenix: Office of the Attorney General.

Olsen, L. 1997. *Made in America: Immigrant students in our public schools.* New York: New York Press.

Pérez, E. 1993. Sexuality and discourse: Notes from a Chicana survivor. In MALCS (Eds.), *Chicana critical issues* (45–69). Berkeley: Third Woman Press.

Quintana, A. 1996. *Home girls: Chicana literary voices.* Philadelphia: Temple University Press.

Rosaldo, R. 1993. *Culture and truth: The remaking of social analysis.* Boston: Beacon Press.

Rumbaut, R. G. 1997. Paradoxes (and orthodoxies) of assimilation. *Sociological Perspectives,* 40 (3), 483–511.

Saenz, B. S. 1997. In the borderlands of Chicano identity there are only fragments. In S. Michaelsen and D. E. Johnson (Eds.), *Border theory: The limits of cultural politics* (68–96). Minneapolis: University of Minnesota Press.

Saldívar-Hull, S. 2000. *Feminism on the border: Chicana gender politics and literature.* Los Angeles: University of California Press.

Sánchez, R. 1994. *Chicano discouirse: Socio-historic perspectives.* Houston: Arte Público Press.

Sandoval, C. 1991. Feminist theory under postmodern conditions: Toward a theory of oppositional consciousness. *Sub/Versions,* 1, 1–6.

Springball, J. 1998. *Youth, popular culture and moral panics: Penny gaffs to gangsta-rap, 1830–1996.* New York: St. Martin's Press.

Villenas, S. 1996. The colonizer/colonized Chicana ethnographer: Identity, marginalization, and co-optation in the field. *Harvard Educational Review,* 66 (4), 711–731.

# MISSION DENIAL

## THE DEVELOPMENT OF HISTORICAL AMNESIA

## Carl Gutiérrez-Jones

### THE STRUGGLE FOR A VOICE

As the first Mexicano to gain a public voice through radio—specifically through his 1928–1934 Spanish-language "Earlyrisers" variety show—Pedro González plays a crucial role in defining what is at stake in representations of politically active Chicanos and Mexicanos because his experience suggests the complex pressures which may come to bear as such personalities become symbolic figures in their own right for hundreds of thousands of listeners. The most extended and detailed account of González's life comes to us through the film documentary *Break of Dawn* (1988), directed by Isaac Artenstein.[1] As the film's three-way crosscutting indicates early on, González's life was most strongly determined by his commitment to improving the conditions of his community, by his resistance to the staunch repatriation-oriented racism in the 1930s that defined all Mexicanos as wetbacks, and by his survival of six years of confinement and torture in San Quentin—a period which was followed by thirty-two more years of legally imposed exile in Mexico.[2] In response to the repatriation drives (which affected approximately half a million Latinos), and in the face of intimidation by the Anglo political establishment of Los Angeles, González used his groundbreaking Spanish radio show to argue for intensified political response from the Mexicano community, a community which heretofore had remained essentially invisible as far as the city's politicos were concerned.[3]

Reacting to González's efforts, District Attorney Buron Fitts's office harassed González constantly, arresting him on misdemeanor charges that were consistently dropped for lack of evidence and similarly threatening on several occasions to revoke his broadcasting license (Parlee and Espinoza 37). Finally, these authorities fabricated a statutory rape case which garnered the radio personality a fifty-year prison sentence, a sentence which was amended

Carl Gutiérrez-Jones: "Mission Denial: The Development of Historical Amnesia," first published as Chapter 2 of *Rethinking the Borderlands: Between Chicano Culture and Legal Discourse*. Berkeley: University of California Press, 1995.

by the presiding judge so that González might, by an admission of guilt, win his parole at the expense of his public voice. Although the principal collaborating witness in the case, Rosa Mazon, contradicted herself blatantly while on the stand, and although Dora Versus, the alleged rape victim, recanted her testimony shortly after the trial (claiming that she had been blackmailed into testifying by the police when she was caught in violation of a curfew), González won a parole only much later (without admission of guilt), thanks largely to the protest organized by Maria González, Pedro's wife, who helped build a combined defense committee membership of more than 100,000 people. This parole-in-exile lasted thirty-two years, finally rescinded only by virtue of a change in California's political leadership. As the film notes at its conclusion, to this day no official recognition of the legal travesty has been granted; González has yet to be fully pardoned although he has been allowed to return to the United States and continues his political activism.[4] As happens with so many of the Chicano narratives, we find here a study of the legal system, a study critically examining how the institution has managed to partially admit its error through its very own confusion but only after effecting disenfranchisement.

*Break of Dawn* suggests that González's only crime was the crime of transgressing public space, of seeking a public voice which could speak its own language.[5] When González gained this voice, the initial reaction of the opportunist Anglo establishment was to co-opt it. Such action promised the political control of the otherwise untilled, entirely dislocated community. Although the establishment represented in the film was at the same time busy scapegoating the Mexicano community in order to capitalize on the racist sentiments of the broader Anglo public, the promise of political gain clearly outweighed any moral considerations of this contradiction that these leaders might betray. However, when it became apparent that González saw through these machinations and that he would use the radio to expose them, these politicians, and particularly the film's district attorney—given the name Kyle Mitchell—attempt to put the genie back into the bottle by stuffing González into the insular, isolated space that he and the rest of his community initially occupied. The nature of this containing effort is in turn brilliantly captured throughout the documentary, as the viewer continually moves back and forth between González as a public actor and González as a prisoner in solitary confinement at San Quentin.

What remains most powerful about this film is the way in which it demonstrates how popular Anglo constructions of the Mexicano ultimately seek a systematic cultural and physical containment. This critique of containment is reflected in the stylization of the film itself, especially in the repetition of scenes one would associate with clichéd postcard representations of downtown Los Angeles; these scenes, developing a "staged" position for the viewer, suggest a symbolic or allegorical level of interpretation that undercuts southern California's cultural fantasy of Anglo (Spanish) purity. The stylization is just self-conscious enough to make viewers uncomfortable with the images of Los Angeles's tourist-oriented self-representation and thereby warns viewers to read mediums of communication with care—a warning very much in keeping with the film's larger goal of exposing the manipulations behind radio as a burgeoning political tool. This emphasis on the politics of style, in turn, helps call attention to the crucial implications of González's "invasion" of the radio waves. Specifically, the emphasis foregrounds the very effective manner in which González creates a new and powerful affiliation between Mexicano and Anglo cultural forms that is directed at an urban Mexicano population eager for greater enfranchisement.

To understand González's full impact on his chosen medium, it is worthwhile recalling that radio played an important role in refiguring the illusion of the "neutral" and monological information fashioned previously by newspapers. Hence, we find González explicitly framing his advertisements and endorsements as a way of "speaking for" others. His technique projects a self-conscious multivocality and a clear sense that transmissions are mediated. Information may thus be marked as passing through a Mexicano worldview. Were this not enough of a revolution, the film also emphasizes the manner by which radio creates a new, intimate contact with its audience. By watching González slip in and out of his roles as entertainer and product promoter, we thus become keenly aware of how advertising mixes with subject matter to affect desires, to entice buyers.

As a consequence, the film's viewers are sensitized to the great stakes that attended González's success. As a medium that was effective to the extent that it violated earlier barriers between the public and private domains, radio was made all the more potentially transgressive as Mexicano voices gained the power to "seduce" listeners. The technology's alteration of popular libidinal dynamics reinforced new cross-racial linkages like that portrayed in the movie between the Anglo district attorney and the Mexicano assistant district attorney. Hence, the homosocial elements evident in the relationship between these men are very much tied up with gaining control of the radio. As people like González and the assistant district attorney are "courted" by power brokers and then rejected, relationships develop that are given strong overtones of sexual infidelity. This larger suggestion of a libidinal dynamics thus becomes the context within which viewers may read the strategic "appropriateness" of the statutory rape allegations: these accusations manipulate this libidinal economy because the political struggle as a whole is informed by it.

Working with this notion of González's context, I take issue with apologists for the legal system (who too easily dismiss the scapegoating of Chicanos as an aberration, a localized fluke within an essentially just system of social interaction) and with neoconservatives (who see the Chicano narratives as the tainted testimony of discontents who would threaten the United States' political unity with subjective, even separatist criticism); instead, I argue that stories like those of Henry Reyna and Pedro González have everything to do with the threat posed by Chicano access to largely male-controlled public discourse. This chapter focuses in turn on two Anglo texts which have had a broad impact on the popular representation of Mexicanos/Chicanos, two works which might be said to have contributed significantly to a national amnesia with regard to Mexicano and Chicano worldviews: the novel *Ramona* (1884), written by Helen Hunt Jackson, and the film *Giant* (1956), directed by

George Stevens.[6] As reformist works—works putatively committed to assimilationist stances that would bring the disenfranchised squarely into the mainstream—*Ramona* and *Giant* attempt to "work through" rather than repeat the scapegoating dynamics they single out for criticism.[7] Despite these reformist intentions, in both *Ramona* and *Giant* these public struggles are collapsed into private spaces. Such spaces, removed from the sphere of legal enfranchisement, thus become the only site where Mexicano political desire might be imagined, a fact that is intimately related to the overhasty priority given to assimilationist unity put into motion by Jackson and Stevens. Ultimately, these artists did not sufficiently think through dynamics of social interaction and therefore the larger institutional blocks to equality; hence, the retreat to private space, which these works posit as the only ground for political resolution, uncritically duplicates the message delivered by the Anglo establishment in *Break of Dawn*. As I will argue, the political implications of *Break of Dawn* which could be developed in *Ramona* and *Giant* are replaced in these reformist works by a legally inflected domestic romance that effectively sentences Mexicanos to a silent, withdrawn existence—to a "solitary confinement" that may well appease Anglo audiences who want to identify with, and thereby share, the experience of victimization in a manner that does not expose their complicity in the initial or ongoing disenfranchisement.

It follows that a study of Pedro González's attempt to win a public voice for his community, of the resistances which he calls forth, and of his filmic re-presentation points toward a critical approach to the specifically legalistic rhetoric that informs *Ramona* and *Giant*. In fleshing out this legal context, we may begin by noting that both *Ramona* and *Giant* are about rights to service, if service is taken to be respect for larger civil rights supposedly guaranteed to Mexicans by the Treaty of Guadalupe Hidalgo. In a most basic sense, such rights begin with the protection of a public voice, something subtly yet effectively denied in the reformist Anglo texts studied here. Of course, *Break of Dawn* posits a similar loss of voice, but it does so critically, and inasmuch as the film is a product of a multi-faceted Chicano collaborative effort, it becomes its own counterexample: its politics are not insulated in a romantic or sentimental way but rather remain irreversibly public. Any doubts about this fact are challenged immediately in the film. The opening scene—a confrontation between González and a prison official over González's use of Spanish in letters written for his fellow inmates—resonates deeply with current debates about English as an "official'" language.[8] At issue in these debates, and in the prison scene, is the question of how our institutions will accommodate the process of cultural translation which must occur whenever Chicanos and Anglos interact, and perhaps more important how institutions will control the transmission of Chicano public discourse, especially in its Spanish medium. "English-only" proponents (the U.S. English organization in particular) often evade these issues of translation and control by falling back on arguments about the danger posed to national unity by a policy supporting multiculturalism, a strategy that clearly recalls the scapegoating tendencies illuminated in films like *Zoot Suit* and *Break of Dawn*.[9] Such English-only approaches fail to recognize that we need to examine dominant attitudes about biculturalism in the United States as historically and culturally specific moments always contending with ideological interests.[10] Viewed as such, these attitudes tell us much about the acceptance of Chicano/Mexicano public voicings and about the difficulties of representing or effecting such enfranchisement through cultural products like novels and film.

Although bilingual education saw a resurgence in the Southwest during the 1960s—largely a result of gains made by the civil rights movement (gains which were translated into law in the 1968 Bilingual Education Act and the 1974 Supreme Court decision in *Lau v. Nichols*), more recently the bilingual mandate has been open to erosion, particularly in the courts. As a response to the revitalized bilingualism of the 1960s and 1970s, and the rapid growth of Latino populations in the Southwest, the 1986 California English Language Amendment likewise erodes gains that would break through the U.S. historical amnesia that underdevelops Chicano voices. Unlike similar laws, the amendment specifies a process of enforcement that allows private individuals to sue the state. The function of this "process" is far from clear in the law's apparently contradictory statement of purpose: "English is the common language of the people of the United States and the State of California. This section is intended to preserve, protect and strengthen the English Language, *and not to supersede* any of the rights guaranteed to the people by this Constitution" (my italics). Perhaps the most ambiguous question raised by the law is how the institutional delegitimation of a social group's language can avoid impinging on that group's rights; to take the most obvious example, plans have already been made to terminate bilingual voting ballots, violating the United States Voting Rights Act (1965).

Various battles have of course been waged concerning the larger effects of such legislation.[11] But, as James Baldwin has suggested, haggling over statistics and policy details may become a means of avoiding more dangerous issues regarding race and culture, issues that are placed in relief in both Chicano and Anglo art.[12] Rather than recognizing the rights of various cultures within our national boundaries, a recognition which would in turn raise questions about mutual responsibility, the posture of national defense (preservation, protection) promotes nothing less than a scapegoating of Spanish public discourse. Where proponents of such legislation argue that this movement is about the promotion of political unity, most Chicanos know all too well that the stakes are much different, that they are about "rights to service" in the phrase's various senses, and that for many survival hangs in the balance. In broadly political terms, such amendments ensure the cultural insularity symbolized by *Break of Dawn*'s prison scenes of solitary confinement; in addition, this sort of law—by guaranteeing the demise of essential programs—threatens the viability of public forums for the majority of Chicanos.

Hence, from the outset when González is portrayed confronting the legal system on this score, *Break of Dawn* throws light on the insulation of the Mexicano/Chicano voice, making the buried goals of the English-only movement and similar efforts an issue of public confrontation; like most Chicano narratives, this film announces itself as an intervention that stands in opposition to previous reformist undertakings and their "Mission" influences, influences which have come to shape the popular (mis)understanding of Chicano communities. But to fully appreciate this crucial aspect which informs so many Chicano projects, we must consider carefully those cultural precedents which have helped shape the interaction between Chicano and Anglo culture, including those which ask us to "step inside" Anglo fantasy, or, as I suggest in the final part of this chapter, inside the giant's castle.

## THE MESTIZA WITHIN

Conceived by Helen Hunt Jackson as a complement to Stowe's *Uncle Tom's Cabin* (1852), the novel *Ramona* was intended to fuel a similar outrage which would likewise ignite political reform, this time in the name of the "Mission Indians" (Jackson's phrase). What actually took place was far from Jackson's intention. Instead of provoking an outcry over treatment of Native Americans, the novel won the affection of many faithful readers for its romantic plot, a plot which eventually reunites the title character, a cultural and biological mestiza, with her foster brother, the pure-blooded Spanish *hacendado* Felipe Moreno. Further, the novel frames its description of Native American life (caricatured as this representation may be) with a high-caste *Californio* environment befitting a courtly drama in any number of historical romances. This is not to say that the novel entirely fails in conveying the political message that Jackson intended. Her evaluation of the conditions faced by the Native Americans at the time are explicitly rendered through various reflections by her characters. Yet as the reception of the novel has demonstrated, readers may grant the romantic elements such importance that all other considerations become virtually invisible.

Packaged as a "romantic best-seller," the Avon edition of *Ramona* underscores the displacement of historical and reformist tendencies in the work by refusing to note the novel's original context; from the information provided on the cover and title page, a reader without previous knowledge would have no reason to doubt 1970—the only publishing date offered—as the novel's origin. This manipulation of historical context is, however, in line with an important aspect of the novel, one which dominated its original reception as well. As a result of its romantically oriented Spanish framing, *Ramona* ultimately became a lodestar for the re-creation of a historically distanced, and therefore both culturally insulated and politically secure, ethos, Spanish colonial California. With this new notion of "colonial" heritage, turn-of-the-century California—dependent on outside investment because of overzealous infrastructure development—constructed a base for tourism that would manifest itself in such institutional forms as Mission Revival architecture and festivals like the much-noted Fiesta Days held in Santa Barbara.[13]

While it is impossible to know for certain why Jackson left the novel so open for the romantic reading, particular facts are suggestive. Most obviously, Jackson wished to touch the United States's popular consciousness in a way that she had failed to do in her previous book-length invective against U.S. Native American policy, *A Century of Dishonor: A Sketch of the United States Government's Dealing with Some of the Indian Tribes* (1881). This earlier reformist argument offers a series of case histories, differentiated by tribes. The collection is in turn framed by a carefully crafted legal polemic, claiming legitimacy for Indian nationhood on the basis of international law. Although Jackson's careful, rational style in *A Century of Dishonor* makes it clear that her rhetorical strategy will appeal to traditional legal and moral argument grounded in precedence—she explicitly rejects a sentimental stance toward the policies and their results—she nonetheless points out at the close of the work that her reform can be achieved only by touching popular sentiment. Readers may thus find Jackson writing herself into the romance intervention even as she attempts to convince the populace to exercise its influence on the legislature.

Reflecting on this desire and on the failure of the first book, which went largely unread, we may conjecture that Jackson might have been drawn too far toward the popular forms of her day in her desire to move her audience. But can we ultimately assume that this question of form was so completely miscalculated by Jackson, or is there some more complex relation between the romance's reception and the issues she wished to confront? Once finished with the novel, she certainly did not consider it a failure as a reformist effort; however, it was not until years after her death that the novel reached its zenith as an influence on neo-Spanish "revival." For Jackson, this project—as described in one of her letters—was wholly written for the "Mission Indian" cause, as distinct from her own desires. For a good portion of the time she was writing, the manuscript title was "In the Name of the Law," a title in keeping with this explicit desire to give fictional form to a legal argument for compensation already set forth in *A Century of Dishonor*.

Given that *Ramona*'s creation marks a translation from legal to literary realms, a translation that inevitably carries vestiges of the old into the new, we may consider why certain assumptions in Jackson's original legal argument lead her to the wholesale importation of a romanticism that ultimately denies the very issues Jackson hoped to enliven. Examining *A Century of Dishonor*, we find that Jackson cautiously aligns herself with those reformers who seek full enfranchisement and legal citizenship for Native Americans. While she warns that an overly hasty transition, especially in terms of citizenship, would jeopardize more than aid Native American living conditions, she nonetheless endorses a statement made by the Indian Affairs Office in 1857: "The utter absence of individual title to particular lands deprives every one among them of the chief incentive to labor and exertion—the very mainspring on which the prosperity of a people depends" (*Century of Dishonor* 341). This stance is complicated by the fact that government policy had long maintained a significant measure of control over the Native American population precisely by granting individuals ownership of properties on the condition that those who accepted sever their ties with their tribes; as Valerie Mathes points out, the provisions of the Homestead Act of 1862 were extended to Native Americans to weaken larger tribal claims.[14] Even for those reformers who could embrace an entirely assimilationist agenda, this method suggested little improvement once the effects of subsequent taxation were considered, taxation which virtually always ensured that Native Americans would be left landless and without other resources. To Jackson's credit, she recognized this impasse and did not attempt an oversimple solution. In effect, she counsels in *A Century of Dishonor* immediate responses to the most obvious outrages and a continued commitment thereafter to holistic reform. Of these immediate actions, she devotes her greatest energy to revivifying the treaty promises made by the U.S. government.

Employing a variety of classical legal statements, *A Century of Dishonor* presents a clear argument for the fundamentally salutary role of freely given consent in social interactions. Jackson thus attempts to make U.S. legal institutions live up to their ideological claims and therefore support the primacy of consent over force. However, Jackson perhaps inevitably uses the concept of volition in a very strained manner, inasmuch as she acknowledges that Native Americans were legally conceived of as wards of the state during her time. Such assumptions were very strong during this period and were often built on the encouragement given women reformers to pursue their activities, encouragement offered by male legal practitioners, among others, who understood Native Americans as children benefiting from women's "nurturing" proclivity. Given such assumptions about the inabilities of the Native American treaty subjects, we can begin to appreciate the primary cultural work that Jackson's argument neglects. This fundamentally necessary work would include attempting to transpose the treaty issues into a Native American perspective to gain some sense of "agency" and "volition" as those concepts might be conceived by the alternative culture. Instead, Jackson acts out a problematic assumption about social interaction, thereby limiting the reformist power in both her legal history and her novel. Ultimately, this failure set the stage for nothing less than a legacy of historical amnesia as entrepreneurs throughout the Southwest took advantage of the romantic elements of the novel to build a newly exoticized "Mission" culture.

Working from the assumption that "just" interaction between peoples is defined by the resolution of consensual agreements among autonomous individuals, Jackson grounds her legal polemic in *A Century of Dishonor* on the tenet that nations (tribes included) must respect one another as individual people would. With this approach, Jackson simply avoids confronting the racism and stereotypes which existed in the minds of her readers. An apparent victim of what Kelman defines as synthetic individualism, Jackson does not argue that the concerns of nations should supersede other interests. Instead, she explicitly conflates nationhood into personhood. Nations are therefore significant only insofar as they are models for, or are composed of, consenting individuals. In *Ramona* these assumptions lead to two principal failings. First, the Native Americans most central to the plot do not evidence any sustaining links to their community because from the outset they are portrayed as exceptions to their race and to the group logic which obliquely defines it as such. Second, the Mexicanos—who are thoroughly imbricated in a hierarchical caste system—become too much of a focal point for Jackson, indicating a shift in the narrative's overall designs. Led by the desire to present the Mission Indians as *potentially* full-fledged citizens, citizens capable of exercising respected contractual decisions, Jackson creates exceptional Native American characters who are described as standing apart from their race as much as representing it. In the Southwest, where oral and otherwise "informal" Mexican government contracts, especially concerning land, were consistently ceded by U.S. courts to Anglo challengers, written law and the ability to read and write English became a critical sign of transition for Native Americans; those who were literate could, in the eyes of reformers, not only act as intermediaries but also serve as symbols of "positive" potential assimilation. In particular, it appears likely that Jackson wished to exploit this latter aspect when she created Alessandro Assis, a Native American who gains entry into the principal locale of the novel, the Moreno hacienda, by virtue of his "European" musical talents (specifically, his skill with the violin), and who later steals away with Ramona, the mestiza ward of the household (a representative of the blending of Anglo, Native American, and Spanish colonial heritages).

Alessandro's initial success with the Morenos is premised on the exceptional training he received from his father, a training which his own people felt ambivalent about since they found him "a distant, cold boy." This problematic relationship to his village of Temecula "had come, they believed, of learning to read, which was always bad. Chief Pablo had not done his son any good by trying to make him like white men" (53). Ramona as well is repeatedly said to stand apart as a representative of her Native American race, a misnomer throughout the novel since she is undeniably a mestiza (biologically the product of Scottish and Native American blood, culturally a mix of Anglo, Mexicano, and Native American legacies). Her adopted family conceals her heritage from her until she threatens to marry Alessandro. Although Señora Moreno, the matriarch of the hacienda, hopes that the weight of Ramona's high-caste Mexicano upbringing will sway her thinking, the young woman ventures forth with her lover against the señora's commands, trusting instead to her unshakable Franciscan faith.

When Ramona and Alessandro resettle, their exceptional "training" continues to shape their lives in material as well as spiritual ways. For instance, their impoverished acquaintances marvel at Ramona's ability to decorate the poorest of hovels with a formal sitting-room arrangement. These acquaintances, poor Anglo neighbors named Jeff and Ri Hyer, represent an unsophisticated intelligence in the novel that nonetheless models the change in popular consciousness which Jackson would like to produce. As they come to know the exceptional Ramona and Alessandro, the Hyer family goes through a revolution in their thinking:

> Aunt Ri was excited. The experience was, to her, almost incredible. Her ideas of Indians had been drawn from newspapers, and from a book or two of narratives of massacres, and from an occasional sight of vagabond bands or families they had encountered in their journey across the plains. Here she found herself sitting side by side in friendly intercourse with an Indian man and Indian woman, whose appearance and behavior was attractive; towards whom she felt herself singularly drawn. (277)

This change in the Hyer mentality, and especially in Aunt Ri, reaches its zenith when she expresses the hope that all whites will learn to care for their society's "displaced." As we will see, however, such concern truncates any

responsive political organization by quickly transforming itself into a faith
about natural law and the justice that comes regardless of what people do.

The setting for Ri's "reformist" sentiment is the one context in which Ramona gains unreserved support from her (anonymous) Native American
community: the aftermath of a tragedy in which a local Anglo viciously guns
down Alessandro after claiming that he had stolen a horse. The occasion
brings forth, as Ri describes, a communal response:

> The way the pore things hed jest stripped theirselves, to git things fur Ramony,
> beat all ever I see among white folks, 'n' I've ben raound more 'n most. 'N' they
> wa'n't lookin' fur no pay, nuther; fur they didn't know, till Feeleepy 'n' me cum,
> thet she hed any folks ennywhar, 'n' they'd ha' taken care on her till she died, jest
> the same. The sick allers ez took care on among them, they sed, 's long uz enny
> on em hez got a thing left. Thet's ther way they air raised; I allow white folks
> might take a lesson on 'em, in thet; 'n' in heaps uv other things tew. Oh, I'm done
> talkin' agin Injuns, naow, don't yeow furgit it! But I know, fur all thet, 't won't
> make any difference; 'pears like there cuddn't nobody b'leeve ennythin' 'n this
> world 'thout seein' 't theirselves. I wuz thet way tew; I allow I hain't got no call
> ter talk, but I jest wish the hull world could see what I've seen! Thet's all! (336–37)

Perhaps nowhere is the reformist's motive more clearly (yet unclearly) enun-
ciated in the novel than in this passage, with its rather unfortunate attempt
at dialect. Even so, had the novel concluded on this note, it no doubt would
have been more successful with regard to its reform agenda because at the
very least readers would have been asked to imagine those alternate Native
American social relations that are alluded to, if not explored, as Ri tries to
describe the group. In other words, readers would be asked to reintegrate the
exceptional character back into the community. Instead, the novel pursues
a forced attempt at individualistic romantic closure: Felipe Moreno, Ramona's stepbrother, returns to carry Ramona away as his new bride, thereby re-
creating the context of the Moreno household. As I would suggest by framing
this approach to the novel with a reading of *Break of Dawn*, the forced reentry
of the sentimental domestic conventions effectively models a form of cultural
solitary confinement. The newly contained Ramona reclaims her hacienda
legacy, including the family jewels, and what is Native American (or, more
properly, racially "crossed") in her becomes safely contained in a closing vision of her passive young daughter (a literal infantilization) and in an occasional memory of Alessandro's voice lovingly calling Ramona by her Native
American name, Majella or "Wood Dove." The process, and its assimilationist
assumptions, concludes when Ramona agrees to raise her daughter severed
from the ties of her race; as was the case with Ramona herself, this child will
grow up not knowing her Indian mother.

Although the name Majella may signify Ramona's Native American identity, the novel's narrator uses "Ramona" in all but the most unusual circumstances—that is, when the character ventures angry criticism of U.S. policy.
The final pages bear out this assumption about Ramona's unshifting identity;
hence, the narrator's language marks Ramona's journey into the Native Ameri-

can community as a venture and little more. Ramona's options in the novel only gesture toward the possibility of accepting "Indian" status. As in Alessandro's case, her exceptional upbringing ironically sounds a death knell for her complex heritage, and especially for the recognition of her existence as a mestiza. This latter position is so forcefully written out of the novel that it becomes its missing symbolic center. Between the three idealized families which make up the world of this "historical novel," the Morenos, the Hyers, and the Assis, there exists a rapidly growing population of impoverished mestizos entirely displaced by Jackson. Jackson could not have avoided contact with this population during her visits to California, and she certainly learned of it from the high-caste Californios whom she interviewed; and these Californios were very much aware of the tremendous racially defined changes—inextricably linked to political, economic, and sexual conflicts—that had thoroughly devastated the once securely ensconced hacienda class. In fact, the essential demise of this caste was complete in all but a few enclaves during the period of Jackson's visits to the Southwest. Judging from Jackson's framing of the novel, her romanticization of the caste system is linked to the parallel legal treatment both the Californios and the Mission Indians received at the hands of colonizing immigrant Anglos. However, as the novel's structure suggests, separating as it does the different worlds of Native American and Mexicano experience, this mutual experience of discrimination fractures for Jackson onto radically different historical planes, inasmuch as the Californios' loss of land and power resided primarily in a distanced and therefore insulated epoch.

If Jackson provides readers with a character who exercises economic and social power to attain justice, a character who thereby threatens to speak to the reader's present, it is Felipe Moreno, who attempts to address Alessandro's murder. By contrast, the two potential sources of reform with Native American backgrounds—Alessandro and Ramona—are initiated into the Native American community by virtue of their growing awareness of their almost complete lack of legal status. It is crucial that, for both characters, their ultimate submersion in legal issues—Alessandro's "stealing" of a horse and Ramona's failure to testify about Alessandro's murder—is portrayed as a lapse of intentionality. Before Alessandro's theft, for instance, growing anger over the discrimination his community confronts leads him not to overt political acts of reprisal and protest but to increasingly severe mental lapses, fantasies of chase and flight (fantasies derived from Jackson's model for the character, a Native American similarly gunned down). It is in just such a confused state that Alessandro rides off with a horse belonging to a local Anglo. When this assailant guns him down, Alessandro is trying to explain his illness, his very lack of agency. Ironically, the attack, which concludes with two shots that remove Alessandro's face, inadvertently completes the process Jackson has initiated. This process includes the absenting of Alessandro as a group victim and the creation of a "faceless" though exotic victim, one deprived of agency who may be "inhabited" by Anglo readers without requiring of them a significant effort at cultural translation.

In an apparently rational moment, Ramona greets Alessandro's death as merciful, given his mental deterioration. Shortly thereafter Ramona herself falls into a fever that leaves her incoherent; it is for this reason that she fails to testify at the time of the investigation into the murder. While there is little doubt that her testimony would not have altered the case's outcome, it is important that Jackson has again premised disengagement on incapacity rather than volition. Regardless of the outcome of the case, the public forum offered by the inquest would have yielded an opportunity to air a group-oriented critique and a group-oriented grieving. Yet a danger underlies this narrative option: in such a forum Ramona could well attack the heart of the consensual-individualistic bias of the law, thereby undercutting Jackson's investment in the institution and offending her mainstream audience, which does need to mourn Alessandro but in a manner that conforms to the precepts encoded in the law; hence, he must remain an objectified, faceless loss. Inasmuch as the novel symptomatically repeats the synthetic individualism noted above, Jackson works toward enfranchising Native Americans legally while displacing them as culturally specific actors. That Ramona, as described by Ri, should find her closest link to her community in this critical moment of incapacity only reinforces the notion that tribal ties and group agency are roadblocks to reform as Jackson envisions it; in the novel these ties, as nurturing as they may be, seem to limit Ramona—as does the fever—to a state of preconscious, albeit saintly, victimization.

Insofar as the movement of the novel as a whole is concerned, an ironic passage to a more ideal/idealized past fulfills the reform project. Only the most blatant nostalgia can support the literal movement back into the colonial era and space (the return to Mexico City) that concludes the novel. Rather than attempting to address Jackson's contemporary issues and transformations in a significant fashion, *Ramona* puts these problems in motion only to circumvent them by leaving the most problematic rhetorical assumptions intact. Ultimately, the family romance may have overtaken Jackson's political intentions because her involvement in reform was continually subjected to patriarchal definitions of her project, definitions that always returned to the familial. However, in the end the most striking feature of *Ramona* is its ability both to claim itself reformist and to defer action, especially legal action.

While many characters in the novel understand the law to be almost uniformly unjust, this awareness never underwrites the sort of inversion of just versus criminal acts that takes place in other minority legal critiques—for example, African-American slave narratives like Frederick Douglass's.[15] Politically motivated retribution is the furthest thing from Jackson's mind, as she makes clear by her elisions of agency. The attenuated sense of justice that Jackson does foster at the close of the novel traces a notion of natural justice originally announced at the conclusion of *A Century of Dishonor*. Essentially, this theory supposes that bad actions will bring bad consequences to their perpetrators; most obviously, guilty people—like the judge who ignores Alessandro's murder—will be haunted by memories and imaginings. Along with this supposition, however, we may well assume that the law, imagined in this way, promotes the various forms of denial that make possible such a return of the repressed. Inasmuch as *Ramona* is a legal polemic, it seems only fair to question whether Jackson has gone far enough in thinking through the ways in which the legal machinations she criticizes shape her own novel. As a text positioning itself between an essentially invisible Native American population (invisible inasmuch as Jackson avoids representing it) and a thoroughly anachronistic hacienda caste, I would suggest that *Ramona*'s most fundamental object of denial is the central character's mestiza identity, an identity that has to be reconfigured in the narrative into different periods connoting separate, secure racial natures.

Can it be any wonder that, as the Los Angeles history project has argued, the "Hispanicization" wrought by California's tourist industry traces in large part back to *Ramona*'s reception?[16] When, for instance, Santa Barbara celebrates Fiesta Days each year at the beginning of August, a pervasive yet virtually unrecognized leap takes place in which a fantasized colonial past supersedes virtually any links between itself and the present. First and foremost, the Treaty of Guadalupe Hidalgo and its deterioration are eclipsed. Every effort is made to reconstruct the original myths of Spanish blood purity because the process reinforces a security in the present, one which attempts to institutionally manipulate political changes in the Southwest, particularly in response to the demographic expansion of the Latino population. Thus, the historical gap figured in these ceremonies, and in their textual icon, ensures a denial of reformist transformation by acting out a sentimentalized closure of the mission era and what was to come.

Although the novel's broad reception in this regard is entirely at odds with Jackson's published intentions, it is likely that her assimilationist beliefs allowed little other choice. What Jackson asked was that Ramona be permitted to emulate the Anglo-European conqueror. When denied this opportunity, Ramona, as a form of protest, finds a home in exile. As is evident in *A Century of Dishonor*, Jackson does not significantly challenge the supremacy of the conqueror's cultural position, and although she offers several blanket condemnations of the law, no real threat to its power is envisioned in either work. If anything, the invocation of natural law suggests an acceptance of current institutions, as their wrongs will be righted by a higher source even while we live our lives in the "hit and miss" fashion conveyed through the metaphor of Aunt Ri's rug making:

> "Wall," she said, "it's called ther 'hit-er-miss' pattren; but its 'hit' oftener 'n 't is 'miss.' Thar ain't enny accountin' fur ther way ther breadths 'll come, sometimes; 'pears like 't wuz kind er magic, when they air sewed tergether; 'n' I allow thet's ther way it's gwine ter be with heaps er things in this life. It's jest a kind er 'hit-er-miss' pattren we air all on us livin' on; 't ain't much use tryin' ter reckon how 't 'll come aout. (337)

Thus, by the conclusion of the novel the deconstruction of Jackson's legal premises is complete. The "magic" which will suggest a cultural rallying point for the construction of alternative forms of agency in later Chicano texts, for instance *Zoot Suit* and *The Brick People*, is here a dislocated and universalized concept, essentially devoid of any power to unify a community around action or changes in perception. Instead, *Ramona*'s focus on the family romance vitiates Jackson's declared political agenda. Like Stowe, Jackson hoped to motivate reform by demonstrating the deterioration of families suffering under racism. However, unlike Stowe, Jackson was unwittingly describing a mestizo class, a class like the mulatto, notable in mainstream anxieties not for its relative recognizability but rather for its ability to impersonate, and to a certain extent infect, Anglo (as well as Spanish) culture.

Arguing that American literature plays out obsessively the concomitant search for, and rejection of, father figures, Mary Dearborn has suggested that literature about mulattos—literature which frequently documents incestuous relations between slaveholders and their slaves, who were often half-brothers or half-sisters—constitutes a literal embodiment of larger cultural anxieties about self-definition.[17] As Dearborn's reading suggests, the incestuous nature of Ramona's final consummation of her stepbrother's love may be one crucial sign of the disruption produced when racial categories are thus threatened. Described elsewhere in the narrative as reminiscent of Lot's wife (267), Ramona finds herself caught at the novel's conclusion in a state of frozen somnambulism. She is essentially trapped between the Franciscan invective against grief, which would posit her angry remembrance of Alessandro's murder as a sin, and Felipe's (her stepbrother's) declaration of love. The incestuous overtones are supplanted only by the overtones of necrophilia one gains while considering Felipe's advances from the position of Ramona's "merciful oblivion." Ramona's sexuality thus comes to be equated with a saintly nature extolling the virtues of a family reunited. On another level, the retreat to the family romance also signals a switch from conventionally understood public spaces of political interaction to a "private" space defined by insularity. Taken together, these incestuous, necrophiliac, and insulating tendencies suggest the denial of an entire historical period representing *mestizaje* (the mixing of racial heritages) itself.

In all of this, there also lies a crucial manipulation of attitudes about mestiza sexuality, attitudes that are part and parcel of Anglo-American slanders of mestiza moral character premised on the failings that must come with racial impurity.[18] Jackson's novel is thus situated in a long history of political containment aided by the ideological suppositions of, and control over, sexuality. As Ramón Gutiérrez has demonstrated, this history reaches back to the Spanish colonial institution of marriage among indigenous Pueblo peoples.[19] Prior to colonization by the Spanish, Pueblo women "were empowered through their sexuality" which "was theirs to give and withhold" (17). Erotic behavior was pursued in "myriad forms (heterosexuality, homosexuality, bisexuality)" and did not recognize "boundaries of sex or age." As the colonization process gained ground, tribes like the Pueblos were more or less successfully convinced that sexuality must fall under the rubrics defined by the church, rubrics which conveyed a vehement distrust of love and sexuality as "subversive" sentiments that "glorified personal autonomy" and promoted "passion as an intrinsic desire of the species—natural, free and egalitarian" (227–28).

In more recent epochs, the general strategy has been carried over as stereotypes regarding mestiza sexuality have been mobilized by U.S. ideologues justifying aggression toward the inferior population of Mexico, which from the outset was damned by its racial mixing. In particular, Antonia Castañeda, in "The Political Economy of Nineteenth Century Stereotypes of Californianas," has followed the manner in which stereotypes of Mexicana sexuality ran seemingly contradictory courses as they altered to fit the specific political agendas that were part of the overall expansionist aggression and part of changing attitudes toward race and gender in the nineteenth-century United States. Highlighting the important justificatory role played by stereotypes denoting sexual immorality among Mexicanas prior to the U.S. invasion of 1846–1848, Castañeda surmises that the subsequent adoption of apparently antithetical romanticized stereotypes depicting "pure" high-caste Mexicanas fit a larger systematic subordination of Mexican society wherein certain limited "foreign" negotiations (Anglo marriages into Mexicano land-grant wealth) were valorized even while the majority of such marriages were not. A complex process, overall subordination thus allowed certain stereotypes obliquely representing cooperation between the cultures to take root—although, as Castañeda underscores, these stereotypes were entirely devoid of anything but the most censored acknowledgment of the Mexican social context. Hence, these high-caste Californianas become purely Spanish; such a Californiana would thus find herself divorced "from her racial, cultural and historical reality" (224).

*Ramona* is in fact the predictable extension of this historical trajectory. As the negotiation with the "other" within becomes even more intimate in the colonizing scenario at the end of the nineteenth century, so too does the denial of historical context that stems from the manipulation of sexuality, a manipulation that "succeeds" in Jackson's case by virtue of her exploitation of the romance form. In this manner, the mestiza population and all the potentially threatening sexuality that it represents become the symbolic center of the novel. Ultimately, the habitat for this missing center is situated between the lines of a systematic historical amnesia that would deny the rising mestizo class that Jackson must have walked among.

## IN THE GIANT'S CASTLE

Film involves a kind of therapy with the audience and it must be handled delicately.

George Stevens

The retreat to family romance evident in Jackson's work is mobilized again years later in one of mainstream Hollywood's more explicit attempts to deal with *mestizaje*, George Stevens's *Giant* (1956). Adapted from Edna Ferber's highly popular potboiler novel by the same name (1952), Stevens's film seeks to convey the grandeur of a developing Texas by presenting, among other things, a feast for the eyes. Often remembered in film studies texts for its sheer visual scope, *Giant* is most frequently represented with stills that seem to take in the whole of the Texas countryside.[20] Nonetheless, Stevens wished to maintain a very focused line of narrative action in *Giant*, one in which the audience would become engrossed in "a story about the hazards of the marriage relationship."[21] With regard to the tension between the epic proportions and the film's specific themes, Stevens told another interviewer, "The title embarrassed us when shooting. It's not a big film, it's small. It closes up on things and on people."[22]

Stevens began his career as an actor, then worked as a cameraman before becoming a director; those early experiences are reflected in the mix of dramatic action and virtually sublime visual experience offered by *Giant*.[23] However, while *Giant* pleased critics particularly because it was able to convey an epic scope even while maintaining clear-cut character development and action, the filmmaking process itself was fraught with difficult decisions, as indicated by the 400,000 feet of film used over the course of the production.[24] Although Stevens was certainly not known for an economical use of footage, the tremendous editing task suggests that the film presented Stevens with one of his greatest challenges.

Certainly one issue that could not be divorced from the desire to make the film at least appear big had to do with new market pressures. From the beginning of the project, Warner Brothers was concerned about the new competition posed by the growing popularity of television.[25] Throughout the industry, this concern translated into a pressure to create films that would move significantly beyond the television viewing experience—hence the marketing impetus behind innovative, though often imperfect, techniques such as Cinemascope. Stevens met this challenge in *Giant* by masking the top and bottom of the lens to emphasize the width of his shots, a technique that avoided the distortion—especially in close-ups—inherent in Cinemascope and similar options. He was thereby able to convey as accurately as possible "the small." In addition to these photographic solutions, Stevens and the screenplay authors, Fred Guiol and Ivan Moffat, substantially reworked Ferber's narrative, creating an entirely new conclusion to the story that could more effectively bring together the various themes of the film, particularly the familial, class, and racial matters. In essence, then, this film—most often remembered for its sweeping vistas—enacts a careful negotiation of wide-open spaces and crucial mid to close-up shots, a negotiation that allowed Stevens simultaneously to convey a Hollywood fantasy about the exotic grandeur of Texas and to funnel key dramatic conflicts into circumscribed spaces, as in the final episodes in the Benedicts' sitting room.

The story begins with an impromptu, whirlwind romance initiated during a brief horse-buying visit to Maryland, a visit in which the cattle-rich Texan Jordan "Bick" Benedict meets and marries the outspoken Leslie Lynnton over the course of a few days. In short order Leslie and the audience are introduced to the wide horizons of Bick's home state, horizons that are filled with cattle, at least at the start. One of the principal changes which will confront the political and economic establishment represented by Bick during the twenty-five years spanned by the film is the extensive exploitation of oil reserves, reserves which will later fill the horizons with endless oil derricks. Along with these economic and political jostlings come players like Jett Rink, members of a working class who gain through the discovery of oil a claim to power, thereby unleashing a virtually unbridled resentment between old and new money.

The enveloping scenes of cattle and oil derricks are juxtaposed with intimate shots of familial settings in which the central drama of the narrative is acted out: the ongoing travails of Bick and Leslie Benedict's marriage. The difficulties make themselves felt immediately on the couple's arrival at Reata, the Benedict family ranch. Leslie throws Bick into obvious discomfort as she discourses far too intimately with the Mexicano help as she greets them for the first time. The prophecy embedded in this early scene is borne out as Leslie takes a strong interest in the welfare of the Mexicano workers who are segregated into a nearby barrio.

Stevens exploits the sentimental appeal of Leslie's first visit to this barrio in a number of ways. In the first instance, the entire visit is crosscut with scenes from a savage ride in which Leslie's sister-in-law, Luz, takes out her frustrations with Bick's marriage on Leslie's horse, an episode that leaves both horse and rider mortally wounded. Through this all, there is a clear effort to build on the implied symbolic relationship between Leslie and the horse, both of which are explicitly and repeatedly linked in terms of beauty and independence. Hence, the horse's mistreatment becomes a foil for Leslie's "provocative" actions in the barrio, where her unconventional sympathies compel her to seek medical assistance from the white establishment for a sick Mexicano child, Angel Obregon. The particularly graphic close-ups which document Luz savagely spurring the horse and the ultimate—though unseen—consequences of these actions confer on Leslie a certain sentimental justification to pursue even more forcefully the improvement she would bring to the barrio, although these efforts lead her into a constant struggle against the racist norms supported by Bick. In this vein, the genteel, Eastern-bred woman is appalled throughout most of the film at the treatment meted out to the Mexicanos by her adopted family. Finally, her reactions to Bick's resistance as she seeks help become a partial barometer of their marital decline. Her dismay at his racism contributes to the mounting tensions in their marriage, tensions that culminate when Bick and Leslie's son, Jordy, secretly defies his father by eloping with Juana Villalobos, a Mexicana who, like Leslie, is committed to the betterment of the barrio.

Although throughout the film these racial issues are often distantly juxtaposed to the business wranglings that threaten the Benedicts' cattle-oriented lifestyle, events toward the end of the film suggest that in fact a common thread links the two spheres. This thread becomes apparent when Bick physically confronts his now-oil-rich economic rival, Jett Rink, at a "who's who in Texas" blowout thrown by Jett. The fight is instigated when Jett's Anglo workers refuse hairdressing service to Juana, now Bick's Mexicana daughter-in-law, and when Jett himself mauls Jordy in a less than fair fight over the same incident with Juana. While the spectacular ballroom fight between Bick and Jett (presumably the two giants of the film) is initiated by the racist treatment of Juana, multiple motivations affect Bick, not the least of which includes the battle over whether he or Jett will ultimately control the affections of Bick's daughter, Jett's most recent conquest.

The discrimination issue lives on as Bick and his son Jordy argue again back in their hotel room after the more public altercations. In this episode—where the son proclaims the father every bit the racist that Jett is—we find an unusual rhetorical display: the altercation is distinguished stylistically by the odd manner in which both participants repeatedly tell the other to just "forget it." The consequent dissolution of the racial theme is reinforced in two ways. First, the Juana of the film, unlike the Juana of the novel, remains largely silent throughout these scenes and is certainly not the angry force that she is in Ferber's novel. Second, moving the reaction to discrimination into the intimate sphere of the hotel room reinforces the sense that father and son are rehearsing a feud that does in fact all too easily forget the privilege they enjoy to choose or not to choose reformist action. Hence, the emotions tied up with the initial discriminatory act are funneled into a model of vicarious participation through this scene as well as others. As a result, audience members are more likely to come to terms with, for instance, Jordy's and Bick's anger than to situate themselves in the event of discrimination. Here, then, we find a therapy that would treat not the victim but rather the responsible, or tangentially responsible, perpetrators—the benefactors of the hacienda. Instead of exploring the consequences of the event for the victim, a kind of narrative deferral or dissolution takes place, one akin to that found in *Ramona* and one which likewise softens the experience of racism.

This tendency toward deferral at "moments of great emotion" is in fact a hallmark of Stevens's cinematic style, in which the "camera does tend not to look, or, at least, to back away" at critical junctures (Richie 43). Donald Richie pursues this point by noting that in Stevens's films, "Close-ups are used to make an emotional impact before the emotion-arousing event . . . and the results of the event are shown in a long shot" (43–44). Such is the case in *Giant* when the audience views an extreme close-up of Luz gouging Leslie's horse just prior to the mortal wounding of both. As Richie goes on to argue,

> The effect is that of making us emotionally involved before the fact. After the fact we are deliberately disinvolved. This is elegiac. We experience the emotion but not its consequences. We are not shown [Luz] dead, for example. Instead, an aesthetic appeal is instantly made. Those beautiful shots of the horse wandering off . . . suggest by both their nature and their context that emotion to be experienced is suddenly over. We are invited to contemplate, to feel, and at the same time to refrain from action. (44)

This tendency to enact a "disinvolvement," described here by Richie in terms of style, appears to have influenced, or at least reinforced, Stevens's treatment of the racial themes in the movie as well. For instance, a similar process occurs in the closing episodes of the film, episodes which substantially alter the final events of the novel. Here again we find a process of narrative "softening" in which emotionally charged discrimination issues are developed only to be largely circumscribed in the privatized space of familial dynamics and contract law. In this case the legal discourse only implied by Juana's earlier question about right to service will become a primary topic.

Thus, we find Stevens interrupting the Benedicts' trip home from the Jett Rink "blowout" with yet another fight, this time pitting Bick against a diner owner who first complains vociferously about serving Juana and her son and immediately thereafter attempts to throw out of the diner another Mexicano family that has just arrived. In a moment that defines Bick's newfound commitment, he stands up and protests the treatment of the victimized family. The climax of the seemingly titanic fight that ensues between Bick and the owner is oddly comical and yet profound in its implications. Bick is thoroughly beaten by the cook, who proceeds to hang a "right to refuse service" sign around Bick's neck as he sits on the floor among the remains of a salad. In this scene one of the wealthiest men in Texas is knocked silly, virtually in his own backyard, and the cook's actions are framed as entirely consonant with the laws of the country, laws which define contractual negotiations as primarily private affairs.

As one would expect of a romantic director like Stevens, this turn of events is not without its silver lining. Retreating to the family space, Stevens plays out the vestiges of the racial issues as a grounds for the reconciliation of the marriage; Bick, in a dramatic comeback, has become Leslie's hero by defending the anonymous Mexicano family, a shift of fortune suggesting that although public action may be ineffective, even "indefensible," it still holds value in the private sphere, in the world of the "small." And to underscore the tentative sanctity of this sphere, Stevens leaves us with an image of the two grandchildren, mestizo by Jordy's marriage and Anglo by Juana's, playing together side by side in the near background.

The final turn to the children is worthy of some consideration since Stevens appears here to be building on the theme of "hope in the next generation" that Ferber exploits at the end of her novel. Although the novel never reaches Jett's blowout—at the beginning and end of the narrative, this event looms in the near future—Ferber does describe a diner incident in which service is denied. However, in the novel it is the women and children of the Benedict family on their own who find themselves confronting an owner who has taken exception to their *mestizaje.* Not only does no physical fight ensue, but it is the reformist Leslie who works desperately to avoid letting Bick know about the event at all. Leslie recognizes in her actions exactly the sort of seemingly passive racism she has despised in Bick, yet the best she can do at the end of the novel is to assume that Jordy and Juana represent "a real success at last," presumably because they continue to challenge the discriminatory status quo (447).

In Stevens's version, Leslie of course maintains a much higher level of integrity in terms of her reformist intentions. Unfortunately, the actions she helps Bick toward do not suggest the kind of political consciousness that bespeaks a profound change. As Bick and Leslie sit back at home to discuss both the incident in the diner and their relative successes in life, Bick can only look on his grandchildren in bewilderment, telling the young boy of Jordy and Juana's marriage that he will never be anything other than a "wetback." Defined by the status of "legal alien," mestizos in the film, even in the most private of spaces, maintain a conditional citizenship, a citizenship which asserts that their only security will be found in public silence and in the virtual invisibility represented by retiring characters like Juana.

Juana is nonetheless representative of a kind of activism which, if it is not given a proper voice, is at least liminally recognized by the film. The same may be said of the bit part of the Mexicano doctor who works with these reformists, a character based loosely in both novel and film on the very politically active head of the GI Forum, Dr. Hector García.[26] Yet it seems that the work of these reformists and their principal advocate in the family, Jordy, is actually devalued in the transformation from novel to film as the final focus on the hope offered by the "next generation" turns not to Jordy's work and Juana's anger, as Ferber would have it, but rather to the essentially mute grandchildren. This distinct shift and the dissolution it betrays are only exacerbated when Stevens adds to the final image of the grandchildren a background that includes a black calf and a white lamb. However secure the final familial sphere may seem, Stevens's visual equation of the children with a calf and a lamb suggests that while the desegregation may have its "natural" side, it is also indebted to a commodity system that will ask for the children's sacrifice. Of particular note in this regard is an earlier episode in the film when a Thanksgiving dinner is entirely ruined as the children realize that their favorite pet turkey has been stuffed and baked for the occasion. Sentimentalized pet livestock do not fare well in this film, and the de facto legal rhetoric which intervenes in the Thanksgiving scene imbues the final images with the suggestion that these children have indeed not escaped racism and, further, that such escape may well be impossible.

As a work depicting various forms of discrimination against Mexicanos, *Giant* is certainly a Hollywood landmark; for this reason it can be appreciated for the step it took in promoting the discussion of racial issues as represented in popular culture. At the same time, however, it is crucial that we understand the ways in which the work perpetuates the legacy for Mexicanos of which *Ramona* is a crucial, if not foundational, part. At the close of *Giant*, racial issues are again afforded only the safe environment of private familial space. Recourse to public action appears largely stifled, especially because the final characters speaking to racism are the representatives of a wealth and power purchased through a discriminatory system. And if there were any doubt about this state of affairs, any doubt about the ability of the public to contain the private, it is erased when Bick reasserts the primacy of legal categories in the final reconciliation scene and therefore reinforces the lessons of the right-to-service issues.

In a sense, then, the racial themes that play such an important role in the marital dynamics of the film become encrypted, particularly after the intermission, when the film jumps fifteen years and leaves the viewer in a more retrospective context. This encrypting is acted out literally in one of the film's more memorable scenes, the burial of Angel Obregon, killed in World War II. This scene calls forth a number of historically and politically sensitive valences that merit scrutiny. Bringing these valences together with the dynamics of the funeral, we may learn a good deal about the very deferred reform Stevens offers.

First, Bick and the Anglo establishment in the film recognize and attend the burial, thereby breaking with previous custom: Bick, for instance, has eschewed other contact, claiming that Mexicanos "have their own ways." At the funeral, though, Bick shares in the public grieving. Audience members viewing the film at the time of its initial release would no doubt recall the tremendous international scandal that evolved out of Texas in the aftermath of World War II, when segregated burial proceedings were fought by Mexicanos, including Dr. García and the GI Forum. The refusal of the Rice Funeral Home in Three Rivers, Texas, to accept the body of Felix Longoría in 1949 was perhaps the most famous of these incidents. An argument may be made, then, that a certain distanced remembrance of these struggles is represented in the Obregon funeral; however, it appears as if this funeral becomes a rendition of how things should have gone, not how they did go. In this sense, the scene becomes a reformist fantasy strained by its own reference to how things actually evolved.

A kind of wish fulfillment in which the bigoted Bick tenderly hands the grieving Mexicano family a Texas flag, the burial gives way to one of the more striking visual constructions in the work. Here the camera moves away from the funeral and captures—again in a typically "disinvolved" wide-angle shot—a small Mexicano child playing in a field, his back to the ceremony. Offering the viewer an apparently disinterested and dislocated child, Stevens strives for a sublime effect in this scene by placing the emotional content of the funeral next to the seemingly untouchable power of life moving forward. Yet this child also embodies a kind of independence that is not explicitly written into the kinds of commodity and legal pressures that one finds, for instance, in the scene of the children at the film's close. Instead, a kind of possibility appears to be wrapped up in the image of this lone child, but a possibility that cannot amount to anything until the child turns and engages not only the funeral that escapes his private musings but also the latent political history that is only distantly recalled for the audience as Angel Obregon is laid to rest. In this sense, this boy may come to represent the sleeping giant of the film, the potential for active political involvement and for public voice; however, as he stands in the world Steven creates, he is little more than another mute participant, an infinitely scriptable character waiting for sentimental investment.

These works reveal specific political issues, issues which pertain to gaining access to sites that might sustain public speaking voices—with all of the entitlements such sites confer in this society. However as the title of *Break of Dawn* suggests, these sites remain on the horizon—a point reinforced when González leaves San Quentin in the film's final scene to be greeted by no one, although clearly the expectation of some bonding permeates the situation. Contemporary institutional histories confirm such deferred status for the Chicano public speaker by continuing to obscure the contexts within which Chicanos find themselves. Even in the much celebrated architectural study by Reyner Banham, *Los Angeles: The Architecture of Four Ecologies* (1971), the Mission Revival movement remains a ghostly presence, a treatment strangely at odds with the author's larger aims to clarify the heretofore apparently confused readings of architectural trends in Los Angeles (23). Gesturing toward the unique role played by Mission Revival, Banham notes that for the purposes of the present study, Spanish Colonial Revival will not be treated as an identifiable or conspicuously adopted style, but as something which is ever-present and can be taken for granted, like the weather—worth comment when outstandingly beautiful or conspicuously horrible, but otherwise simply part of the day-to-day climate from which . . . much of modern California architecture derives. (61)

This diaphanous yet clearly fundamental presence masks, however obliquely, the historical pressures noted in the narratives and institutional strategies studied in this chapter, pressures that are both too apparent (a sense underscored by Banham's emphasis on the "conspicuous") and necessarily, though not entirely successfully, denied.

## NOTES

1. Although Artenstein is not a Chicano, I treat this film as a Chicano production because it is clearly indebted to the larger participation of many Chicanos, including actors like Oscar Chavez, Maria Rojo, Tony Plana, and Pepe Serena and numerous others, like Lorena Parlee, supporting the project from behind the scenes. In addition, as a "period piece" with a comparatively small budget, this film depended more than most productions on the generous contributions of those most desirous of having González's story told. It is for these reasons that I choose not to treat Artenstein as an "auteur," although his part—from the original research onward—was obviously crucial.

2. In a preliminary documentary, *Ballad of an Unsung Hero* (directed by Artenstein [1983]), González describes each of these aspects of his life, including the near drowning he endured in a tank of raw sewage at San Quentin—tanks that he and other prisoners were subjected to for days at a time. Despite such treatment, González helped organize a hunger strike at the prison in 1939, a strike which won major reforms in living conditions.

3. Of note in this regard is the "Ballad of Juan Revna," sung by González. The song critiques a widely controversial trial in which Reyna was convicted of killing a Los Angeles police officer.

4. Among other roles, González has acted in recent years as the head of Revolutionary Veterans of California, an advocacy group for participants in the Mexican revolution who now reside in the United States.

5. Of course, it is now commonplace to challenge public/private distinctions like the one I am making use of here. Perhaps the most sophisticated of these critical approaches, Donna Haraway's "Manifesto for Cyborgs," makes a strong case for rethinking such public/private dichotomies by considering instead the myriad social, political, technological, and cultural affiliations which exist in the liminal space between anything we might term purely public and the purely private. Although I acknowledge Haraway's point, I still stand by the strategic purpose of revivifying the dichotomy when it appears to be pertinent to how particular groups read (or misread) their experience. Clearly the introduction of radio as a medium played a large part in challenging the dichotomy as it existed then, and on this score we might recognize that part of the threat posed by González was due to his role in very effectively mining this new liminal ground. Even while González might have gained strength precisely by manipulating this liminality, the responses he evoked from the Anglo establishment may be read as a retrenchment of, and battle over, public versus private domain.

6. Here amnesia is taken to be *an effort* not to remember something which nonetheless cannot be avoided and which, in turn, dramatically shapes psychological and interpretive activity.

7. The psychoanalytic term *working through* is used here in order to suggest a mode of interacting with particularly charged or critical social issues. Drawing from the works of Freud and Dominick LaCapra, I adopt this term to denote a process whereby charged issues (or "materials" in the Freudian lexicon) are engaged in such a manner as to produce alternative perspectives or options that allow a distance from the simple repetition of the initial issue (or the assumptions which dominated its discussion). Such "salutary" options, in turn, allow affected people to find new models of dealing with problems.

8. I would like to thank Amy Rabbino, who has noted in seminar that the English subtitles which appear in the midst of the fight between the official and González take on an irony that is furthered both by their glaring presentation and by their often obvious inadequacy. Ultimately the subtitles, like the other forms of stylization discussed above, highlight the politics of the medium. In this sense, the necessary reduction of text that accompanies the use of subtitles itself becomes an ironic mirror for the Anglo refusal of cultural translation depicted by the film's narrative.

9. For an example of this scapegoating mechanics, see Gary Imhoff and Gerda Bikales, "The Battle over Preserving the English Language," *USA Today* 115, no. 2,500 (January 1987): 63–65. These proponents of English-Only open their article by claiming that "the political forces behind bilingual education are those which promote cultural separatism" (63). The article proceeds by supposing that the promotion of biculturalism will create political chaos in this country, dissolving the glue which holds it together, an approach clearly reminiscent of E. D. Hirsch's in *Cultural Literacy*.

10. No doubt the reaction to European immigration which took place in the 1920s set the stage for the present English-only movement. Not only was bilingual education in existence prior to World War I, but it was often looked on as a national resource. With the 1920s and the Great Depression, however, a growing concern over immigration made it possible for provincialists to sway public opinion against bilingualism by emphasizing the need for national unity. For an overview of attitudes toward U.S. language policy, see Dennis Baron, *The English Only Question: An Official Language for Americans?*

11. For summaries of these battles, see Reynaldo F. Macías, ed., *Are English Language Amendments in the National Interest? A Policy Analysis of Proposals to Establish English as the Official Language of the United States*, and Antonio J. Califa, "Declaring English the Official Language: Prejudice Spoken Here."

12. See Baldwin, "In Search of a Majority" (233), for an elaboration of this point. Within the specific context of the English-only movement, proponents of the law—including, until recently, Linda Chavez, who quit U.S. English when a memo was leaked revealing the organization's politically oriented anti-Latino agenda—argue that forced assimilation will improve the economic status of the groups involved. However, both sides agree that none of the studies of education has shown a linguistic advantage to the English-only approach, otherwise known as the immersion technique; to date it is not apparent that a distinct advantage exists to monolingual over bilingual ESL programs, although there are certainly many practitioners who feel that bilingual education has never had a sufficient chance to prove itself. Meanwhile, the bill's detractors argue that standards beyond English proficiency need to be considered. They ask, How does one measure the loss of science and math instruction in an immersion program? How does one measure the student's sense of self-worth or the student's relationship with family and culture? At the very least we need to be aware that short-term gains may have subtle, long-term effects.

13. As Mike Davis notes in *City of Quartz: Excavating the Future in Los Angeles*, neither oil nor oranges nor movies "provided an adequate economic foundation for Los Angeles's dramatic ascent during the 1920s.... Homegrown wealth and commerce were insufficient to support the region's lavish superstructures of consumption" (117–18). The creation of the All Year Club in the 1920s—a business venture promoting retirement

and travel in California—attempted to sustain absolutely necessary growth by convincing people, primarily Easterners, that life in the Golden State could be both comfortable and culturally rich. Santa Barbara did its part to convince visitors of the latter by initiating the first city laws in the West dictating "Mission style" architecture for its downtown tourist district.

14. For a summary of the policies and their apparent motivations, see Valerie Mathes, *Helen Hunt Jackson and Her Indian Reform Legacy*, 56.

15. For a reading of this aspect of African-American slave narratives, see H. Bruce Franklin, *Prison Literature in America: The Victim as Criminal and Artist*, and especially chapter 1, devoted to Frederick Douglass and Linda Brent.

16. The Los Angeles History Project develops this argument in its video production *Ramona: A Story of Passion and Protest*.

17. See Mary Dearborn's elaboration of this argument in her *Pocahontas's Daughters: Gender and Ethnicity in American Culture*, 131–58.

18. Prescott Webb's work (see esp. *The Great Plains* and *The Texas Rangers*) is perhaps the most infamous example; however, Chicana historiography is now uncovering a systematic manipulation of such stereotypes that infuses Anglo/Mexican relations from well before the Mexican-American War. For example, see the work of Antonia Castañeda (discussed below).

19. Ramón Gutiérrez documents these aspects of colonial life in the first chapters of his latest study, *When Jesus Came, the Corn Mothers Went Away*.

20. See, for instance, the photograph of the Reata barbecue used in a full two-page reproduction by Donald Richie in his *George Stevens: An American Romantic*, 74–75.

21. Stevens was interviewed on this point by Richard Dyer MacCann: see his "Giant in Preparation: George Stevens Bringing Novel on Texas to Screen," *Christian Science Monitor*, 18 September 1956.

22. The interview with Joe Hyams is cited in Bruce Petri, *A Theory of American Film* (185).

23. For a brief summary of Stevens's career, see the introduction to Petri.

24. Fred Hift's article from *Variety* offers an example of this positive critical response (qtd. in Petri 186). The elaborate editing process is also detailed in Petri (185).

25. Petri sums up the situation and Stevens's response when noting, "Because of the frantic efforts in Hollywood to offer wide-screen entertainment that could not be approximated by television, Stevens was under immense pressure to photograph *Giant* in Cinemascope, or a similar process. In fact, the initial publicity for the film announced that it would be filmed in Warner SuperScope. Although the vast sweep of the novel would seem to make it a natural for the wide screen, Stevens held out against the pressure" (187).

26. Arnold García, Jr. records this relationship in his newspaper article "Hispanic Champion Battles Against Bias: Passion for Equality Burns in Hector García," *Austin American Statesman*, 15 December 1985: D1, D12.

## REFERENCES

Artenstein, Isaac, dir. 1983. *Ballad of an Unsung Hero*. Cinewest.

———. *Break of Dawn*. Platform Releasing, 1988.

Baldwin, James. 1985. "In Search of a Majority." *The Price of the Ticket*. New York: St. Martin's / Marek, 229–36.

Banham, Reyner. 1971. *Los Angeles: The Architecture of Four Ecologies*. New York: Penguin.

Baron, Dennis. 1990. *The English-Only Question: An Official Language for Americans?* New Haven: Yale University Press.

Califa, Antonio J. 1989. "Declaring English the Official Language: Prejudice Spoken Here." *Harvard Civil Rights–Civil Liberties Law Review* 24: 294–348.

Castañeda, Antonia. "The Political Economy of Nineteenth Century Stereotypes of Californianas." Del Castillo, *Between Borders*, 213–36.

Davis, Mike. 1990. *City of Quartz: Excavating the Future in Los Angeles*. New York: Random-Vintage.

Dearborn, Mary. 1986. *Pocahontas's Daughters: Gender and Ethnicity in American Culture*. New York: Oxford University Press.

Del Castillo, Adelaida R., ed. 1990. *Between Borders: Essays on Mexicana / Chicana History*. Encino: Floricanto Press.

Ferber, Edna. 1952. *Giant*. New York: Doubleday.

Franklin, H. Bruce. 1989. *Prison Literature in America: The Victim as Criminal and Artist*. New York: Oxford University Press.

Gutiérrez, Ramón A. 1990. *When Jesus Came, the Corn Mothers Went Away: Marriage, Sexuality and Power in New Mexico, 1500–1846*. Stanford: Stanford University Press.

Haraway, Donna J. 1985. "Manifesto for Cyborgs: Science, Technology, and Socialist Feminism in the 1980s." *Socialist Review* 80: 65–108.

Hirsch, E. D., Jr. 1988. *Cultural Literacy: What Every American Needs to Know*. New York: Random.

Imhoff, Gary, and Gerda Bikales. 1987. "The Battle over Preserving the English Language." *USA Today* 115, no. 2,500 (January): 63–65.

Jackson, Helen Hunt. 1881. *A Century of Dishonor: A Sketch of the United States Government's Dealings with Some of the Indian Tribes*. Boston: Roberts Brothers.

———. 1970. *Ramona*. New York: Roberts Brothers, 1884. Rpt. New York: Avon.

Macías, Reynaldo, ed. 1989. *Are English Language Amendments in the National Interest? A Policy Analysis of Proposals to Establish English as the Official Language of the United States*. Claremont, Calif.: The Center.

Mathes, Valerie Sherer. 1990. *Helen Hunt Jackson and Her Indian Reform Legacy*. Austin: University of Texas Press.

Parlee, Lorena, and Paul Espinoza. 1983. "Ballad of an Unsung Hero." *Caminos* 5.11: 35–37.

Petri, Bruce. 1987. *A Theory of American Film: The Films and Techniques of George Stevens*. New York: Garland.

*Ramona: A Story of Passion and Protest*. (Videotape.) Princeton: Films for the Humanities, 1990.

Richie, Donald. 1970. *George Stevens: An American Romantic*. New York: Museum of Modern Art.

Stevens, George, dir. 1956. *Giant*. Warner Brothers Studio.

Webb, Walter Prescott. 1931. *The Great Plains*. Boston: Ginn.

———. 1935. *The Texas Rangers*. Cambridge: Houghton.

# ALIENS IN HETEROTOPIA:
# AN INTERTEXTUAL READING OF THE
# BORDER PATROL MUSEUM

## Eduardo Barrera

Heterotopias are places where "all the other real sites that can be found within the culture are simultaneously represented, contested, and inverted" (Foucault 1986, 24). The museum is the best example of a heterotopia. The border has been theorized as a heterotopia that becomes a trope—the trope du jour—of the "postmodern condition." Representations of these topoi have been generated using different narrative strategies and emplotment techniques. This exercise has as a point of departure the Border Patrol Museum, analyzing its discursive practices and including a critical view of the theories about the border as the heterotopia par excellence.

### CRIME AND PUNISHMENT ON THE FRONTIER:
### THE BORDER PATROL MUSEUM

The museum signified "a mythological setting inhabited by the nine goddesses of poetry, music, and the liberal arts" (Findlen 1989, 60) and is a deci-mononic heterotopia described by Bennett as "that space of representation as a rational and scientific one, fully capable of bearing the didactic burden placed upon it, by differentiating it from the disorder that was imputed to competing exhibitionary institutions" (1995, 1).

In the mid-1990s, the Border Patrol inaugurated the Border Patrol Museum and Memorial Library in El Paso. This city was selected because the agency was created here, and there are national training centers here for agents and for dogs. This facility is divided into two wings and consists of artifacts used

Eduardo Barrera: "Aliens in Heterotopia: An Intertextual Reading of the Border Patrol Museum," first published as Chapter 7 of *Ethnography at the Border*, edited by Pablo Villa. Minneapolis: University of Minnesota Press, 2003.

by migrants and agents, displays that re-create scenes, a video screen that continually plays different productions by the agency, and a gift shop. This internal ordering and conjugation of the separate but related components produces meaning and constitutes the poetics of exhibiting (Lidchi 1997). The politics of exhibiting articulate the objects that are appropriated and displayed to preexisting discourses, reinforcing the scientific credibility of discursive formations (Lidchi 1997). A common theme of all the artifacts on display and on sale is the threat that the immigrant, as a criminal because of his or her illegal status, poses to American society.

The southern wing has, among other artifacts, a display of plates with the names of agents who have died while on duty. It is a replica of what first welcomes a visitor to the office of the head of the Border Patrol in the area. The allusion to death frames the issue as a mythical opposition, as a situation of life and death, where two subjects are engaged in a conflict that can only be solved through reduction by annihilation or assimilation. This theme is repeated in other displays that re-create scenes that use visual and textual metaphors of war, the frontier of Westerns, and hunting. One display depicts a scene of an agent with a snowmobile and hunting gear; another one uses the conventions of campfire scenes of a Western, with haystacks and horse-back-riding gear. This discourse to the outside is reproduced inside the institution, through the "John Wayne Ethos" throughout the training of future agents, where a violent reaction becomes a reflex act that is desirable in an environment constituted as being full of threats. This Western imagery is in direct continuity with the image of the Kineños or Texas Rangers, the first "lawmakers" who policed the territory taken away from Mexicanos (Paredes 1958). The use of images of horseback riding elicits ambivalent reactions among migrants: "They use horses by Anapra, they looked really cool, very elegant, with uniforms . . . that's how they feel, like dogs waiting to attack." The snowmobile scene is titled "The One That Got Away" and provides the visitor with a text that describes it:

THE ONE THAT GOT AWAY

In many instances, Border Patrol Agents will miss capturing an illegal alien, due to the terrain or lack of manpower. In the background, the snow scene depicts a setting near Houlton, ME, where an agent missed capturing an alien by a few hours. An agent will now rely on his schooling and prowess in trying to locate signs (tracks) to follow. If the signs are fresh enough, the agent may be able to locate a person within a day.

The narrative style bears an obvious resemblance to the hunting scenes of nature magazines and TV documentaries. These narratives naturalize the hunting language with an omniscient and scientific tone.

Besides the displays of helicopters, patrols, and firearms used by the agents, there are two rudimentary boats used by Cuban refugees. The boats have texts that explain the Cuban migration in an essentialist manner, with liberty being the powerful magnet that makes refugees risk their lives in fragile boats.

The narratives about migration from other countries offer different explanations. Narratives by the INS and other sources range from a voluntarism
that uses the individual and his or her psychological characteristics as the unit
of analysis, typically by behavioral scientists and ethnographers, to structural
explanations where the actions of individuals are explained as mere effects
of macroeconomic forces by demographers and economists. This spectrum
also has at one end those theories that privilege the push forces, that is, the
socioeconomic conditions of the country of origin. Governments tend to emphasize the dynamics of the other country as the ultimate cause.

Ideological and academic discourses can be classified in any of the four
categories that result from the interaction of the two axes discussed. Mexican
officials tend to accuse migrants of lack of nationalism and for "choosing a
handful of dollars over their contribution to build a better Mexico, as former
governor of the state of Coahuila Oscar Flores Tapia would say. Behavioral
scientists base their explanations on the motivations and personality traits
of the individual migrant. Scholars in the field of economic anthropology
argue that peasants supplied the urban centers with food at low costs during the 1940s and 1950s, which made possible the industrialization that employed them as workers. The extraction of resources from rural communities
did not allow their reproduction, and rural-urban migration coincided with
the oversupply of labor in the 1960s. International migration became an option favored by peasants with enough resources to finance the costs of border crossers (Arizpe 1985). Neoconservatives make an essentialist argument
by constructing "liberty" as the dream that magnetically attracts the human
spirit from "nondemocratic" societies (Hauser 1990). Critical economists and
demographers point out that certain sectors of the U.S. economy actually
need the low-wage workforce of undocumented migrants to remain competi-
tive (Bustamante 1988; Sassen 1988). An undocumented worker pointed out,
"We're here to work, to do them a favor."

On the same north wing, there's a display of what are mostly household
knives labeled as "Weapons Seized from Illegal Aliens." Two artifacts that
stand out from the dozens of common ice picks, screwdrivers, scissors, and
kitchen and utility knives are a ring and a fourteen-inch knife with an exotic
leather cover with the word "Guatemala." The ring has a text that reads: "This
'James Bond' type weapon was taken from an illegal alien by Border Patrol
Agents E. Flores and Gordon on 5/9/74. Subject was wearing the ring and
claims that it is a .22 cal. pistol." These artifacts, rudimentary and allegedly
"hi-tech," are explained only in the context of their possible use against Border Patrol Agents, which reinforces the mythical opposition.

A museum is a heterotopia that reveals as much by what and how it includes as by what is excluded. There is no reference about these objects' possible use to cut paper, nails, or hair (scissors), to eat (knives), or to fix things.
When the objects are used as weapons, no mention is made of the threat posed
by others besides Border Patrol agents: muggers, wild animals, and so forth.
As an undocumented worker says, "Sometimes one carries something to protect yourself against gang members, muggers . . . the 'migra' is just prepared
to fight." The "hi-tech" weaponry is on the side of the army of illegal aliens,

while the Border Patrol is romanticized as Western law-and-order agents with a rugged lifestyle and accessories. All the pictures in leaflets and other literature depict the agents riding horses, and not their usual passenger trucks. Other transportation modes displayed in the museum represent some form of danger to the agent (i.e., helicopter). Conspicuously absent is any reference to the "hi-tech" military surveillance technology such as long-range infrared nightscopes, low-level-light television cameras, ground sensors, encrypted two-way radio, and positive identification systems to track recidivism (Andreas 1995; Dunn 1996).

The souvenir shop displays T-shirts and sweatshirts, mugs, paperweights, trading cards depicting the dogs that smell drugs, playing cards, and books. The violence theme repeats in some of those artifacts that bear the legend "Mean Green," a rhetorical strategy that moves the agency from a defensive to an offensive position. This shift can also be seen in the new motto "American Frontline," which is more reminiscent of the frontier than of the border. Products sold to children include the dog cards and coloring books. Both items articulate the work of the Border Patrol with the War against Drugs more than with halting undocumented migration. This operation works by reversing the two elements of a synecdoche. The undocumented worker becomes the part that represents the whole, which are the drugs. This subject, according to a Gallup Poll, is displaced from what is perceived as the fourth most important problem (curbing illegal migration, 72 percent) to number one (flow of illegal drugs, 89 percent) (Andreas 1995). The illegal alien now wears the face of the illegal drug.

Most of the books sold there are about the Border Patrol, except for a well-edited hardcover book titled *Illegal Aliens* (Hauser 1990) with a foreword by Daniel Patrick Moynihan. The cover has the series title on top: "The People of North America," flanked by the flags of the United States and Canada. At the center of the cover, it shows a photograph of three Mexican undocumented aliens discovered while being smuggled under the false bottom of a truck. Nobody could complain that any of the three countries that signed the North American Free Trade Agreement is excluded.

Racism is a complex problem full of ambiguities. Whereas a Mexican American student reads the museum as a strategy "to remind us who has the power," UTEP students from Ciudad Juárez point out that Anglo agents are not as despotic as Mexican American agents. An undocumented worker stated that Mexican American agents "didn't suffer, their parents and grandparents did . . . they think like us, they ask questions where they know they're going to get you, those of your own race can be much more suspicious." Undocumented workers also build redemption myths, where an Anglo agent is touched by divine forces and does the paperwork needed by a woman who had her family in Michigan.

The most recent activity organized by the Border Patrol in the area is a series of awareness seminars to the public. According to a fellow professor doing research on organizational communication at Customs and the INS, participants in those seminars have the same profile of paramilitary organizations throughout the United States.

## THE DIVINE EPIC: RETABLOS AND MURALS

Undocumented migrants are interpellated by the legal framework, the mainstream media, and the texts of the Border Patrol Museum as illegal. Some of their representations about themselves that resist that position are the *retablos* or *exvotos*. *Retablos* are a centuries-old tradition from Spain that was appropriated and adapted by Mexican Catholics (González 1994). These artifacts are small rectangles, no bigger than eight by twelve inches, by which the faithful give thanks for, and testimony about, a miracle or a blessing. They were made out of wood in Spain but were replaced by tin in Mexico (Durand and Massey 1990). Usually the topics of *retablos* are related to health or financial problems, but the theme of migration is increasingly important. These paintings usually include images of the migrant, a Virgin—mainly that of Saint John of the Lakes—and elements depicting the situation: trucks, rivers, buses, hospital beds, et cetera, and a written text below. Some representative texts are:

> I dedicate this retablo to Holy Virgin of St. John of the Lakes for saving me from a Texan of taking me, I hid under a tree with my little brother by the side of the highway. (Durand and Massey 1990, 24)

> Being lost in Chicago I put myself in the hands of the Virgin of St. John of the Lakes asking her to lighten the way I was looking for and thank her for granting me what I asked. That's why I dedicate this retablo as a tribute. (33)

> My Mother of St. John of the Lakes I thank you infinitely for the miracle of orienting and guiding me to Brackville Ranch, Texas, without me knowing. For that reason miraculous Dear Virgin I give testimony of the miracle and dedicate this retablo. (34)

Although Durand and Massey say that the reason behind a *retablo* is "the need to testify a miracle or give thanks for a favor" (1990, 6), González goes further, pointing out first that "the history of the defeated, told by themselves their way . . . doesn't just narrate the instant itself but a series of social, psychological, economic and environmental elements, which in each exvoto and the whole set constitute a popular history of what happens to the people" (1994, 106), and second that those *retablos* "are not a minor artistic genre, but an instrument of communication . . . they materialize a notion of life, faith and the world, a notion that is different and opposed to official religion" (118–19). The favorable outcome of a difficulty is the result of divine action, that is, a logic in which migration itself is legitimated by the "sacred donor" (virgin or saint). In sum, the migrant opposes natural law to the inferior positive law that labels him or her a criminal.

*Coyotes* and *pateros* produce other texts with epic overtones. They are the people who get migrants across the border for a fee. They have painted murals on the concrete walls of the Rio Grande on the sides of the Downtown International Bridge between El Paso and Juárez. These murals have an epic tone to them that depicts *pateros* as heroes who help their fellow Mexicans and are victims of acts of brutality on the part of the Migra (Border Patrol agents).

## MIGRANTS AS ART-E-FACTS: CHICANO ART

What do cultural studies in the North and the South have in common when they discuss the border? The view of the border as an ungrounded communal base was borrowed from the work of performance artist Guillermo Gómez-Peña. Although his performance art is not easily confined to traditional museums as heterotopias, there are other works and photographs that are. In the work of this artist, there seems to be an essence of a syncretic culture that radiates from the border and reaches the cultural centers:

> All major metropolis[es] have been fully borderized. In fact, there are no longer visible cultural differences between Manhattan, Montreal, Washington, Los Angeles or Mexico City. They all look like downtown Tijuana on a Saturday night. . . . In this new cartography where the East-West Coast cultural axis is being replaced by a North/South one . . . the North is Third-Worldized, the border becomes an omnipresent nomad center. (Gómez-Peña 1992, 60)

According to Fox (1993), the performances by this artist have become increasingly decontextualized and less site-specific as he has moved from Southern California to the East Coast. Although Gómez-Peña rejects the label "postmodern" in favor of "intercultural," he does so as a strategic move to focus on the border without subordinating it as an appendix to the established discourse of power centers in art circles.[1] He had already differentiated himself from " 'deterritorialized' Latin American artists in Europe and the United States [who] have opted for 'internationalism.' . . . I, on the other hand, opt for 'borderness' and assume my role . . . the chilango . . . who came to 'El Norte' . . . gradually integrated itself into otherness . . . the border became our house, laboratory, and ministry of culture (or counterculture)" (Gómez-Peña 1993, 37).[2]

This positioning of his texts through strategic labeling was a movement that created a "resistance capital" that was finally cashed in by a second move to those centers physically. By reclaiming the autonomy of the voice of the border, Gómez-Peña appropriates it. This type of ventriloquism is criticized by Haraway because the appropriated others are "carved out of one collective entity and relocated in another, where they are reconstituted as objects of a particular kind—as the ground of a representational practice that forever authorizes the ventriloquist. Tutelage will be eternal. The represented is reduced to the permanent status of the recipient of action, never to be a co-actor in an articulated practice among unlike, but joined, social partners" (Haraway 1992, 362). The tutelage by appropriation strategy is not exclusive of art and is present in academe, where publication titles interpellate "other" academics from the border, claiming the exclusivity of the object of study.[3]

## TELLURIC IDENTITIES VERSUS ESSENTIAL "OTHERS": MEXICAN ACADEME

The literature on the cultural identity of migrants is not as broad in Mexico as that about the border they cross. In an exhaustive review of the Mexican literature dealing with culture on the border in the last few decades, Zuñiga

(1992) found that these analyses could be collapsed into three broad visions: (1) the border as a cultural desert, (2) the border as a cultural edge, and (3) the border as a cultural trench.

The first depiction implies a hierarchy of cultures, combining simultaneously the elitist distinction of high culture and popular culture and the more anthropological distinction between culture of exotic societies and psychology of Western societies.[4] The former distinction was due to the contrast between the artistic and cultural infrastructure of Mexico City, with its museums of history, anthropology, and modern art, among others, the Palace of the Fine Arts and other concert halls and theaters, conservatories and art schools, with the almost nonexistent facilities in the border, which leaves a second-class popular culture implicit in the other distinction. The latter distinction is not stated explicitly but refers to the lack of grandiose pre-Columbian ceremonial centers, and colonial architecture, which take these studies to the logical conclusion that the border lacks the cultural heritage and the exotic element that makes a society worthy to be studied.

The last vision depicts the border as the site of cultural penetration on the part of the American "frivolous" and "alienating" mass culture. This is largely based on the telluric position of the second view, which assumes that the essence of Mexico will radiate from its political center, and that the border population are either traitors or passive victims of the song of the Boreal Siren.

There is a fresh body of literature that affirms that national identity on the border is even stronger than in the interior because we live side by side with the "other." This view positions the border as the new site that radiates the essence of that new Mexicanness (Barrera 1996). Bustamante argues:

> The goal of reducing or eliminating the inequality with the neighbor implies a strong motivation . . . an historical conscience. . . . Vis-à-vis the otherness of the neighbor, the border inhabitant relies on the reaffirmation of traditional values learned from the elders and which is reproduced in family relations. Relying, perhaps intuitively, on the values of his/her own definition of Mexicanness, stimulated by the contrast with the cultural otherness with which he/she is interacting. (1992, 99-100)

He substantiates this with the measurement of "national cultural identity" on the border and then compared to nonborder cities, showing that it is stronger in the former.

This position is a step ahead of the earlier visions of the border by eliminating the telluric character of Mexicanness but still has some limitations to overcome: (1) the reification of "otherness," (2) the negative conception of identity, and (3) the emphasis on the "residual" elements of cultural activities.

The "other" is reified through a process of singularization that erases the possibility of differences. This leaves the true and only "other" as the WASP U.S. citizen. Minorities, including Mexican Americans, do not constitute others. This is a severe limitation in theory as in practice as can be observed in the work of Vila (1994, 2000), who shows the tensions and differences between

Mexican Americans, undocumented and intra-Mexican migrants, and the rest of the border population. He found many cases in Ciudad Juárez where

> Mexican Americans are regarded as the principal other, while for poorer Juarenses sometimes the dividing line lies between their poverty with dignity and the poverty without dignity of Mexican Americans. On the other hand . . . some Mexican Americans . . . tried to distinguish themselves from Mexican nationals by constituting them as the stigmatized "other." . . . They revindicate their Mexican heritage, but stressing that they are proud of the Mexico of the past, not the "corrupt, poor, violent, and machista" Mexico of the present. On the other hand, they separate themselves from the contemporary Mexicans, who are not recognized as their own people. . . . And this Mexico of the present from which these interviewees want to separate themselves, to preserve their identities as "Mexicans" of the past, is felt as so strange that it is characterized as being "a completely different world" . . . from which there is no bridge that can close the gap, they feel separates them now from what was united before. (Vila 1994, 213-15)

The second limitation is the negative conception of identity; that is, cultural identity is what is left after we isolate the other. Valenzuela points out that collective identities are constructed through a process of differentiation from the "orher."[5] This view implies an intrinsic subordination of the identity that is constructed negatively. As Eagleton points out, the "other" "is always anterior to us and will always escape us, that which brought us into being as subjects in the first place. . . . We desire what others . . . unconsciously desire for us; and desire can only happen because we are caught up in . . . the whole field of the 'Other'—which generates it" (1983, 174).

Stam, Burgoyne, and Flitterman-Lewis (1992, 129) summarize the construction of identity in the Lacanian mirror stage as the " 'other' perceived as a whole, it mistakes this unified, coherent shape for a superior self." Bustamante ameliorates the negative nature of this process, but only by essentializing a historical conscience, which is only triggered by the "other."[6] The third limitation is the definition of Mexicanness by equating it with "traditional values" operationalized by Díaz Guerrero as the alignment with a gender division of labor or the subordination to figures of authority. This means that there cannot be a Mexican feminist or a Mexican revolutionary. Adherents of this position, particularly Bustamante, privilege the reliance on residual elements and consider subcultures such as *cholismo* as "a nationalism expressed in manifestions of popular culture" (Bustamante 1992, 103). Valenzuela does give more space to emergent elements but anchors them in class rather than nationalism.

The argument about reinforcement of national identity through friction is not shared by everybody. Monsiváis asks the rhetorical question "Will Mexico become a nation of Chicanos?" and responds: "In a period of changes that will become permanent transformations, in a moment where the most proven form of being rooted is a form of nomadism, there is an increase in the interest about tactics of resistance and adaptation. And in the recomposition of nationalism (which subsists despite everything) what is Chicano is a cultural version indispensable to observe" (Monsiváis 1993, 515).

## THE SEMIURGIC NOMADS IN CULTURAL STUDIES

Fox (1993) points out how the border has been appropriated by post-structuralist theorists and artists who replace the use of the border as the synecdoche of the nations it divides with a metaphor of liminal spaces and the coexistence of symbolic systems, in other words, a heterotopia.[7] This trope is giving way to its correlate of migrancy, nomadism, or diaspora (Hall 1987; Chambers 1991; Bhabha 1994). Although the liminality refers to the transformation through the intertextuality of signifying practices, the literature has reduced the supporting evidence to formal "intertextuality" or to the "intertextuality" of border writers and artists. The nonhyphenated word refers to "a set of signifying relations that is alleged to be manifest within a text, the product of the permutation of texts it deploys," and the hyphenated term refers to "the ways in which the relations between texts are socially organised within the objective disposition of a reading formation" (Bennett and Woollacott 1987, 86). The voices that are privileged in cultural studies are those of "enlightened migrants" such as Gómez-Peña. García Canclini's title *Culturas hibridas* (1990) and the notion of the border as a lab of postmodernity are clearly taken from the 1987 text "Documented/Undocumented" (published in Gómez-Peña 1993). Chambers (1991) and Bhabha (1994) also prove their arguments by citing the voice of the same enlightened migrant.

Lawrence Grossberg criticizes the border as a trope for "ignoring the fragmentary and conflictive nature of the discourses of power; ignoring the heterogeneity of power and reducing it apparently to discourses of representation and ignoring their material realities: ignoring the positivity of the subaltern. . . for supposing a privileged subjectivity of the subaltern" (1996, 92). The migrant as a traveler whose main struggle is to make sense of the semiotic environment is taken to the extreme of disappearing completely from the new marketplace of tropes. In the taxonomy by Bauman (1996), the pilgrim of modernity has as postmodern successors the stroller or flaneur, the vagabond, the tourist, and the gambler. The migrant doesn't fit the vagabond, who "doesn't have a fixed destination . . . depends on the generosity and patience of residents" (Bauman 1996, 28), or the tourist, who "moves with a purpose . . . they want to submerge in a strange and bizarre element . . . their world is structured completely and exclusively by aesthetic criteria (29-30). The uncomfortable sweat of the migrant is replaced by mere cognitive processes that, more than trying to survive, are trying not to get bored. The materiality of the migrant has thinned down to the extreme of disappearing altogether.

## THE VIOLENCE OF EXCLUSION: WHEN THE TROPE IS OVER ...

Aliens have been replaced by their incarnation as tropes of drugs and dwellers of heterotopias. The use of tropes in theoretical discussions has pushed the image of the migrant to a status of a disincarnate essence, an ambulatory and omnipresent phantom in a heterotopia. The imagery generated by the migrants themselves is a strategic discourse of survival that is an integral part of their strategy of material survival. While the border and the migrant became postmodern spaces of contestation in the North, these images became the paradigm of modernized post-NAFTA Mexico. The new theories of cultural identity by border scholars in Mexico articulated, and were strategic in, the marketing of NAFTA. This framework stands vulgar Marxism on its head by promoting economic integration while assuring readers that Mexicanness can only become stronger; national sovereignty is reduced to an issue of cultural identity, which becomes the new last instance. These theories also suffer from an overemphasis on difference, neglecting the key role of mimicry (Bhabha 1994), the simulation as a subaltern strategy when they are not on their own turf. This allows the migrant to break the positive rules by strategically nullifying his or her identity. Perhaps academics should enhance the border-related glossary by introducing the notion of smuggling. This trope would allow for the permeability of signifying practices and elements between territories and identities.

The texts by Gómez-Peña are informed by poststructuralism and at the same time serve as evidence for the literature that uses the migrant as an epitome of postmodern culture. This creates an incestuous circularity that in the end excludes over half a million Mexican migrants each year. The border has become a simulacrum that is crossed by semiurgic migrants who have replaced the economic agents and their material circumstances. Migrants suffer from a double exclusion: the one enforced by the Migra, and the other from the coupling of academics and semiurgic migrants who have appropriated their existential surplus value. When the trope is over, you can't just turn off the light.

## NOTES

1. Another difference from postmodern artists is his modernist production of manifestos. With respect to manifestos, Cagle writes, "unlike Dadaists or Surrealists . . . didn't offer specific manifestos or alternatives . . . not engaged in the credible procedure of working on a 'critical' problem" (1995, 10).

2. Originally "Documented/Undocumented" (1987).

3. Jorge Bustamante is one among those scholars at border cities who use this strategy frequently.

4. For a discussion of this anthropological distinction see Rosaldo 1989.

5. Valenzuela 1992. Although Bustamante and Valenzuela share the centrality of the "other," the former analysis is founded in the Webberian notion of social interaction and in Mario Ojeda's thesis of power asymmetry, while Valenzuela bases his in the theories of new social movements of Touraine, Melucci, and Smelser.

6. The development of a cultural identity through a process of paradigmatic differentiation evolves genealogically from Saussurian linguistics to Lacanian psychoanalysis to contemporary scholars who work within a framework that includes the axes of ethnicity, gender, and class such as Homi Bhabha (1994). However, not only is there the possibility of "positive" identities through differentiation, but an important distinction should be made between these accounts of "horizontal-secular" processes of differentiation and the "vertical-natural" processes. The former are based on the differences between the material and signifying practices of the everyday lives of

social actors. The latter is more noticeable in precapitalist/premodern societies, where eschatological founding myths narrate the process of differentiation from divine elements and grounding the social actors in question to their habitat, and where ethnicity, gender, and class are secondary effects. Telluric accounts can be found in Mexican border cities such as Nuevo Laredo (Ceballos 1992) and Tijuana (Díaz Castro 1992). The creation of a Free Trade Zone regime for the border (with renewed variants throughout several decades) can be regarded as the founding myth for the whole region that constituted the new border subject who is so important in this emerging view.

7. For an analysis of these uses of the U.S.–Mexico border see Fox 1993. Fox's paper cites as examples D. Emily Hicks, *Border Writing: The Multidimensional Text*, Iain Chambers, *Border Dialogues: Journeys in Postmodernity*; Henry Giroux, *Border Crossings: Cultural Workers and the Politics of Education*; Trinh T. Minh-ha, *When the Moon Waxes Red: Representation, Gender, and Cultural Politics*; Maggie Hymm, *Border Traffic: Strategies of Contemporary Women Writers*; and Renato Rosaldo, *Culture and Truth: The Remaking of Social Analysis*. Predecessors include Jacques Derrida's "Living On: Border Lines" and "The Parergon."

# REFERENCES

Andreas, Peter. 1995. "The Retreat and Resurgence of the State: Liberalizing and Criminalizing Flows across the U.S.–Mexico Border." Paper presented at the Latin American Studies Association Nineteenth International Congress, Washington, D.C., 28–30 September.

Arizpe, Lourdes. 1985. *Campesinado y migración*. Mexico, D.F.: SEP.

Barrera, Eduardo. 1996. "The U.S.–Mexico Border as Post-NAFTA Mexico." In *Mass Media and Free Trade: NAFTA and the Cultural Industries*, ed. Emile McAnany and Kenton T. Wilkinson, 187–217. Austin: University of Texas Press.

Bauman, Zygmunt. 1996. "From Pilgrim to Tourist—or A Short History of Identity." In *Questions of Cultural Identity*, ed. Stuart Hall and Paul du Gay, 18–36. London: Sage Publications.

Bennett, Tony. 1995. *The Birth of the Museum: History, Theory, Politics*. London: Routledge.

Bennett, Tony, and Jane Woollacott. 1987. *Bond and Beyond: The Political Career of a Popular Hero*. London: Macmillan.

Bhabha, Homi. 1994. *The Location of Culture*. New York: Routledge.

Bustamante, Jorge A. 1988. "Migración de indocumentados de México a Estados Unidos." In *Documentos de Trabajo*. Mexico, D.F.: Friedrich Ebert Foundation.

———. 1992. "Identidad y cultura nacional desde la perspectiva de la frontera norte." In *Decadencia y auge de las identidades: Cultura nacional, identidad cultural y modernización*, ed. José Manuel Valenzuela Arce, 91–118. Tijuana: El Colegio de la Frontera Norte.

Cagle, Van M. 1995. *Reconstructing Pop/Subculture Art, Rock, and Andy Warhol*. Thousand Oaks, Calif.: Sage.

Ceballos Ramírez, Manuel. 1992. "La epopeya de la fundación de Nuevo Laredo: El nexo entre la tradición y la historia." In *Decadencia y auge de las identidades: Cultura nacional, identidad cultural y modernización*, ed. José Manuel Valenzuela Arce, 99–107. Tijuana: El Colegio de la Frontera Norte.

Chambers, Iain. 1990. *Border Dialogues: Journeys in Postmodernity*. London: Routledge.

———. 1991. "Migrant Landscapes." *Strategies* 6 (6): 50–69.

Derrida, Jacques. 1979a: "Living On: Border Lines:" In *Deconstruction and Criticism*, ed. Harold Bloom et al., trans. James Hulbert, 75–176. New York: Seabury.

———. 1979b. "The Parergon." *October* 9 (summer 1979): 3–41.

Díaz Castro, Olga Vicenta (Sor Abeja). 1992. "La tía Juana." In *Decadencia y auge de las identidades: Cultura national, identidad cultural y modernización*, ed. José Manuel Valenzuela Arce, 109–33. Tijuana: El Colegio de la Frontera Norte.

Dunn, Timothy J. 1996. *The Militarization of the U.S.–Mexico Border, 1978–1992*. Austin: CMAS Books.

Durand, Jorge, and Douglas S. Massey. 1990. *Doy gracias: Iconografia de la emigración Mexico–Estados Unidos*. Guadalajara, Mexico: Programa de Estudios Jaliscienses.

Eagleton, Terry. 1983. *Literary Theory: An Introduction*. Minneapolis: University of Minnesota Press.

Findlen, Paula. 1989. "The Museum: Its Classical Etymology and Renaissance Genealogy." *Journal of the History of Collections* 1 (1): 59–78.

Foucault, Michel. 1986. "Of Other Spaces." *Diacritics* 16 (1): 22–27.

Fox, Claire F. 1993. "Mass Media, Site-Specificity, and Representations of the U.S.–Mexico Border." Paper delivered at the Conference *The Border* organized by the Whitney Museum, New York, April.

García Canelini, Néstor. 1990. *Culturas hibridas: Estrategias para entrar y salir de la modernidad*. Mexico, D.F.: Grijalbo.

Giroux, Henry. 1992. *Border Crossings: Cultural Workers and the Politics of Education*. New York: Routledge.

Gómez-Peña, Guillermo. 1992. "The New World (B)order." *High Performance* 55 (summer–fall): 58–59.

———. 1993. *Warrior for Gringostroika*. Saint Paul, Minn.: Graywolf Press.

González, Jorge. 1994. *Más (+) Cultura(S): Ensayos sobre realidades plurales*. Mexico, D.F.: Conaculta.

Grossberg, Lawrence. 1996. "Identity and Cultural Studies—Is That All There Is?" In *Questions of Cultural Identity*, ed. Stuart Hall and Paul du Gay, 87–107. London: Sage Publications.

Hall, Stuart. 1987. *The Real Me, Post-modernism, and the Question of Identity*. London: ICA.

Haraway, Donna, 1992. "The Promise of Monsters: A Regenerative Politics for Inappropriate/d Others." In *Cultural Studies*, ed. Lawrence Grossberg, Cary Nelson, and Paula Treichier, 295–337. London: Routledge.

Hauser, Pierre. 1990. *Illegal Aliens*. New York: Chelsea House Publishers.

Hicks, Emily. 1995. *Border Writing: The Multidimensional Text*. Minneapolis: University of Minnesota Press.

Hymm, Maggie. 1991. *Border Traffic: Strategies of Contemporary Women Writers*. New York: St. Martin's.

Lidchi, Henrietta, 1997. "The Poetics and the Politics of Exhibiting Other Cultures." In *Representation: Cultural Representations and Signifying Practices*, ed. Stuart Hall, 151–208. London: Sage Publications.

Monsiváis, Carlos. 1993. "¿Tantos millones de hombres no hablaremos inglés? (La cultura norteamericana y México)." In *Simbiosis de culturas: Los inmigrantes y su cultura en Mexico*, ed. Guillermo Bonfil Batalla, 455–516. Mexico, D.F.: Fondo de Cultura Económica.

Paredes, Américo. 1958. *With a Pistol in His Hand: The Ballad of Gregorie Cortez*. Austin: University of Texas Press.

Rosaldo, Renato. 1989. *Culture and Truth: The Remaking of Social Analysis*. Boston: Beacon Press.

Sassen, Saskia. 1988. *The Mobility of Labor and Capital: A Study in International Investment and Labor Flow*. Cambridge: Cambridge University Press.

Stam, Robert, Robert Burgoyne, and Sandy Flitterman-Lewis. 1991. *New Vocabularies in Film Semiotics*. London: Routledge.

Trinh T. Minh-ha. 1991. *When the Moon Waxes Red: Representation, Gender, and Cultural Politics*. New York: Routledge.

Valenzuela Arce, José Manuel. 1992. "Identidades culturales: Comunidades imaginarias y contingentes." In *Decadencia y auge de las identidades: Cultura nacional, identidad cultural y modernización*, ed. José Manuel Valenzuela Arce, 49–65. Tijuana: El Colegio de la Frontera Norte.

Vila, Pablo, 1994. "Everyday Life, Culture, and Identity on the Mexican-American Border: The Ciudad Juárez—El Paso Case." Ph.D. diss., University of Texas at Austin.

———. 2000. *Crossing Borders, Reinforcing Borders: Social Categories, Metaphors, and Narrative Identities on the U.S.–Mexico Frontier*. Austin: University of Texas Press.

Zuñiga, Victor. 1992. "La política cultural hacia la frontera norte: Análisis de discursos contemporáneos." Paper presented at COLEF II, Tijuana, Mexico, 22–24 October.

# PART II
# TESTIMONIES

# Great River

## Paul Horgan

"… Since I offered to narrate the story, I shall start at the beginning, which is as
follows."

—Pedro de Castañeda, or Náxera

### CREATION

Space.

Abstract movement.

The elements at large.

Over warm seas the air is heavy with. moisture. Endlessly the vast delicate
act of evaporation occurs. The seas yield their essence to the air. Sometimes
it is invisible, ascending into the upper atmosphere. Sometimes it makes a
shimmer in the calm light that proceeds universally from the sun. The upper
heavens carry dust—sea dust of salt evaporated from ocean spray, and other
dust lingering from volcanic eruption, and the lost dust of shooting stars that
wear themselves out against the atmosphere through which they fly, and dust
blown up from earth by wind. Invisibly the volume of sea moisture and dust
is taken toward land by prevailing winds; and as it passes over the coast, a
new condition arises—the wind-borne mass reflects earth temperatures that
change with the earth-forms inland from the sea. Moving rapidly, huge currents of air carrying their sea burdens repeat tremendously in their unseen
movement the profile of the land forms over which they pass. When land
sweeps up into a mountain, the laden air mass rolling upon it must rise and
correspond in shape.

And suddenly that shape is made visible; for colder air above the mountain
causes moisture to condense upon the motes of dust in the warm air wafted
from over the sea; and directly in response to the presence and inert power of
the mountain, clouds appear. The two volumes—invisible warm air, immov-
able cold mountain—continue to meet and repeat their joint creation of cloud.
Looking from afar calm and eternal, clouds enclose forces of heat and cold,

Paul Horgan: "Great River," first published as Prologue in *Great River: The Rio Grande in
North American History*, by Paul Horgan. New York: Rinehart & Co., 1954.

wind and inert matter that conflict immensely. In such continuing turbulence, cloud motes collide, cling together, and in the act condense a new particle of moisture. Heavier, it falls from cold air through warmer. Colliding with other drops, it grows. As the drops, colder than the earth, warmer than the cloud they left, fall free of cloud bottom into clear air, it is raining.

Rain and snow fall to the earth, where much runs away on the surface; but roots below ground and the dense nerve system of grasses and the preservative cover of forest floors detain the runoff, so that much sky moisture goes underground to storage, even through rock; for rock is not solid, and through its pores and cracks and sockets precipitation is saved. The storage fills; and nearing capacity, some of its water reappears at ground level as springs which find upward release through the pores of the earth just as originally it found entry. A flowing spring makes its own channel in which to run away. So does the melt from snow clinging to the highest mountain peaks. So does the sudden, brief sheet of storm water. Seeking always to go lower, the running water of the land struggles to fulfill its blind purpose—to find a way over, around or through earth's fantastic obstacles back to the element which gave it origin, the sea.

In this cycle a huge and exquisite balance is preserved. Whatever the amount of its element the sea gives up to the atmosphere by evaporation, the sea regains exactly the same amount from the water which falls upon the earth and flows back to its source.

This is the work, and the law, of rivers.

## GAZETTEER

Out of such vast interaction between ocean, sky and land, the Rio Grande rises on the concave eastern face of the Continental Divide in southern Colorado. There are three main sources, about two and a half miles high, amidst the Cordilleran ice fields. Flowing from the west, the river proper is joined by two confluents—Spring Creek from the north, and the South Fork. The river in its journey winds eastward across southern Colorado, turns southward to continue across the whole length of New Mexico which it cuts down the center, turns southeastward on reaching Mexico and with one immense aberration from this course—the Big Bend—runs on as the boundary between Texas and Mexico, ending at the Gulf of Mexico.

In all its career the Rio Grande knows several typical kinds of landscape, some of which are repeated along its great length. It springs from tremendous mountains, and intermittently mountains accompany it for three fourths of its course. It often lies hidden and inaccessible in canyons, whether they cleave through mountains or wide level plains. From such forbidding obscurities it emerges again and again into pastoral valleys of bounty and grace. These are narrow, at the most only a few miles wide; and at the least, a bare few hundred yards. In such fertile passages all is green, and the shade of cottonwoods and willows is blue and cool, and there is reward for life in water and field. But always visible on either side are reaches of desert, and beyond stand mountains that limit the river's world. Again, the desert closes against the river, and the gritty wastelands crumble into its very banks, and nothing lives but creatures of the dry and hot; and nothing grows but desert plants of thirsty pod, or wooden stem, or spiny defense. But at last the river comes to the coastal plain where an ancient sea floor reaching deep inland is overlaid by ancient river deposits. After turbulence in mountains, bafflement in canyons, and exhaustion in deserts, the river finds peaceful delivery into the sea, winding its last miles slowly through marshy bends, having come nearly one thousand nine hundred miles from mountains nearly three miles high. After the Mississippi-Missouri system, it is the longest river in the United States.

Along its way the Rio Grande receives few tributaries for so long a river. Some are sporadic in flow. Reading downstream, the major tributaries below those of the source are Rock Creek, Alamosa Creek, Trinchera Creek and the Conejos River in Colorado; in New Mexico, the Red River, the Chama River, and four great draws that are generally dry except in storm when they pour wild volumes of silt into the main channel—Galisteo Creek, the Jemez River, Rio Puerco and Rio Salado; and in Texas and Mexico, the Rio Conchos (which renews the river as it is about to die in the desert), the Pecos River, the Devil's River, (another) Rio Salado and Rio San Juan. The river commonly does not carry a great volume of water, and in some places, year after year, it barely flows, and in one or two it is sometimes dry. Local storms will make it rush for a few hours; but soon it is down to its poor level again. Even at its high sources the precipitation averages only five inches year-round. At its mouth, the rainfall averages in the summer between twenty and thirty inches, but there the river is old and done, and needs no new water. In January, at the source the surface temperature is fourteen degrees on the average, and in July fifty degrees. At the mouth in the same months the averages read fifty and sixty-eight. In the mountainous north the river is clear and sparkling, in the colors of obsidian, with rippling folds of current like the markings on a trout. Once among the pastoral valleys and the desert bench terraces that yield silt, the river is ever after the color of the earth that it drags so heavily in its shallow flow.

Falling from so high to the sea, and going so far to do it, the river with each of its successive zones encounters a new climate. Winter crowns the source mountains almost the whole year round, in the longest season of cold in the United States. The headwaters are free of frost for only three months out of the year, from mid-June to mid-September. Where the river carves its way through the mesas of northern New Mexico, the seasons are temperate. Entering the Texas desert, the river finds perennial warmth that rises in summer to blasting heat. At its end, the channel wanders under the heavy moist air of the tropics, mild in winter, violently hot in summer.

## CYCLE

Landscape is often seen as static; but it never is static. From its first rock in the sky to its last embrace by the estuary at the sea, the river has been surrounded by forces and elements constantly shoving and dynamic, interacting to produce its life and character. It has taken ocean and sky; the bearing of winds and the vagary of temperature; altitude and tilt of the earth's crust; underground waters and the spill of valleys and the impermeable texture of deserts; the cover of plants and the uses of animals; the power of gravity and the perishability of rock; the thirst of things that grow; and the need of the sea to create the Rio Grande.

The main physical circumstances of the Rio Grande are timeless. They assume meaning only in terms of people who came to the river.

# Nothing to Declare: Welcome to Tijuana

## Juan Villoro

### NORTH-BY-NORTHWEST

In one of their best parodies, Adolfo Bioy Cásares and Jorge Luis Borges invented a writer so caught up in his own internal reality that he could only describe what was happening on the north-northeast corner of his desk. Being less sensible than that character, I agreed to write about Tijuana in the north-northwest corner of Mexico.

The biggest disadvantage of being from Mexico City is that your origins are obvious to everyone. Chilangos are so disparaged in the rest of the country that we should perhaps stay in our own area. In fact, Tijuana is the place where journalist El Gato Félix began a "Chilangos, Go Home" campaign before he was assassinated—not by one of us, as far as we know.

In my defense, I should say that the Great Customs House of Baja California Norte dispels all provincialism. It is the most crossed border in the world, where the city limits of the Global Village change landscape as if by remote control. It's the duty-free store that traffics reality and dreams. For anthropologist Nestor García Canclini, it is one of the largest laboratories of the post-modern experience. For Tijuana writer Luis Humberto Crosthwaite, "It's an invented city, malleable and with many faces."

One of the typical products of this Mecca of syncretic culture is the Caesar Salad. Mexicans who make their pilgrimages to the Vatican are usually surprised that nobody offers them the antipasto we assume to be an Italian favorite. The answer to this mystery is simple—the Cesar for whom the salad was named was not one of the Roman Caesars, but was César Cardin, a Tijuana restaurateur disposed to culture smuggling.

As Mexico's most cosmopolitan of cities, Tijuana is the primary point of contact we have with the most powerful nation in the world, and this complexity requires multifaceted investigation. On the flight there, I thumbed through

Juan Villoro: "Nothing to Declare: Welcome to Tijuana," translated by Antonio Garza, first published in *Puro Border: Dispatches, Snapshots, and Graffiti from La Frontera*. El Paso: Cinco Puntos Press, 2003.

Aeroméxico's in-flight magazine to find the usual map of Mexico. It made me think of an ancient atlas with Aeolus, his puffed-out cheeks representing the directions of the winds, and an inscription that signaled the end of the world—*Hic sunt leones/There are lions here.* It showed an unexplored horizon that promised wild beasts. Now that lions yawn for a living at the circus, we must look for other animals to represent the unknown. What animal embodies the borderline condition of Tijuana? Through my headphones I hear Manu Chao's voice:

> Welcome to Tijuana
> tequila, sexo y mariguana
> con el coyote no hay aduana.

The lyrics advertise my travel destination as a City of Vice for sinners on a budget. In this deeply mythical folklore, the coyote is omnipresent. The problem is that it's about a person corrupted into a beast—a being who pronounces marvelously the two languages he speaks poorly and who has access to the secret passageways that let Mexicans enter into the United States. The coyotes have sent so many Oaxacans to San Diego that the city is now often called Oaxacalifornia.

Another creature that might symbolize this border-area is the seal, an animal torn between sea and land. It's no accident that Federicio Campbell chose to analogize his villagers to seals in the novel *Everything about the Seals* (*Todo lo de Focas*). All these creatures aside, nothing compares to the hybridized farm animal Tijuana dreamed up—burros painted like zebras. For reasons I can't understand, tourists love getting their picture taken next to this veterinary perversion.

The first thing a visitor sees upon landing in this city where donkeys masquerade as zebras is a metal wall, the same metal wall that the U.S. Army used as a road to advance in the dunes during Desert Storm. Placed here as a means of control, the wall is ridiculous. It has slits that act as rungs, and the wall isn't very high. Wade Graham in *Harper*'s magazine compares this symbolic wall to Christo's installation work.

Running a fence along the border that extends 30 meters into the ocean doesn't stop the illegals, but it does warn them that they *will* be stopped. The worthless scrap iron functions merely as advertising. It foretells the horrors that the adventurous may suffer. It's no coincidence that the landscape is ugly. Since October 1994, when Operation Gatekeeper was implemented, approximately 400 Mexicans have died trying to reach that temporary heaven we call *el otro lado* (the other side).

## THE INVISIBLE CHINESE

According to Crosthwaite, "President López de Santa Ana was the largest real estate agent in history." Thanks to him, we Mexicans lost half of our land; the border dropped down to Tijuana and it was attacked by little Century 21 signs. Land value is measured by its proximity to the empire. The city has grown so far north that it rubs up against the barbed wire fence where that which is Mexican becomes suspect. But on the American side, San Diego has its back to the border and its houses face the Pacific Ocean.

What could possibly unite these two disparate cultures? Before my trip, I talked to Daniel Sada, a writer from Mexicali who'd just finished his invigorating contribution to the Mexican novel, *Porque parece mentira la verdad nunca se sabe* (*Because It Looks like Lying, the Truth Is Never Known*). Daniel took me out to a Chinese restaurant on Bucareli Street in Mexico City. The restaurant belongs to Lin May. She's the Amazonian woman with breast implants who did stripteases at the Esperanza Iris Theater. Although the place was empty, and the décor was nightclub-esque, a Chinese waiter handed us lunch menus. We ate our chop suey by the dance stage like gangsters out of a Scorcese movie who had just shut down the place so they could chow down on some noodles.

"Do you know what culture brings Mexico and the United States together?" Daniel half-shut his eyes like a pitcher on the mound and hurled his answer—"Chinese food."

Mexicali was founded in a basin below sea level, in the middle of the desert. The Chinese were welcome there because the terrain was considered uninhabitable. With the secretiveness of a people used to living in kitchens, they spread throughout the border. The nights in Mexamerica are aglow with neon Chinese characters. In Tijuana, there are almost 300 Chinese restaurants and a consulate which keeps up with the immigration paperwork of this populous but invisible people who cook so much food.

In the movie "Pulp Fiction," set in Los Angeles, a criminal holds up a cafeteria by shouting, "Get the Mexicans out of the kitchen!" If the scene had occurred a few miles south, he would have shouted, "Get the Chinese out!" This would have permitted us to see them for the first time.

In Tijuana, Luis Humberto Crosthwaite also took me to an amazing restaurant that serves the local cuisine, Chinese food. Because he's lived in Tijuana since his birth in 1962, he knows many people, including some Chinese folks who hide amid the steam of their pots. This liking for secrecy has led them to open little clandestine cafes where their customers arrive like guests invited to a home. Luis Humberto made me try shrimp glazed in coconut and other Tijuanan marvels, delicacies that surely Marco Polo tasted as he traveled along the Great Wall. But he didn't consider me worthy of membership in that fraternity of people who hide in order to eat glazed duck. Only those who already know some of these people-in-hiding can belong to the brotherhood. I don't know the exact number of people you need to know. All I know is that I don't yet qualify.

These invisible Chinese restaurants are as interesting as other forms of local commerce. The informal economy in Mexico has produced strange merchandise, but someone seems to be buying it. You see masks of the former president Salinas de Gortari. Before the border toll booths, cars stop to buy even weirder handicrafts. This is the only place in the Western world where plaster sculptures of Bart Simpson, the size of dorm refrigerators, are considered decoration. You can choose from Power Rangers, Pocahontas or Aladdin. These artisans keep up with Hollywood trends. Currently they're engrossed in Tarzan. The rough mold will be painted with acrylic paints thus ensuring the result will be grotesque. And yes, it's a complete success. You even see people walking across who buy them and then carry them home piggyback.

Tijuana has the greatest concentration of pharmacies on the planet. That says two things about Americans: either they're very sick people or very self-indulgent hypochondriacs. Prescription drugs so vigilantly controlled in the U.S. can be bought here without prescription.

Dentists, dermatologists and plastic surgeons are the biggest beneficiaries of the border's cheap unregulated medicine. On a good day, you'll bump into a pack of clinical tourists. And if you're lucky, you'll see these humanoids with cherry-red faces fresh off the plastic surgeon's table.

From greyhound races to lobster tacos, the mercado that is Tijuana has it all in stock. In this emporium of transactions, the poet Robert L. Jones proudly boasts of having crossed the bridge carrying "one undocumented rose." But of course, love isn't the only motivation for such lyricism. Above a border toll crossing you can see a billboard that reveals the consequences of this international commerce: *Herpes? Call 800-336-CURE.*

## EROTIC MATINEE

The Mexican Consulate in San Diego and the Colegio de la Frontera Norte organized a field trip for a group of writers and journalists so we could see the real Tijuana. There were to be no pictures of sightseers with brooms in hand standing next to striped burros. We had to take an interactive tour as participatory as the one taken by the head of the Colegio, Jorge Bustamante. He experienced the reality of the border by crossing the border just like a wetback.

As soon as I got into the school's minibus, a professor started railing against an unexpected byproduct of capital-chauvinism.

"Have you ever noticed that the weather man on chilango-TV points out the weather for places in central Mexico, and the whole time his head is covering the entire peninsula of Baja California?"

"No, uh, I hadn't noticed *that.*"

"That's how cruel centralization can be."

I sat there shamefacedly keeping quiet until we got to our first stop: an enormous statue of a nude woman. It was so large that it was up there with the largest statue of Lenin in the old Soviet Union. The size of this giant wasn't as significant as the fact that the sculptor lived inside of her. It was oddly oedipal; he can look onto the world from a balcony that comes out of his loved one's stomach. And he has hung out a FOR SALE sign.

After contemplating the statue, simultaneously womb and condo, we traveled along the Mexican side of the border. Our colleagues from the Colegio referred to it as la línea—the line.

The closer you get to the U.S., the poorer the city becomes. Half of the construction is made of the ever-present tire. Houses are erected on top of tire pillars, like beach huts on piers. On hills of loose soil often visited by earthquakes, these tires act as both a foundation and a shock absorber.

I saw walls, swings and bricks made from tires. In this refuge for nomads, the tire, the emblem of mobility, is stationary.

It was 11 in the morning when our van went in an unexpected direction—Coahuila Street. It was late for many things, but it was a bit too early to visit a night club.

"The greatest inconvenience of being executed is that it's always done at dawn." I thought of this line by Carlos Fuentes as we entered the cabaret with people from the Colegio. The darkness of the place created a sense of suspended time, an eternal midnight which regulars in Las Vegas and at Hugh Hefner's mansion know well.

I sat down between two academics to contemplate this erotic failure. A woman stripped on the catwalk, fondled by drug-laden eyes. Down front, two customers in cowboy hats stared at the bottles covering their table. It seemed like they'd been in that position for a week.

There are people who go to strip joints to get turned on, and there are others who go to get excited by those who are turned on. "You've got to go to El Bambi," a friend tells me, "and you can see soldiers kissing each other." This reporter is not as engrossed by the exposed breasts as much as he is by the reactions of audience members. Sticking bills of money in a woman's g-string is commercialized eroticism, but it's no less sordid being a nosy observer.

The woman on my right pointed at the stripper getting off amid thin applause: "Don't worry, the other girls are better. What would you like them to do to you?"

My purple chair turned out to be a great spot for fretting. It felt like Tijuana time was standing still at 11 o'clock. My companion was disturbing me more than the dancers. A harsh announcer called out the next victim—Yadira or Yasmine or Yesina, something like that. The professor sitting next to me crossed her legs. OK, I haven't said this before, but she was wearing very short shorts and was sporting an ankle bracelet, attire not so uncommon in this 100-degree border heat, but unthinkable on a university campus in Mexico City. My neighbor asked for a double shot of tequila, but what they brought her looked more like a triple. She took a looong drink. I could see the tequila enter her throat, and I knew I saw too much. I asked my other colleague something, the one who hates the meteorologists blocking Baja California. She could not explain reality without statistics. By the time I took a sip from my tequila, the short shorts professor had already finished hers. The woman on my right was talking as if her suffering were linguistic. She explained the women's routines, what men got off on, what Americans' tastes were. She neither condemned nor celebrated the sex industry. That was life, hard, broken and monotonous. There was something irresistible in her impartiality in the face of everyone else's frenzy. I quit looking at the stage. I could only see the woman who was checking out the stage.

"Do you want a dance?" she asked.

It was at a Tijuana matinee. The stripper was moving towards my table or my lap. I asked for the check.

We got back to sun-baked Coahuila Street. The professors were refreshed and glowed as if we had just had some invigorating juices.

I was reminded of another trip I once took to Tijuana. I went with my wife and I asked a taxi driver to drive us around for an hour. We circled around statues of different heroes, a planetarium decorated by a model of a small dinosaur and a place where an impresario built a miniature model of Mexico. It had been closed because of a dearth of visitors.

"People aren't very patriotic," complained the driver.

I wondered if the desire to see a shriveled motherland was a test of patriotism, but I couldn't keep up my train of thought: we were on Coahuila Street and the driver was pointing out the whores.

"Here come some cheap hookers. Poor girls." He turned to my wife: "Sorry ma'am, but you told me to drive around for an hour, and, well, after twenty minutes we're bound to bump into some hookers."

I got back into the Colegio van. Time went back to normal. It wasn't 11 o'clock anymore, the hour held back for desire. Where were we going? I'd find out in twenty minutes.


## THE BAD WEED

After the Cold War, the U.S. was unable to tout its virtues without reference to an archetypal enemy. The Latino drug lord replaced the devouring communists. Drug trafficking prospers throughout the continent because of organized crime networks. Of these networks, very little is known of the drug lords who operate on the northern side of the American continent. By contrast, unrelenting propaganda keeps us up to date with the intimate lives and detailed misdeeds of each and every Latin American drug cartel.

The most crossed border in the world is an irresistible magnet for the drug traffickers who have built their homes along the border. They are part banking fortresses and part arabesque mansions full of megalomaniacal grandeur.

In 1994 Luis Donaldo Colosio, the PRI presidential candidate, was assassinated in the Tijuana suburb of Lomas Taurinas. In his book, *Sorpresas te da la vida* (*Life Hands You Surprises*), Jorge G. Castaneda offers an explanation for the crime. President Salinas, he argues, broke his non-aggression pact with the narcotraficantes by signing the NAFTA agreement with the U.S. and Canada, so the regional cartel took matters into their own hand.

Most Mexicans know about Lomas Taurinas from TV footage. We saw a dusty valley filled with party faithful in jackets and a sad crowd where Colosio was finished off point blank. The sequence become the oracle that we could watch a thousand times without finding a single clue.

By now, the crime scene qualifies as a "place of interest." The city government has touched up the gorge. A little memorial commemorates the assassination and a few offices put in enough energy to erect a pistachio-green wall, but none was able to fill the wall with something of value.

In its civic poverty, Lomas Taurinas shows the uneven battle between the legal authorities and the audacious lawbreakers. To say that the crime was because of drug traffickers is almost like saying, "It was in the hands of God." Organized crime is impenetrable and the losses it incurs come only from inside the organizations. Like suddenly a drug lord (or his double) dies on the operating table while undergoing liposuction, or he's found dead in the trunk of a car with enough stab wounds to insure the job was done right. Only someone in the Brotherhood can get close to those colorful Versace shirts and the golden spoons that hang from around their necks.

These famous ghosts incriminate themselves in the pursuit of pleasure with certain kinds of cars, certain restaurants, and a specific type of woman: Grand Marquis, seafood from Los (N)Arcos Restaurant, women in spandex with flaming red hair.

The most important cultural manifestation of narcotraficantes is heard in the songs which have changed the repertoire of norteño bands. Although not all members of this norteño New Wave pay their respects to Camelia la Texana in these drug epics, rhythmic accordion plays still churn out the narco hit parade, singing about Cessnas on hidden air fields, farm workers who pack AK-47s and drugs being smuggled to the U.S. The city of the Caesar Salad hasn't produced as many narcocorridos as Culicán, the real Motown of this music craze, but Tijuana does its part:

Unos perros rastreadores
Encontraron a Yolanda
Con tres kilos de heroína
Bien atados a la espalda

Drug-sniffing dogs
Found Yolanda
With three kilos of heroin
Tied tight on her back

So sing the Los Incomparables de Tijuana. Also singing their share are Los Aduanales (The Customs Agents):

Salieron de San Isidro
Procedentes de Tijuana
Traían las llantas del carro
Repletas de hierba mala

They left San Isidro
Coming out of Tijuana
Their car tires
Stuffed with the baddest weed

## ALIENS

It's summer and on the empire's terraces, they are serving three-colored noodles and fragrant cappuccinos. In these areas of controlled enjoyment—where cigarette smoke sets off fire alarms—wine enjoys an excellent reputation. North Americans need pleasures that are medically certified. And this alcoholic grape regulates hypertension.

Each bottle of California wine has a label which chronicles its epicurean attributes. But those who raise wine glasses in support of Napa Valley red wine overlook the work it took to produce it.

It all begins in the burning Mexican desert. Near the Tijuana border crossing, plaster heads of Bart Simpson are stored in whitewashed stalls. Not far from there, in the nearby dry hills, other figures stick out. Men are waiting for the perfect moment. Unmoving, crouched down, they wait to advance. Their posture is a testimony to the heritage of the poverty—no Mexican of Spanish blood could "rest" in such a hunkered position.

I imagined it would be hard to talk to them, but on the Mexican riverbank, before being spotlighted by helicopters, these undocumented ones talk incessantly.

A 50-year-old man wearing a baseball cap and sneakers begins to tell me, "I have my three children on the other side. I was also there but I had to go back to Oaxaca for the youngest one."

The border is an enormous depository of stories. These accounts prove that crossing is possible. The fact that Rubén, Chucho, Carmen and Ramona are already working in strawberry fields and grape orchards means that they have dodged the helicopters which they call "mosquitoes" and a heat-sensing device they refer to as "the eye of the tiger." Soon, one of them will be a happy alien in the U.S.

But pessimism is also plentiful. "I have been bounced back more than 30 times," said one young man who seemed to have been born trying to cross.

The trick is perseverance. Sooner or later, the tide cannot be contained. The migra only send out 20 men on searches. If they send you back to Mexico, you must endure one more day of hunger with blistering noon heat and cutting wind at daybreak—one more try. On the other side, after a 20-minute walk, yellow taxis are there ready to give you a ride down Interstate 5, on the yellow brick road to jobs.

"The motherfucking government can go fuck itself," yells a strong 20-something man. He is wearing a black t-shirt with a gothic logo of some rock group. "We need another Pancho Villa." He kicks some rocks. "Does it seem right that I can get time for begging? It's okay to lock me up for robbing but not for panhandling. They're fucks."

Apparently, Mexican police stop people from begging near the Immigration Office. Others look at him, fed up with his loud mouth.

"What we need is democracy and justice," an old man explained.

"And a fucking gun to kill those assholes," added the fanatic.

I wondered how the old men were going to jump the barricades and run, but they didn't seem worried. It was worse to stay where they were. All of them came from far away—Zacatecas, Morelos, Aguascalientes.

At night, the waiting men suck on tequila-soaked oranges to keep warm. They cover themselves with cardboard boxes, and when they wake up, they burn the boxes.

"Why?"

"Because it's the law," they answer.

Mexamerica is a country with its own rules. For $700, a coyote will take you to San Francisco, a crazy expense for immigrants who are trying to avoid the $27 passport fee. They might as well be renting a limo with that money.

In 1991, 65.5 million people crossed through the Otay Point of Entry by legal means. Near by in San Ysidro, 40,000 cars cross daily. No one keeps statistics for those illegals who were successful in crossing. Only the rejected are counted—1,700 a day in the San Diego area.

The rules of Mexamerica are absurd. On the other side, jobs are waiting but the manual laborers must go through initiation rites to satisfy the most demanding of tribes.

In this theatre of bilateral posturing, the U.S. government strengthens its stance to win the racist vote (including any Chicanos who already have the proper paperwork). In turn, the Mexican government makes good use of the harassment to carry out its own foreign policy, to do what it cannot do in Mexico. Our countrymen suffocate in boxcars, their bones found under brush; others die from the xenophobic actions of the Los Angeles Police Department. These events permit even the most undemocratic of countries to protest in the name of human rights.

While people are drinking summer wine on terraces in the U.S., Mexicans are picking grapes in the Napa Valley. Not far from there, in a Hollywood basement, the *Alien* movie poster preserves a cool glowing message: "In outer space, no one can hear you scream."

## CODA

On my final passage through customs back to Mexico, I take the line marked NADA QUE DECLARAR. This slogan shields those journeying with legal baggage. But it also protects those who are returning filled with confusion.

# WITH THE SMOOTH RHYTHM
# OF HER EYELASHES

## Luis Humberto Crosthwaite

A baby cries every day at four in the morning. This demanding child does not miss an opportunity to chastise her parents, especially when they're late to tend to her needs. Zombiefied, the father gets up to take the baby from the crib and puts her in the arms of her sleeping mother.

Thirty minutes later, groggy, in a daze, the father gets up to take the baby back to the crib.

The mother is pensive. She's worried about her daughter's future. She's already three months old and doesn't have a visa. She can't enter the United States like any other normal person. The father is also worried. Baseball season has started and the daughter needs to feel the thrill of watching the king of sports.

As if it were his morning civic duty, the father dials a phone number. He is notified that there is a 12-pesos-per-minute charge for the call. "I want to apply for a visa for my daughter." On the other end of the line, a woman speaks slowly, explaining each step in the process. The woman takes down the child's name, but the father is certain that he should tell her more. "She's not just a name, Miss, she's a person. You should see her sweet face, listen to her cry. Cough. Burp. It's amazing." Patiently, the woman listens to the man's rambling (at 12 pesos-per-minute). Then she tells the proud father not to forget Questions #33 and #34 when he fills out the application. They're the most important questions.

It's a solemn obligation (and a government requirement) that both parents appear at the administrative hearing for the conferring of the visas. But on the day of the appointment, the mother can't get permission to get off of work. The father is forced to attend alone. He carries his baby like an Olympic torch, and, unable to help himself, he shows her off to the hordes in the line. The hordes all certify that she is a beautiful, healthy baby.

Luis Humberto Crosthwaite: "With the Smooth Rhythm of Her Eyelashes," translated into English by Antonio Garza, first published in *Puro Border: Dispatches, Snapshots, and Graffiti from La Frontera*. El Paso: Cinco Puntos Press, 2003.

The first stage in the process requires the filling out of the application.

The father is overjoyed in the discovery that they don't just require this little person's name, but also her eye color, hair color, complexion, religion, race, date of birth, blood type, names of parents and grandparents. The father waltzes to the edge of the earth as he fills in the blanks, until he abruptly arrives at Question #33.

It's not just one question but a whole series.

*a. Have you ever been involved in a terrorist organization? Yes / No*

Who would answer yes to this question? Could there be honest terrorists? A terrorist not wanting to jeopardize his entry visa?

*b. Have you crossed contraband into the United States? Yes / No*

Even though it's illegal to cross the border with agricultural products, as American customs laws clearly state, the father remembers one time when he brought two apples to a baseball game. In any case, there was no room for comments on the application.

*c. Have you ever been imprisoned for committing a crime? Yes /No*

The last thing America wants is people with prior convictions. The father remembers that one time . . . but that was a long time ago. In any case, these questions refer to the baby, and she's definitely done nothing wrong that he knows of.

*d. Have you ever assisted another person to enter the United States with false documents? Yes /No*

The father thinks this may be a trick question. False is an ambiguous adjective and with regards to the baby, no.

And that was just Question #33. Question #34 is much more simple.

*a. Are you entering the United States with the intent of participating in acts or intended acts of terrorism? Yes / No*

The father is shocked that it's even possible to participate in such organizations in the United States. The only thing on his mind is baseball. His wife just wants to hit the clothes and shoe sales.

The father looks at his little girl with her gray eyes, sweet smile, curly hair and angelic face. No. No. No, no, and no. The father releases his anger every time he checks off the No box. His daughter is not and will not ever be some kind of Patty Hearst. How could she ever possibly become one? Sadness fills him when he imagines baby Patty's dad answering a similar application. What would he have answered?

The father looks into his baby girl's eyes, looking for some indication. And his daughter opens her eyes with the smooth rhythm of her eyelashes.

There's no reason to ask such questions. There should be another application especially for cases such as these. They should be telling him, "You are the father of a beautiful baby girl, so you need to fill out Form 24B, not 25H."

Question #34 on Form 24B:

a. *Do you think that your daughter will fulfill all your hopes and dreams?*

b. *Do you think your daughter will one day marry a good-for-nothing punk?*

c. *Do you have reason to believe that your daughter will one day, when you least expect it, break your heart?*

These questions would be much more appropriate. And on any of these forms, no, no and no. No to it all.

The second step in the application process requires the father to have a brief interview with a consular agent.

"Are you her father?"

*Yes.*

"How about the mother?"

*No, she's not here.*

"Where is she?"

*She's far away.*

"How far?"

*Very far.*

"Occupation?"

*The mother's?*

"No, yours."

*I write. Odd jobs from time to time. I write.*

By sheer coincidence, this blond man also has a 3-month-old baby. He shows pictures of his baby son. As if accepting a challenge to duel, the father draws his own snapshots. Photo against photo. Two cardsharks pulling ace after ace from their sleeves. Baby: naked on the bed. Crying baby. Baby in need of diaper change. Bathing baby cries with shampoo in baby's eyes.

Question #35:

*Do you think it's possible that someday your daughter will fall in love with the son of a consular agent? Yes / No*

Life is full of uncertainty.

As a goodbye, the agent hands the father a sheet of paper that says "Congratulations! You have been approved for a Laser-Visa to enter the United States of America, the most powerful nation in the world."

The father goes home with visa in hand, and a heavy feeling bearing down on his heart. He, after all, got what he wished for.

# TALKING TO THE RÍO GRANDE

## Cecilio García-Camarillo

Siempre regreso a ti, my source, you gnarled piece of liquid leather. When I feel good or reventado you're always there for me. Solamente your indifference tiene la capacidad de entender the outpourings of my soul. As a child in Laredo I knew you as the powerful divider of a people who were once one and the same, y ahora de aquel lado están los mexicanos, y acá, nosotros, los tejanos. You flowed on doing your own thing, not caring about the weird games men play. I swam in you and your dark waters mixed with my blood. Toda mi vida he permanecido cerca de ti 'cause I have the need to reveal myself to you so that I can cope con todas las chingaderas de la vida. Listen to me old one, and help make her love me once again . . .

¿Pero cóma jodidos le hago para resolver la situación? Old river, how can I reject with my body la maña of wanting to own her? ¿Cómo puedo dejar de ser lo que soy? How? I'd have to die and be reborn. If I were a rattlesnake and could change skins, I'd be renewed. I'd be young with a glistening new skin. I'd drink your waters with a new soul. Maybe then I wouldn't have the need of wanting her by my side. I'd even be able to forgive my father. To be renewed, but first I'd have to die.

I almost died once, remember? Yes, I was in junior high, and my friends from school and I played hooky, and I took them in my old car to the family ranch. Man, aquellos sí eran tiempos locotes. And then I showed them something special, la noria, so deep and mysterious. I remember my cousins Kiko and Pepe digging it years before, and I was always afraid to get close to it. But now my friends were right up to the rim of the well, and they saw some snakes at the bottom. They got all excited and started shooting at them with .22-caliber rifles. I yelled no, son víboras negras, they're harmless. Estan alla abajo porque hay ratas y se las van a comer. But they just kept shooting like maniacs. Then they argued about who was going to go down the ladder to get the snakes so we could take them back to Laredo and scare the shit out of people, but nobody had the guts to volunteer. Then someone said I should go down 'cause after all it was my ranch and I was used to those kinds of things,

Cecilio García-Camarillo: "Talking to the Rio Grande," first published in *Selected Poetry of Cecilio García-Camarillo*. Houston: Arte Público Press, 2000.

and they circled me and called me joto, miedoso, chicken shit, and pussy. My heart started jumping all over the place, but I decided to go down anyway. I'd show them que mi verga estaba más gruesa than all of theirs put together.

I started going down and it felt warm, with a tightness and then a release, as if the dark and damp well were pulsating. There was a thick old smell all around. I could barely see the bottom, but I knew the snakes were dead, probably killed twenty times over. I went lower, trying to focus on the snakes. The well now felt cool and exhilarating. Suddenly, I saw movement all around me. I couldn't believe that the dark walls were moving all around me. Then I realized there were thousands of crickets living there and the shooting had agitated them. I stood still and looked at them for a moment. They were like a black blanket moving in waves. Then my friends again me rayaron la madre and even threw stones, and I felt so alone and scared. The crickets got even more excited when my foot slipped and I almost fell. With one hand I braced myself against the wall of the well, but when I did that the crickets began jumping. I felt their cool and spiny legs all over my body, and then they started chirping, first a few chirping softly, then more. I had my balance now, then by the thousands the crickets were chirping louder and louder all around me. Their song relaxed me, and I did not feel scared of them anymore. It seemed as if they were playing their cricket song so that I wouldn't hear my drunk father or my friends yelling obscenities. I didn't care about falling off the ladder or about the snakes. The rhythm of the crickets' song kept coming into me, filling up my mind and every part of my body like a soothing dream. I knew my face was smiling, yes, I was at peace with myself for the first time in my life, and at that moment that is all that mattered in the world. The song of the crickets and I became one.

# Pocho Pioneer

## Richard Rodriguez

It is appropriate that I come to this distinguished encuentro as something of a naysayer. It is appropriate, though ironic, that I sound a sour note in the midst of all your talk about "a new moment in the Americas." As a child I grew up in blond California where everyone was optimistic about losing weight and changing the color of her hair and becoming someone new. Only my Mexican father was dour and sour in California—always reminding me how tragic life was, how nothing changes, reminding me that everything would come to nothing under a cloudless sky.

Mexicans speak of "el fatalismo del Indio"—the sadness at the heart of Latin America. As a child, when I looked South, I shuddered at the Latin sensibility. I turned away from it, spent my childhood running toward Doris Day and Walt Disney.

You cannot imagine the irony with which I regard this meeting. My Latin American colleagues have travelled several thousand miles north to speak about the new democratic spirit in their countries, the new spirit of individualism. We of the north, by contrast, have become a dark people. We do not vote. We have lost our optimism. We are besotted with individualism and we have grown lonely. We, in California, now sound very much like my Mexican father.

I end up a "pocho" in the United States, reflecting on the tragic nature of life.

Clearly, I am a freak of history. I carry this Indian face; I have a Spanish surname; my first name is Richard (*Ree-cherd*, Mexico calls me). The great Octavio Paz, in *The Labyrinth of Solitude*, has a chapter concerned with the "pachuco"—the teenaged gangster in Los Angeles. For Paz the gang kids of California represent the confusion within the Mexican-American—caught between two cultures. The child does not know where he belongs. The child has lost his address. The child no longer belongs to Mexico, neither does he fit into the United States. The Mexican-American is a tragic figure, a pathetic

Richard Rodriguez: "Pocho Pioneer," delivered as a speech in November 1994 at a White House Conference, "A New Moment in the Americas." First published in *The Late Great Mexican Border: Reports from a Disappearing Line*, ed. Bobby Byrd and Susannah Mississippi Byrd. El Paso: Cinco Puntos Press, 1999.

one. Señor Paz is right about Mexican-Americans, but he is also arrogant and wrong about us.

Consider these the reflections of a pocho. . . .

You know, we sit here in this elegant room, talking about the new moment in the Americas as though the moment has just happened, today—November 12, 1994. We act as though we are the witnesses of its happening. In fact, the so-called moment, the discovery of the Americas by Americans, has been going on for nearly a century. But the discovery has been mainly by peasants. They were the first Americans who trespassed American borders.

I speak of the hundreds of thousands of migrant workers who have been coming to the United States since the turn of the century. The two largest groups: Puerto Ricans and Mexicans. Back and forth they went, across borders, time zones, languages, faiths. Between Puerto Rico and New York, between Los Angeles and Mexico.

The Puerto Ricans found themselves, at the end of the nineteenth century, suddenly part of the United States. The Mexicans found themselves in places like Arizona and California, which used to be part of Mexico. The Mexicans and Puerto Ricans were like no other immigrant group the United States had ever seen. There was something wrong with us.

And yet I would like to argue that we were the first Americans—Americans, that is, in the sense we are talking today. The peasants of Puerto Rico and Mexico were the first people who saw the hemisphere whole.

Oh, there is President Salinas de Gortari today with his Harvard degrees, as there are the new "technocrats" of Latin America with their Ivy League degrees. Business executives and government officials in the United States sigh with relief at meeting this new class of Latin Americans.

"At last, Señor Salinas, we understand you. You speak our language. You are our kind of Mexican. Let's talk business."

Do not listen to the flattery of the United States, Señor Salinas. I am sorry to have to tell you that you have been preceded North to the United States by several decades, by millions of peasants.

Mexican-Americans, Puerto Ricans—we were a puzzle to the United States. We were people from the South in an east-west country. (The United States has written its history across the page, east to west. The United States saw its manifest destiny unfolding in the western migration.) Land was the crucial metaphor for possibility in the United States' scheme of things. As long as there was land, there was possibility. As long as you could move West, you had a future. As long as you could leave Maryland for Nebraska, then you could change the color of your hair, change your religion. As long as you could leave Kansas for Nevada, you could drop your father's name or shorten it. You could drop the embarrassing "ini" or "izzi" or "stein." You could become someone other than your father.

I am going to California to become Tab Hunter. Yes, I like that name. Me llamo Tab Hunter.

The crisis in California today is due to the fact that the United States has run out of land. The metaphor of the west has been exhausted. The end had been decades in coming. As early as the 1860s, there were premonitions of finitude in California. In the 1860s, when California was newly U.S. territory, environmentalists reached the coast with a sense of dread. John Muir stood at the beach in the 1860s and announced to the United States that he had come to the edge of possibility: America is a finite idea. We have to start saving America. We have to start saving the land. Conserving America. The message went back—west to east—back to the crowded brick cities of the East Coast.

I grew up in the 1950s when California was filling with people from Nebraska and Minnesota. People arrived from Brooklyn, or they came from Chicago. They came for a softer winter. They came to re-create themselves.

But shortly we ran out of land. Los Angeles got too crowded and needed to reinvent itself as Orange County. Then Orange County got too crowded and had to reinvent itself as north county San Diego. Then north county San Diego got too crowded. Now Californians are moving into the desert. We don't have enough room any more, we say.

Suddenly foreign immigrants are coming. They are pouring into California from the South. ("We are sorry to intrude, señor, we are looking for work.") They come from Latin America, talking of California as "el Norte," not the West Coast. El Norte is wide open. The West Coast is a finite idea. *Whose map is correct?*

There are planes landing in Los Angeles today, planes from Thailand, from Hong Kong, planes from Seoul and from Taiwan. People getting off the planes say about California, "This is where the United States begins." Those of us in the United States who believe in the western route to California say, "No, no. California is where the United States comes to an end." *Whose myth is true?*

People in the United States used to say, "Go West, young man." We meant, go West toward possibility. Now that we have hit against the wall of the coastline, we start talking about going East. "Go East, young man!"

"I'm leaving California; I'm going to Nebraska."

"I'm leaving California; I'm going to Colorado."

And, for the first time, today Californians speak of the North and the South. Not because we want to. Not because we are accustomed to looking North and South. It's only because the West is a finite idea.

"I'm going to get a condominium in Baja California. You know, there are condos throughout Baja where everyone speaks English. We're going to make Baja our national park."

Or, "I'm leaving California for Canada. I'm going to Vancouver. There are too many ethnics in California. I'm going to Canada where the air is cleaner."

Go North, young man.

Puerto Ricans, Mexicans—early in this century we were a people from the South in an east-west country. We were people of mixed blood in a black and white country. America's great scar, its deep tear, has always been the black and white division. Puerto Ricans and Mexicans tended to be of mixed race. Hard, therefore, for the United States to classify or even see.

For the last thirty years in the United States, Hispanics have impersonated a race. We have convinced bureaucrats in Washington—bureaucrats who knew nothing about us and cared less—that we constituted a racial group. It was essential, if the United States were ever to recognize us, that we be a racial group, people subject to "racial discrimination."

The only trouble is, Hispanics do not constitute a racial group. But what does the United States care? There we are in the ponderous morning pages of *The New York Times*, listed on a survey alongside black, white, Asian.

Puerto Ricans, Mexicans—we were Catholics in a Protestant country. And millions of us were Indians in a country that imagined the Indian to be dead. Today, Los Angeles is the largest Indian city in the United States. All around the city, you can see Toltecs and Aztecs and Mayans. But the filmmakers of Hollywood persist in making movies about the dead Indian. For seven dollars, you can see cowboys kill the Indians. We are sorry about it. We feel the luxury of regret from our swivel seats.

On the other hand, I remember a chic dinner party in Mexico City. (You know, rich Mexicans can be very polite when they say cruel things. It is their charm.) One Mexican, a drink in his hand, said to me, "You are a writer? Very interesting. Your work has been translated in Mexico?"

I replied, "Well, not much."

He said, "Well, we Mexicans are not going to know what to make of you as a writer." He said, "We're not accustomed to writers who look like you."

Seriously, let me apologize. I must *apologize* for not being able to speak to many of you in your own language. I suffer from this strange disability. I can understand spoken Spanish, can read it. But I can't speak Spanish with ease. I walk through Latin American cities like a sleepwalker, comprehending everything but unable to join the conversation.

How shall I explain my disability? Elena Castedo, in her wonderful essay on the United States, suggested that we in the United States are afraid of foreign languages. That is true, but not quite right. Better to say that we are obsessed with foreign languages. Most of us in this country are one or two generations from a grandparent who scolded us for losing her language. There is an enormous guilt in the American soul.

I want you to know that I have been haunted by Spanish for most of my life. I understand your jokes and your asides. I hear your whisperings. I smile feebly in response. I feel so guilty about not being able to join you. It is because I have taken this new lover, American English, this blond lover of mine has taken my breath away.

Hispanics in the United States turn into fools. We argue among ourselves, criticize one another, mock one another for becoming too much the gringo. We criticize each other for speaking too much Spanish or not enough Spanish. We demand that our politicians provide us with bilingual voting ballots, but we do not bother to vote. We are, as Señor Paz observed decades ago, freaks of history.

I have heard Mexicans of the middle class say to their children when their children head for the United States to go to college, "Stay away from those Chicanos, whatever you do. Stay away from them because they're crazy. They think of themselves as 'minorities.' "

We are Mexico's Mexicans. Everything Mexico loathes about herself, she hates in us. We lost our culture to a larger power. Mexico lost her tongue to

Cortés. For us Cortés is Uncle Sam. If I go back to Mexico, Mexico comes closer to me, breathes in my ear. "Hijito, háblame en español," Mexico says.

I say, "Ay, Madre, no puedo. No más un poquito."

"Un poquito. Un poquito. ¡Tu propio idioma...!"

Then, POCHO.

Michael Novak was speaking last night about what unites the hemisphere. What unites us as Americans, he said, is our willingness to say goodbye to the motherland. We say to Europe, farewell. And there is bravery in that cry of goodbye.

The only trouble is that adiós was never part of the Mexican-American or the Puerto Rican vocabulary. We didn't turn our backs on the past. We kept going back and forth, between past and future. After a few months of work in New York or Los Angeles, we would cross the border. We were commuters between centuries, between rivals. And neither country understood us.

Abuelita didn't understand us because our Spanish was so bad. On the other hand, people in the United States would wonder what was wrong with us. Why do you people need to keep going back home? (In a country that believes so much in the future our journey home was almost a subversion.) The United States said to us, "When my parents left Sweden, they didn't keep going back to Sweden. But you—you keep turning back. What's the matter with you? Are you a mama's boy?"

Pocho.

Someone said last night that the gringo had hijacked the word "American" and given it to himself with typical arrogance. I remember my aunt in Mexico City scolding me when I told her I was from America. Didn't I realize the entire hemisphere is America? Listen, my Mexican aunt told me, "People who live in the United States are norteamericanos."

Well, I think to myself—my aunt is now dead. God rest her soul—but I think to myself, I wonder what she would have thought when the great leaders—the president of Mexico, the president of the United States, the Canadian prime minister—signed the North American Free Trade Agreement. Mexico woke up one morning to realize that she's a norteamericana.

I predict that Mexico will have a nervous breakdown in ten years. She will have to check into a clinic for a long rest. She will need to determine just what exactly it means that she is, with the dread gringo, a North American.

Meanwhile, peasants keep crossing the border. The diplomats keep signing the documents. But has anyone ever met a North American? Oh, I know. You know Mexicans. And you know Canadians. But has anyone met a North American?

I have.

Let me tell you about him, this North American. He's a Mixteco Indian who lives in the Mexican state of Oaxaca. He is trilingual. His primary language is the language of the tribe. He speaks Spanish, the language of Cortés, as a second language. Also, he has a working knowledge of U.S. English.

He knows thousands of miles of dirt roads and freeways. He commutes between two civilizations. He is preyed upon by corrupt Mexican police who want to "shake him down" because he has hidden U.S. dollars in his shoes. He is pursued as "illegal" by the U.S. border patrol. He lives in a sixteenth-century village where his wife watches blond Venezuelan soap operas. There is a picture of La Virgen de Guadalupe over his bed. He works near Stockton, California, where there is no Virgin Mary but the other Madonna—the rock star.

This Mexican peasant knows two currencies. But he is as illegal on one side of the border as he is an embarrassment to his government on the other side of the line. He is the first North American.

People in the United States have always been wary of Mexican water. We love your beaches and your pre-Columbian ruins. But we are afraid to sing in the shower at the hotel. On the other hand, we have always trusted Canadian water. We drink gallons of it. We also assumed that Canadian water was clean.

But there is a virus in Canadian water called "multiculturalism" which is making its way into the United States' blood stream. The most interesting thing we think to say about one another now in the United States is that we are multicultural. But, of course, when people in the United States talk about multiculturalism, they mean, like the Canadians, culture to signify only race or ethnicity. In fact, culture means many other things, too.

Culture means region. What part of the world, what sky governs your life? I come from California.

Culture means age. The old man looks at the young boy with incomprehension.

Sex is culture—that great divide between the male and female, their delight and their frustration.

Religion. The United States is a Protestant country though we do not like to describe ourselves in that way.

We are a Puritan country.

A friend of mine, Pico Iyer, who writes of the confusion of cultures in the U.S. metropolis, speculates about the inevitable confusion that results when so many races, so many languages, altars, meet in modern Los Angeles. I think the more interesting dilemma for the post-modern citizen of the city is that she feels herself multicultural within herself: *How shall I reconcile the world within my own soul?*

My father remembers a Mexico that no longer exists. My father remembers a village. "Where is it, Papa? Show me where, in the state of Colima, you were a boy. Where?"

He explores the map with his finger. The city of Colima has swallowed up the village. The city has grown bloated, has larded itself over the countryside, obliterating the village.

"It is not there," he says.

We Mexican-Americans end up like the British Columbians. If you go to British Columbia, you can visit houses and see the Queen of England on the wall. People use tea cozies in British Columbia. They remember an England that is nothing like the Britain of blue-haired soccer punks who beat up Pakistanis on Saturday nights. The British Columbians remember an England that exists nowhere on earth but on a faded post card.

My father remembers a Mexico that used to be a village.

A friend of mine, a European, was a hippie in northern Mexico during the 1960s. Recently my friend took his son back to Mexico to look for the villages where he was a bohemian.

My friend phoned me the other night with chagrin. He said, "Everything has changed. The little towns—no one hangs out anymore. All the Mexicans are working at the local maquiladora." And he says, "Thirty years ago, Mexicans used to walk around these small towns wearing guns. Now nobody wears guns."

I say to my friend, "If you want to see Mexicans wearing guns, go to East Los Angeles." My relatives in Mexico City, they watch ESPN. My niece in Mexico City is inordinately proud of her tee-shirt which proclaims HARD ROCK CAFE. My relatives in Mexico City have wandered away from Roman Catholicism in favor of Buddhism. My relatives in Mexico City are divorced.

At this moment, about this time in the afternoon, there are minibuses going South—Jehovah's Witnesses, Mormons. This is the great moment of conversion in the Mormon world. By the end of the century, half of the world's Mormon population will be Spanish-speaking, at which time what will we think of Salt Lake City? And of course, here come the evangelical Christians. They are converting Latin America. The great soul of Latin America is turning toward the Easter promise of Protestantism. "You are redeemed! You can change! You can become a new man! You can put away the old ways, become something new, praise the Lord! Hallelujah!"

A Lutheran pastor I know in San Francisco works with immigrants from Central America. He often notices that, without even asking, without even thinking too much about it, the immigrants convert to Protestantism as they settle in the United States. The conversion becomes part of their Americanization. They seem to sense that in becoming Americans, they should also become Protestant.

On the other hand, the other day in Tijuana, Mexico, I met three boys from an evangelical church called Victory Outreach. (Victory Outreach works with kids who suffer from serious drug problems.) The kids said they are coming to the United States this year—502 years after Columbus—to convert us back to our Protestant roots. The youngest one said, "Those Americans are so sad."

Someone once asked Chou En-lai, the Chinese prime minister, what he thought of the French Revolution. Chou En-lai gave a wonderful Chinese response. He said, "It's too early to tell."

I think it may be too early to tell what the story of Columbus means. The latest chapter of the Columbus story might be taking place right now, as the Hispanic evangelicals head north.

The kids on the line tonight in Tijuana, if you ask them why they are coming to the United States of America, will not say anything about Thomas Jefferson or notions of democracy. They have not heard about Thomas Paine or the *Federalist Papers*. They have only heard that there is a job in Glendale, California, at a dry cleaners.

They are going back to Mexico in a few months, they insist. They are only going to the United States for the dollars. They don't want to be gringos. They don't want anything to do with the United States, except the dollars.

But then a few months will pass, and they will not go back to Latin America. What will happen, of course, to their surprise, is that the job in Glendale will make them part of the United States. (Work in the United States is our primary source of identity.)

People in this country, when they meet one another, do not ask about family or where the other comes from. The first thing people in the U.S. ask each other at cocktail parties is what the other does for a living.

The hemisphere, the story of the hemisphere, began with a little joke about maps and the fact that Columbus, our papasito, our father, got it all wrong. He imagined he was in some part of the world where there were Indians. He thought he had come to India.

We laugh today because papi didn't know where he was. But I'm not sure we know where we are, either. We are only beginning to look at the map. We are only beginning to wonder what the map of the hemisphere means.

The story of the Americas began with a cartographer's whimsy in the Renaissance: *Is the world flat?* And to the delight of the mapmaker, the explorer set out on the sea to discover the great human possibility of roundness.

Mexican-Americans, Puerto Ricans—we ended up in the United States city. We are people from the village. We ended up in the city. We ended up with a bad knowledge of English, a failing knowledge of Spanish. Yet we were remarkable people. We travelled many thousands of miles, some of us on foot. We ended up cooking for the United States or making beds or gardening. We have become the nannies of North America. We take care of the blond children of Beverly Hills and Park Avenue—these children will become the next generation of Hispanics. We have subverted, invaded, the wealthiest homes in America.

The kids in East LA, the kids that Octavio Paz was talking about forty years ago, the pachucos have turned murderous against one another. Several months ago I was talking to some gang kids in Los Angeles about New York. The photographer working with me was from New York. I asked one of the gang kids, "Would you like to see New York some day?"

The littlest one piped in response, "Not me, man."

I said, "Why not? Don't you want to see where Joe, the photographer, comes from?"

"Not me, man! I'm Mexican. I belong here."

Here? This boy lives within four blocks. If he goes a fifth block he's going to get his head blown off because he doesn't use the right sign language or he is wearing the wrong color today. This Mexican kid couldn't even find his way to the beaches of Los Angeles.

The odd thing, the tragic irony, is that many times our fathers and grandfathers who were so brave, who travelled so many thousands of miles, trespassed borders, end up with grandchildren who become Chicanos, timid children who believe that culture is some little thing put in a box, held within four blocks.

One of the things that Mexico has never acknowledged about my father, I insist that you today at least entertain—the possibility that my father and others like him were the great revolutionaries of Mexico. They, not Pancho Villa, not Zapata, were heralds of the modern age. They went back to Mexico and changed Mexico forever. The man who worked in Chicago in the 1920s returned one night to his village in Michoacán. The village gathered around him—this is a true story—and the village asked, "What is it like up there in Chicago?"

The man said, "It's okay."

That rumor of "okay" spread across Michoacán, down to Jalisco, across Jalisco into Oaxaca, from village to village to village.

There are now remote villages in Latin America that have become the most international places in the world. Tiny Peruvian villages know when farmers are picking pears in the Yakima Valley in the state of Washington.

We talk about the new moment in the Americas. The moment has been going on for decades. People have been travelling back and forth.

I am the son of a prophet. I am a fool. I am a victim of history. I am confused. I do not know whether I am coming or going. I speak bad Spanish. And yet, I will tell you this: to grow up Hispanic in the United States is to know more Guatemalans than if I grew up in Mexico. Because I live in California, I know more Brazilians than I would know if I lived in Peru. Because I live in California, it is routine for me to know Nicaraguans and Salvadorans and Cubans—as routine as meeting Chinese or Greeks.

People in California talk about the "illegals." But there was always an illegality to immigration. It was a rude act, the leaving of home. It was a violation of custom, an insult to the village. A youthful act of defiance. I know a man from El Salvador who has not talked to his father since the day he left his father's village. (It is a sin against family to leave home.) Immigrants must always be illegal. Immigrants are always criminals. They trespass borders and horrify their grandmothers.

But they are also our civilization's prophets. They, long before the rest of us, long before this room, long before this conference was ever imagined, they saw the hemisphere whole.

# I Could Only Fight Back in My Poetry

## Guillermo Gómez-Peña

*Performed live as "El Quebradito," a flamboyant vaquero from northern Mexico, dressed in a fake zebra-skin tuxedo. He looks tired and crestfallen, and his voice is raspy. Soundbed: Music by guitar maestro Antonio Bribiesca plays on a ghetto blaster; the irritating voice of an evangelist preacher can be heard in the distance.*

it was the spring of '87 in the city of Arlington
I tried to explain to you in my very broken English
that Texas had once been a Mexican ranch
& that truth was not a "gringo-bashing ideology"
but you had seen too many Stallone films
& felt obliged to let me have it, ¿qué no?
so you tried to beat the Meskin out of me
of course, since you were a foot taller & 85 lbs.
    heavier
& not that skilled in cross-cultural diplomacy
I could only fight back in my poetry
in fact, I'm fighting back right now
you claimed you hated my accent & my arrogance
but the real reason you despised me
was that your wife was just about to leave you
& hit the road to sexy Mexico
to escape the Texan nightmare, your inflexible arms,
your smelly feet & psychotic eyes
so Mexico became the source of all your fears
the red-light district where gringos are poisoned by
    midget whores
the mountain of trash where kids with typhoid make
    holes to sleep in

Guillermo Gómez-Peña: "I Could Only Fight Back in My Poetry," included in *The New World Border: Prophecies, Poems, and Loqueras for the End of the Century*. San Francisco: City Lights, 1996.

the bus that keeps breaking down on your way to
    some generic jungle
the gentle mariachi who touched your wife like you
    never did
you saw all these images in my eyes before you broke
    my ribs
& I could only fight back in my poetry

P.S. #1   I don't harbor any resentments but I sure
    hope one of these days you learn to read &
    write

P.S. #2   See, I told you culero, I win most fights in
    the streets of my poetry

P.S. #3   I heard you joined the militia movement
    last month. . . . I must say that you are
    consistent in misplacing your anger, man

# A Dream

## Ilan Stavans

I had a pleasant dream in which I saw the future in our Americas. According to my abstruse calculations, it took place in the year 2061, more than a couple of centuries after the Treaty of Guadalupe Hidalgo. Made of disconnected halves, the dream took place in bizarre, almost-unrecognizable locations—the set of the first half looked like Santa Barbara, California, and the other was a tropical setting, probably Havana. For inexplicable reasons, during the whole dream I longed for the ugly metropolitan landscapes of my Mexican childhood, which I was able to invoke in brief conversations with a waitress I saw at a college cafeteria.

Ultramodern architecture, without the slightest hint of baroque style, was in the background in the first location in my dream. A gigantic clock was mounted in the top of a brick tower. While I sat on a glorious beach next to a majestic academic institution, a polite old lady, almost fluent in what sounded at first like my mother tongue, Spanish, and with what appeared to be an Arabic accent, came to me offering a rotten, yellowish pear. I politely rejected it. She asked me what had brought me to the place. I answered that I had come to research the life and times of Oscar "Zeta" Acosta, a militant lawyer of the hippie generation who befriended Hunter S. Thompson. His papers were in archives at the University of California at Santa Barbara. She smiled and began feeding dry bread to hungry seagulls. She assured me that no such place still existed. It had been relocated to the East Coast, somewhere in New England. I laughed, partly because I had trouble understanding her. She then reflected on historical events and discussed revolutions and gradual social changes.

Decades after the North American Free Trade Agreement, also known as the Tratado de Libre Comercio, was signed by the United States, Canada, and Mexico, in late 1993, she assured me, the region north of the Rio Grande, by then known as the Tiguex River—a name first used around 1540—had changed fundamentally. A high-speed highway had been built between Los Angeles, the capital of the Hispanic world and the metropolis with the most Mexicans, some 78 million, and Tenochtitlán, whose name now substituted for the standard appellation: Mexico City. Poverty was still ubiquitous in

Ilan Stavans: "A Dream," first published as "Prologue" of *The Hispanic Condition: The Power of a People*. New York: HarperCollins, 2001. Reprinted by permission of the author.

numerous rural areas and urban ghettos, even after politicians' repeated attempts to abolish it. In fact, at the end of the previous millennium, Mexico had undergone a bloody civil war, which was led by unhappy Indian soldiers of Mayan descent, who belonged to the Ejército Zapatista de Liberación Nacional. The civil war had begun in the southern state of Chiapas and spread throughout the Yucatán peninsula and Veracruz. Inequality was no longer based on racial lines. Anglos had slowly been alienated from society and now lived on the fringes, unequivocally resented.

In my dream a new global culture had indeed emerged, one with Latino, French, Portuguese, and Anglo elements intermingled. Other nations, including Chile, Argentina, and Colombia, had joined the trade pact originally set forth in North America, and neglected diplomatic boundaries dividing North America had quickly vanished. No more Monroe doctrines, no more Good Neighbor policies; the Anglo-Saxon and Hispanic worlds had finally become one. With the fall of Communism in China, a monumental influx of industrious Asian immigrants settled first in Los Angeles, then in Tenochtitlán, and finally in Piedras Negras. Children of mixed marriages, part Asian and part Hispanic, had increased in considerable numbers. Even for those who constantly rejected change, ethnic and cultural purity were totally irretrievable. *Caliban's Utopia: or, Barbarism Reconsidered*, an epoch-making book published in 2021 by Dr. Alejandro Morales III, a theoretician at the University of Ciudad Juárez, claimed that a new race had been born: *la arroza de bronce*—the Bronze Race of the Rice People.

My Arab interlocutor, referring to the volume as "prophetic," explained Morales's thesis. Based on José Vasconcelos's early-twentieth-century volume about *la raza cósmica*, a triumphant mix of European and Aztec roots, the volume argued that Asian Hispanics, as true superhumans, had been called to rule the entire globe. The author based his argument on the new function of the Rio Grande, which he called Río de Buenaventura del Norte: Once an artificial division, it had become "just another Mississippi River," a natural sight, a commercial avenue, a tourist spot. And, indeed, in 2020, after the War of Mannequins between Cuba and the United States, an agreement was signed by all governments in the region to dismantle all North American borders and establish a single hybrid nation of nations, simply called the New World.

People originally thought the tongues of Shakespeare and Cervantes would share the status of "official language," but a strange phenomenon took place— Spanglish became an astonishing linguistic force. Television, radio, and the print media soon modified their communication codes to accommodate the new dialect, a sort of Yiddish: English with a phonetic Iberian spelling. A vast quantity of what sounded to me like unrecognized words circulated.

Suddenly, I was transported to the next scene in my dream—the cafeteria, still in Santa Barbara. I had finished eating and was sitting next to the fire, rereading a story by H. G. Wells, but I forget which one. The Arab woman was seated next to a Filipino waitress, who reminded me of a woman I met at age eighteen and whom I loved deeply. After much quick talk that, once again, I had trouble understanding, the waitress, for some mysterious reason, mentioned Edna Ferber's *Giant*, set in Texas. I told her I had recently been recalling the scene in the book in which a handful of Mexicans are vilified at a bar. The conversation moved to another topic: my love for and hatred of Mexico. She also referred to Morales's *Caliban's Utopia* and handed me the copy she happened to be carrying in her purse. When I opened it, I realized its pages were totally virginal—blank.

During most of my dream's second half, I wandered through the labyrinthine historical streets of a downtown Caribbean capital. By then I was seventy-six years old and was walking with the help of a cane. Curiously, in spite of the balmy, temperate heat, a heavy snowstorm had fallen the night before. At some point, I met Henrick Larsen, a mature man who was ready to act as a *lazarillo*, guiding me around. His name was stamped in my mind because of its resemblance to a character by the Uruguayan writer Juan Carlos Onetti, "Years, Christmas, and the Fourth of July no longer exist; there are no watches or calendars. Time, with a capital *T*, has ceased to be counted. Our present is eternal," he said. As we walked, I had the impression of being on a film set. Street lamps were lighted, and buildings had been re-created to give the impression of accumulated decay. Even a passerby or two walked as if framed by a movie camera. A tourist heaven, I thought. I soon realized I was witnessing the Hispanic future. The colonial vista surrounding me had been frozen, immobilized forever, turned into a magisterial museum. Henrick Larsen and I entered a print shop, where a few men were busy making engravings. One of the men, who had a big belly, looked like José Guadalupe Posada, the legendary south-of-the-Rio-Grande lampooner during the revolution of 1910 that saw the participation of Pancho Villa and Emiliano Zapata. I approached him. He told me that his trade was the preservation of the collective memory through cartoons. I sensed a Cuban accent in his voice, but most of his words were unintelligible.

"He is the silent genius, a personality of Olympian virtuosity," Larsen whispered in my ear.

"What?" I asked. I barely understood his message.

"He nurtures a desire and determination to record the collective history, to prove that our past is well documented, widely known, at least within ethnic circles, and administered as a stimulating and inspiring tradition for coming generations."

I still felt puzzled. His sentences had a Borgesian tone. Had I read these same words somewhere before?

"The last grain of sand in our hourglass has brought us a reminder. In a fashion similar to the way all the faithful are called to prayer in the East, we are called to render an account of our stewardship. The problem of the twenty-first century is the problem of miscegenation."

At that point I woke up, uneasy, bewildered, with Nietzsche's dictum in my mind: Only the past, neither the future nor the present, is a lie. What also crossed my mind was an unspecified scene from the film *Blade Runner*, a favorite of mine, based on a haunting novel by Philip K. Dick, that dealt with, as Kevin Star once wrote, the fusion of individual cultures into a demonic polyglotism that is ominous with unresolved hostilities. As I opened my eyes, I managed to see, lost in darkness, a copy of *Caliban's Utopia* on the bedroom table. I also thought I felt the hands of the gigantic clock on Santa Barbara's brick tower move behind me.

# Selected Bibliography

Anzaldúa, Gloria. *Borderlands/La Frontera*. Introduction by Sonia Saldívar-Hull. 2nd edition. San Francisco: Aunt Lute Foundation, 1999.

Bejarano, Cynthia L. *¿Que Onda? Urban Youth Culture and Border Identity*. Tucson: University of Arizona Press, 2005.

Byrd, Bobby, with Susannah Mississippi Byrd, eds. *The Late Great Mexican Border: Reports from a Disappearing Line*. El Paso: Cinco Puntos Press, 1999.

Crosthwaite, Luis Humberto, with John William Byrd and Bobby Byrd, eds. *Puro Border: Dispatches, Snapshots, and Graffiti from La Frontera*. El Paso: Cinco Puntos Press, 2003.

Fox, Claire F. *The Fence and the River: Culture and Politics at the U.S.–Mexico Border*. Minneapolis: University of Minnesota Press, 1999.

Fregoso, Rosa Linda. *MeXicana Encounters: The Making of Social Identities on the Borderlands*. Berkeley: University of California, 2003.

Gómez-Peña, Guillermo. *The New World Border: Prophecies, Poems, and Loqueras for the End of the Century*. San Francisco: City Lights, 1996.

Gutiérrez-Jones, Carl. *Rethinking the Borderlands: Between Chicano Culture and Legal Discourse*. Berkeley: University of California Press, 1995.

Irwin, Robert McKee. *Bandits, Captives, Heroines, and Saints: Cultural Icons of Mexico's Northwest Borderlands*. Minneapolis: University of Minnesota Press, 2007.

Miller, Tom, ed. *Writing on the Edge: A Borderlands Reader*. Tucson: University of Arizona Press, 2003.

Saldívar, José David. *Border Matters: Remapping American Cultural Studies*. Berkeley: University of California Press, 1997.

Stavans, Ilan. *The Hispanic Condition: The Power of the People*. New York: Rayo/HarperCollins, 2001.

———. *Q&A: Latino History and Culture*. New York: Collins, 2007.

Torrans, Thomas. *The Magic Curtain: The Mexican-American Border in Fiction, Film, and Song*. Fort Worth: Texas Christian University Press, 2002.

Villa, Pablo, ed. *Ethnography at the Border*. Minneapolis: University of Minnesota 2003.

Wood, Andrew Grant, ed. *On the Border: Society and Culture between the United States and Mexico*. Lanham, MD: SR Books, 2004.

# Index

# About the Editor
# and Contributors

## EDITOR

**Ilan Stavans** is Lewis-Sebring Professor in Latin American and Latino Culture and Five College–Fortieth Anniversary Professor at Amherst College. A native from Mexico, he received his doctorate in Latin American Literature from Columbia University. Stavans' books include *The Hispanic Condition* (HarperCollins, 1995), *On Borrowed Words* (Viking, 2001), *Spanglish* (HarperCollins, 2003), *Dictionary Days* (Graywolf, 2005), *The Disappearance* (TriQuarterly, 2006), *Love and Language* (Yale, 2007), *Resurrecting Hebrew* (Nextbook, 2008), and *Mr. Spic Goes to Washington* (Soft Skull, 2008). He has edited *The Oxford Book of Jewish Stories* (Oxford, 1998), *The Poetry of Pablo Neruda* (Farrar, Straus and Giroux, 2004), *Isaac Bashevis Singer: Collected Stories* (3 vols., Library of America, 2004), *The Schocken Book of Sephardic Literature* (Schocken, 2005), *Cesar Chavez: An Organizer's Tale* (Penguin, 2008), and *Becoming Americans: Four Centuries of Immigrant Writing* (Library of America, 2009). His play *The Disappearance*, performed by the theater troupe Double Edge, premiered at the Skirball Cultural Center in Los Angeles and has been shown around the country. His story *"Morirse está en hebreo"* was made into the award-winning movie *My Mexican Shivah* (2007), produced by John Sayles. Stavans has received numerous awards, among them a Guggenheim Fellowship, the National Jewish Book Award, an Emmy nomination, the Latino Book Award, Chile's Presidential Medal, and the Rubén Darío Distinction. His work has been translated into a dozen languages.

## CONTRIBUTORS

**Eduardo Barrera**: Professor of Communications at the University of Texas in El Paso.

**Cynthia L. Bejarano**: Assistant Professor of Criminal Justice at New Mexico State University. Author: *¿Que Onda? Urban Youth Culture and Border Identity* (2005).

**Luis Humberto Crosthwaite**: Fiction writer and essayist. Author: *El gran preténder* (1994), *The Moon Will Forever Be a Distant Love* (1997), and *Instrucciones para* *cruzar la frontera* (2002). Co-editor: *Puro Border: Dispatches, Snapshots, and Graffiti from La Frontera* (2003).

**Mike Davis**: Scholar and social commentator. Author: *City of Quartz: Excavating the Future in Los Angeles* (1992), *Magical Urbanism: Latinos Reinvent the US City* (2000), *Late Victorian Holocausts: El Niño Famines and the Making of the Third World* (2001), and *Planet of Slums* (2006).

**Claire F. Fox**: Associate Professor of English and International Studies at the University of Iowa. Author: *The Fence and the River: Culture and Politics at the U.S.–Mexico Border* (1999).

**Mario T. García**: Professor of History and Chicano Studies at the University of California in Santa Barbara. Author: *Desert Immigrants: The Mexicans of El Paso, 1880-1920* (1981) and *Mexican Americans: Leadership, Ideology, and Identity, 1930-1960* (1989). Editor: *Border Correspondent: Selected Writings of Ruben Salazar, 1955-1970* (1995), *Luis Leal: An Auto/Biography* (2000), and *The Gospel of César Chávez: My Faith in Action* (2007).

**Cecilio García-Camarillo**: Chicano poet and activist. Author: *Selected Poetry of Cecilio García-Camarillo* (2000).

**Guillermo Gómez-Peña**: Performance artist. Author: *The New World Border: Prophecies, Poems, and Loqueras for the End of the Century* (1996), *Dangerous Border Crossers: The Artist Talks Back* (2000), and *Ethno-techno: Writings on Performance, Activism, and Pedagogy* (2005), edited by Elaine Peña.

**Carl Gutiérrez-Jones**: Professor of English at the University of California, Santa Barbara. Author: *Rethinking the Borderlands: Between Chicano Culture and Legal Discourse* (1995) and *Critical Race Narratives: A Study of Race, Rhetoric, and Injury* (2001).

**Paul Horgan**: Essayist and fiction writer concentrating on the Southwestern United States. Author: *Great River: The Rio Grande in North American History* (1954) and *Lamy of Santa Fe* (1974).

**Robert McKee Irwin**: Associate Professor of Spanish at the University of California in Davis. Author: *Bandits, Captives, Heroines, and Saints: Cultural Icons of Mexico's Northwest Borderlands* (2007).

**Richard Rodriguez**: Essayist and TV commentator. Author: *Hunger of Memory: The Education of Richard Rodriguez* (1983), *Days of Obligation: An Argument with My Mexican Father* (1992), and *Brown: The Last Discovery of America* (2002).

**Juan Villoro**: Mexican essayist. Author: *La casa pierde* (1999), *Efectos personales* (2000), and *El testigo* (2004).